Camping Florida

Hookups   WES   C (cable)

Cedar Key

Camping Florida

A Comprehensive Guide to Hundreds of Campgrounds

Rick Sapp

FALCON GUIDES

GUILFORD, CONNECTICUT
HELENA, MONTANA

AN IMPRINT OF GLOBE PEQUOT PRESS

FALCONGUIDES®

Project Editor: David Legere
Layout Artist: Kevin Mak
Maps by Trailhead Graphics © Morris Book Publishing, LLC

Interior photos by Rick Sapp.

Library of Congress Cataloging-in-Publication Data is available on file.
ISBN 978-0-7627-4447-3

Printed in the United States of America

10 9 8 7 6 5 4 3 2 1

Contents

Counties: Escambia, Santa Rosa, Okaloosa, Walton, Holmes,
Washington, Jackson, Calhoun, Bay, Gulf, Gadsden, Liberty, Leon,
Wakulla, Franklin, Jefferson

Counties: Madison, Taylor, Hamilton, Suwannee, Lafayette, Dixie,
Columbia, Gilchrist, Baker, Union, Bradford, Alachua, Levy, Nassau,
Duval, Clay, Putnam, Marion Citrus

Counties: The St. John's River Basin—St. Johns, Flagler, Volusia,
Lake, Seminole, Orange, Brevard, Osceola, Polk, Indian River

Counties: Hernando, Sumter, Pasco, Pinellas, Hillsborough,
Manatee, Sarasota, Hardee, DeSoto, Highlands, Glades, Charlotte,
Lee, Monroe, Collier

Counties: Okechobee, St. Lucie, Martin, Glades, Hendry,
Palm Beach, Broward, Monroe, Dade

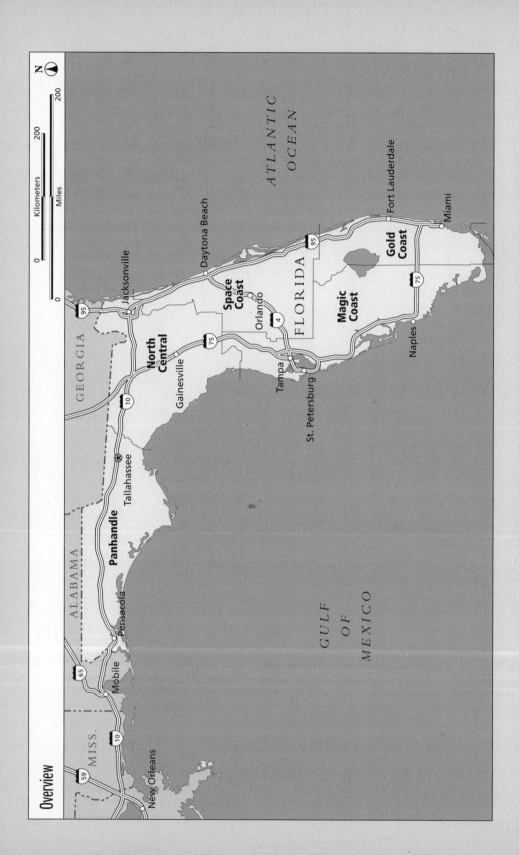

Acknowledgments

I must thank the staff and volunteers who make Florida's splendid public parks, forests, and wildlife areas work at all levels: federal, state, county, and municipal. Without these often underpaid and under-appreciated professional staff who love the outdoors, the Sunshine State would not have its world-class park system; without the unpaid volunteers who devote countless hours to such mundane tasks as picking up litter and painting signs and removing invasive flora and fauna, our parks, wetlands, and forests would not have their customary elegant feel, sometimes primitive and sometimes simply comfortable. *Muchas gracias. Obrigado. Merci beaucoup. Danke schöen.* Thank you.

Introduction

No place in the world beats Florida for being wonderful and crazy—at the same time. Here are a few facts (and pseudo-facts) from various books, brochures, and internet sites such as www.stateofflorida.com:

- A museum in Sanibel owns 2 million shells and claims to be the world's only museum devoted solely to mollusks.
- The U.S. city with the highest rate of lightning strikes per capita is Clearwater.
- Dr. John Gorrie of Apalachicola invented mechanical refrigeration in 1851—and died penniless, unknown, and unrecognized.
- Miami installed the first bank automated teller machine especially for in-line skaters.
- Florida is the only state that has two rivers with the same name: Withlacoochee in north central Florida (Madison County) and Withlacoochee in central Florida (enters the Gulf between Levy and Citrus Counties).
- Distance from Pensacola to Key West: 792 miles by road
- Coastline: 1,197 statute miles, but the tidal shoreline is 2,276 statute miles
- Number of lakes greater than ten acres: approximately 7,700
- Number of first magnitude springs: 27 (more than any other state)
- Number of islands greater than ten acres: approximately 4,500 (Florida is second in the nation by this measure; only Alaska ranks higher)
- Number of people who move to Florida each day: 1,000
- Number of hotel rooms: more than 370,000
- Number of campgrounds: 700 (100,000 campsites)
- Number of people who camp in Florida each year: 6 million

If you are a camper at heart, recognize that Florida offers magnificent landscapes, from coral reefs to dry highlands, from bright, sugar-sand beaches to swamps teeming with gators. The weather varies almost as much, from summers with 100-degree-plus temperatures to winters occasionally bringing snow. Of course, the image most people have of Florida's sunny and humid camping is right too. But you have to fill out the picture: We have beautiful and unspoiled beaches. We have cold, clear springs. We have shady oak hammocks where you can hang out and feel the cares of the world slip away. And we have miles of Everglades and nature trails, kayak trails, and multiuse trails.

When you camp here, look for the rare crocodile and the elusive ivory-billed woodpecker, long thought to be extinct, but . . . maybe not. Shiver in the springs and build sand castles by the ocean. Snorkel in the Keys and hike the restored longleaf highlands, fragrant with the scent of pine. Watch rockets take off and complete your bird lists. Hunt deer, catch fish, and pedal our multiuse trails.

Please do come for a visit. Toss up your tent and swing up the RV awning as soon as possible. We're ready to show you around. Then, go home and tell your neighbors to come for a visit. I am convinced that once you experience the real Florida, the essence of this lovely state, you will want to help preserve and protect it for generations to come.

How to Use This Guide

Camping Florida zeroes in on public campgrounds and parks. The lists and descriptions are close to exhaustive. Along with the developed sites, I've included primitive places where you must pack in or canoe in with food, water, and camping gear—and then take everything out when you leave. I also mention youth and group sites, cabins, yurts, and tepees. Florida emphasizes diversity in its campgrounds and you will find one of everything—many of everything, in fact—in our marvelous state.

Why focus only on public campgrounds, not private? There are hundreds of fine privately owned campgrounds in Florida, perhaps thousands. There must be that many to accommodate the six million campers the state receives each year. Private campgrounds supplement public camping and sometimes provide the necessary magic that allows campers to fully appreciate an area. Most are well managed, clean, quiet, in conformity with state and local laws, and corporately conscious of Florida's inherent fragility. Private campgrounds come and go, however, and are primarily located in high-traffic locations. They also change owners and Web sites with some regularity. Their ultimate job is not to preserve the sensitive diversity of the peninsula's landscape or even to make sure you have a good time, but to make a profit.

Public campgrounds, on the other hand, are by and large here to stay. While they close occasionally for repairs, you can count on their continued availability, and their fee structure is always reasonable. Additionally, public sites offer access to more of Florida, with locations not just in the most beautiful areas, but also in the remote nooks and crannies of the state, those wild places that can only be reached with effort, on foot or via kayak. Public parks also have a committed staff with volunteers who care about public, rather than private, profit. Campers, kayakers, and hikers understand this.

Choosing a Campground

I have organized this book based on the five regions around which the Florida State Park System organizes its wonderful, award-winning parks. In each of the following sections, parks are organized geographically, moving from northwest to southeast (please note that some large counties overlap regions):

- The Panhandle (roughly Tallahassee to Pensacola)
- North Central (Jacksonville to the Suwannee River)
- The Space Coast (anchored on the Ocala National Forest and the Kennedy Space Center)
- The Magic Coast (Florida's center and southwest, roughly from Tampa to the Everglades)
- The Gold Coast (Palm Beach through Miami to Key West)

Each campground description answers a list of key questions. Because of the dynamic nature of camping in Florida, information may vary or is sometimes incomplete. Brochures and Internet sites go out of date or give incomplete information; parks grow and services change. Even good contacts, such as volunteers with experience on sites, couldn't always supply essential facts, such as the distance to potable water or the number of allowed campers or the maximum RV length for a site.

Nevertheless, I have sought to give the very best information on location, season, the number of sites, maximum RV length, availability of facilities and services, fee per night, the management agency, contact information, how to get there, and what you can expect to see and do once you have put "boots on the ground."

The numbers assigned to parks and campgrounds coincide with those on the regional maps. By consulting the appropriate map and scanning the descriptions, you should be able to select a public campground that appeals to your interest and is most convenient for your travel plans.

Helpful Information

Specific categories of information in the campground sections are location, season, sites, maximum RV length, facilities, fee per night, management, contacts, finding the campground, and about the campground. The following explains the information provided within these categories and provides a few tips specific to camping in Florida.

Seasons: With a mild, subtropical climate, Florida public campgrounds are open throughout the year, with three exceptions:

- The brief public hunting seasons, basically in the fall, during which you may want to wear bright clothing and keep your horses out of the woods.
- When the state is threatened by an emergency such as a hurricane, June through November. These days, given the state's extraordinary drought circumstances, there is also a March through July wildfire season.
- When a campground is receiving an upgrade or renovation.

Campsites: Florida sites are either RV or tent sites. RV refers to a broad class of recreational vehicles, the thousands of motor homes, vans, tent-trailers, and assorted pull-behind campers on the road, even in this era of high and increasing gas prices. Find a campground with amenities, and chances are it accepts RVs.

Tent sites may also have amenities—other than a flat spot. Florida camping areas often provide (or sell for a very small fee) electric hookups, and potable water is generally available. On the other hand, if a site is labeled "primitive," you must carry in all of your food and water—or boil water—and carry out all of your trash. On such sites, the credo to make no permanent mark other than a footprint is The Rule.

Many Florida campgrounds have cabins, and where this is the case, amenities and fees are listed. If you are ground- and sleeping bag–phobic, a woodsy cabin is for you.

Fee per night: The price codes used throughout the book are based on prices listed for 2008. A range is used because prices increase incrementally. The purpose of the symbols is to assist in cost comparisons and provide an idea of out-of-pocket costs.

$	=	Less than $10
$$	=	$10 to $19
$$$	=	$20 or more

The price codes refer to single campsites only. Expect cabins, yurts, or tepees to cost more. Many camps have add-on fees for additional vehicles, tents, special amenities, or extra members of the party.

Reservations: Reservations are required at Florida's state parks; they can be arranged by telephone, e-mailed directly, or obtained through ReserveAmerica.com. In other areas, reservations may be accepted, but in wildlife management areas or national forests, you can usually pick up a no-charge permit when you arrive. Arriving early in the day or telephoning in advance, however, is always better.

Most other campgrounds and especially those on state hiking and kayak trails or those that have primitive sites generally take campers first-come, first-served. Nevertheless, if you can possibly call ahead, do so. I have included local numbers for park managers or attendants. After using this book as a reference, they should be your next point of contact for precise, up-to-the-minute information.

Water: Unless a site notes that it is primitive, potable water should be available. If you are hiking, canoeing, or kayaking, however, you must have a supply available because you just never know . . . and you cannot safely drink from a stream, even if your health insurance is paid in advance.

In the backcountry, be prepared to strain and boil water for drinking. Keep in mind that stream water is still not fit to drink the moment it begins to boil. It needs to boil for more than a minute before you can cool and drink it. (In an emergency, a one-eighth teaspoon of bleach per gallon of water soon kills most disease-carrying organisms.)

Pets: Pets are generally acceptable in Florida's public campgrounds, but there are rules. They must not be left unattended in a site; they must be on short leash; they must not bark excessively; and the owner must clean up after them. Follow the basic rules of neighborliness and people will love you and your pets. Violate them and risk removal from a campground. A pet that is not comfortable around strangers is a pet that should be kenneled, not camped.

Quiet hours: I have found this to be the most frequently abused rule in public campgrounds. Be courteous of your neighbors and keep the noise level down after sunset.

Amenities charts key:
Hookups:

W	=	Water
E	=	Electricity
S	=	Sewer
C	=	Cable
P	=	Phone
I	=	Internet

Total Sites:

T	=	Tents
C	=	Cabins
Y	=	Yurts

Maximum RV Length: Given in feet

Toilets:

F	=	Flush
NF	=	No flush

Recreation:

H	=	Hiking
S	=	Swimming
F	=	Fishing
B	=	Boating
L	=	Boat launch
O	=	Off-road driving
R	=	Horseback riding
C	=	Cycling

Florida's parks have an amazing diversity of recreational opportunities in addition to the above, and in specific cases I have mentioned hunting, snorkeling, in-line skating, and scuba. There are also BMX bicycle tracks, Frisbee golf courses, off-road cycling, swimming pools, and dog parks.

Getting to the campground: The best way to reach your intended campsite is to use the campground directions in conjunction with a detailed state road map such as the *DeLorme Florida Atlas & Gazeteer*, the appropriate Forest Service map, or an online mapping service such as Google Maps. Maps in this book are precise, but be alert, however, as many boat launches and primitive sites or county parks in Florida are in remote locations.

Outdoors in Florida

Gators sunning themselves on fallen logs, red-cockaded woodpeckers waking you to morning coffee, or friends tripping on their tent pegs, you're about to have an unforgettable Florida experience and collect stories you will share and chuckle about for years. So bring your camera, and if you haven't been camping lately, especially camping in Florida, here are a few tips to help you take advantage of this state's remarkable resources and make your stay as easy and safe as it will be memorable.

Camping Refresher Course

A responsible attitude toward enjoying the outdoors, especially at remote campgrounds and trails, is the best way to protect and preserve a quality outdoor experience. It is also the best way to help control campground costs.

The drive: Traveling along major highways poses little problem. These roads are well maintained, a town or passing vehicle is never far off, and your cellular phone's reception is fine.

Backcountry roads—even in Florida—are quite a different story. For this type of travel, it is mandatory that you keep your tires and engine in good repair. Top the gas tank at the last point of civilization and carry emergency vehicular gear: jack, spare tire and belts, tire pump, jumper cables, and emergency lights.

Basic survival gear: Bring water, food, blankets, matches, a first-aid kit, insect repellent, sunscreen, and a flashlight. You may also want to add a collapsible shovel and small bucket to the list. A downed tree or dirt road washout from a thunderstorm should not spoil your trip if you are equipped for an unintended stop. Don't forget a backcountry map, compass, flashlight, and—very important in any search and rescue situation—a whistle. Carry your GPS, your cellular phone, and a flashlight, but remember that they operate on batteries and must be kept dry. And, like ET—phone ahead, phone home, and phone often.

Notification safeguard: Because being stranded or injured in the wild poses a greater problem than similar situations at home, it is critical before any outdoor adventure to notify a responsible party of your intended destination and estimated time of return. Contacting that individual upon return completes the safety cycle. This works in reverse, too: If an emergency occurs on the home front, someone may be able to alert you or help the authorities locate you.

At the campground: Zero-impact camping should be everyone's goal, even at developed campgrounds. Keep your site neat—not fastidiously clean, but in reasonable shape. Do not rearrange the site, pound nails in trees, remove ground cover, or dig drainage channels around your tent. If you build a campfire, keep it manageable and follow the site rules—usually, no scrounging for firewood. Heed all rules on campfires, smoking, and wood gathering.

Setting up: Be courteous. Keep your site orderly and avoid blocking roads, hanging towels from tree limbs, and letting the dog out unattended. If you are not qualified to back up an RV, look for campsites with pull-through spots and hope they are unoccupied when you arrive. Or else, practice . . .

Storing food: Store food in closed containers. At night, be sure food and coolers are stowed away in a vehicle or suspended from a high line or, at a minimum, beneath an overturned canoe. There are hungry raccoons, bears, and cougars in Florida, so in some areas you will need to cover and secure the coolers. Bears have learned that coolers hold food, and they have ripped open car doors and tents to reach them. Camping in any remote area in Florida may bring you face to face with these furry and always-hungry wild critters.

Garbage: Dispose of litter properly and often. If no waste facility is provided, you must, as a matter of ethics and law, pack your trash out with you. Use sturdy garbage bags to collect the debris at your site, storing the bags where they are handy for use but are not an eyesore to fellow campers. At night you should stash the bags inside a vehicle to avoid raids by raccoons or bears. Never put garbage down portable toilets, never leave it in washrooms for someone else to deal with, and never just abandon it in a fire pit. If you did not burn your flammable garbage during your stay, pack it out.

Sanitation: Dispose of your wastewater in the provided sites. Bathing, washing dishes, and personal necessary chores should be done well away from natural waters.

Smoking: Florida is in the middle of an extended drought and now, as I write this, wildfires are out of control in Gilchrist and Volusia Counties. If you are found to be responsible for a fire that requires public assistance to extinguish, you could be held liable for financial compensation. So be ultra-immaculately careful with fire.

Courtesy: Please be respectful to the fact that there is no one to clean up after us in the Everglades or the Corkscrew Swamp.

Fee and permits: Most of the areas where you can camp for free require a government permit. Generally there is no charge.

Gearing Up for the Outdoors

Clothing: From April through October, it is usually hot in Florida—hot and humid. Dress accordingly. Bring deodorant, environmentally safe body wash, and lightweight changes of clothing. Hats are mandatory, and not just the John Deere cap you use when mowing the lawn. The sun will bake you down here in the subtropics so, at the risk of being compared to Indiana Jones, something with a wide brim is immensely preferable. If you are visiting during the winter, realize that temperatures in northern Florida fall into the teens a couple of times every year.

Footgear: Sneakers and socks are appropriate in camp and in town. On the trail, you want sturdy, lightweight boots, boots that have a quick drying time because many if not most of Florida's hiking trails are wet, which is described as "damp" down here. In the RV park, kick back and wear your flip-flops.

Equipment: The quantity and variety of equipment you carry depends on where you are going and how long you will be away. Day packs with padded straps or fanny packs offer convenient storage and portability while keeping hands free. Water, snacks, a poncho, money and identification, keys, all-purpose paper, sunglasses, your camera, and binoculars are fine for short hops. For long hikes, buy specialty gear and work up to carrying or kayaking all of the above plus a tent and bedroll.

Sunscreen, bug repellent, and other protection: Buy it. Use it. Every day. When it comes to SPF—sun protection factor—go for the big number. If you're on the St. John's River and it's hot and you're sweating, reapply sunscreen (and deodorant) frequently. (Please do a little research about UVA and UVB protection. Recent studies indicate that most sunscreen formulations are not effective and may, in fact, be dangerous.)

Bug repellent is a sensitive subject. DEET is effective, but it can be dangerous to your health as well as that of the bugs. Still, if you have ever found yourself in a swarm of mosquitoes or biting flies, you know where the edge of sanity lies. Florida has bugs, and many of them bite, so be prepared. You cannot anticipate our Africanized honeybees (the so-called killer bees), and the very best scientific advice if attacked— and you will know it because they swarm—is to run. Run and do not stop. Generally, several hundred yards are required, but run as far as necessary—especially if you are the least bit allergic to a bee sting.

And there are fire ants, so named because their bite is like the touch of a match and they, too, will swarm. Stay away from their noticeable mounds and you should be fine. If bitten, move away and brush off your feet and shoes carefully and immediately. Then use an after-bite formulation to help decrease the stinging pain.

If you ever get an earache after swimming, don't forget those eardrops. An earache can spoil an otherwise marvelous outing. Finally, carry iodine tablets for water and pepper spray for more dangerous wildlife encounters.

Atlases, maps, and brochures: This is Florida. You could wallpaper your house with the material generated by a single chamber of commerce office. Do you have the correct maps for your trip? If you are kayaking across Florida, unless you are in the Panhandle, you will cross multiple jurisdictions. Call ahead and ask for maps. And did I mention a whistle?

What to Do While You're Camping

In Florida, you won't run out of activities on your camping trip. On a warm summer day, the fishing's good, the water's fine, waterways and trails beckon further into the subtropical landscape. If you come during hunting season, there's more down those trails to tempt you.

Swimming and snorkeling: Swimming areas mentioned in this book are typically managed without lifeguards, so swim at your own risk. Visitors should never swim alone, though. Also, always supervise children; survey the area for hazards beforehand; and use common sense with regard to water levels, flow, and water temperature. Chilly temperatures and undertows can disable even the strongest swimmer. While horseplay is common around playgrounds—isn't that what they are there for—drinking should be discouraged. Watch where you dive, as streams and rivers can be shallow.

Like swimmers, snorkelers are found at or near the surface. The two dangers while someone is hunting for scallops or simply looking at a reef are power boaters and sunburn. There is no license—nor should there be—for swimming or snorkeling, but I have found that a colorful, lightweight life vest will help you enjoy the water because it helps you stay afloat and preserve energy, and yes, attach a whistle to that vest. (A yellow or red vest may not be as sexy as a black one, but if you recall the movie *Open Water* where a couple bobbed in the ocean for days, well, that could happen anywhere. Be visible and be safe.)

Kayaking and canoeing: Wonderful activities for most of Florida's inland and Gulf coastal areas. The pace of the river and of your shoulder power is slow enough to appreciate the gorgeous surroundings that Florida offers. As always, get a good map when you apply for a camping permit, a waterproof map if possible, file a "flight plan" with a friend, and watch for power boaters, who often become a little tipsy on petrol fumes. And it isn't only alligators and the very occasional moccasin that will give you the jitters; watch for the rare jumping sturgeon in the lower Suwannee and the flying skates or rays in the Keys. More than one death has been associated with the always-amazing and coincidental impact of a fish with a head. It's true.

Hunting and fishing: Florida welcomes hunters and anglers. Deer, wild turkey, and feral hogs are plentiful here; ducks and morning dove migrate through the state in great numbers. Licenses and information about seasons are readily available at outdoor products stores, bait shops, mass merchants, and via the Internet. In Florida, hiking and biking and camping are done year-round. Hunters get a month or two, max. So wear a little blaze orange in the fall and you ought to be just fine. For anglers, be aware that Florida's shape as a peninsula gives you access to fresh- and saltwater species. Be properly licensed and informed of seasons and limits before you impale a worm or live shrimp with a hook.

Trails and multipurpose trails: The Rails-to-Trails Program is growing—in miles of normally paved and wheelchair-accessible multipurpose trails—and in thousands of users. Florida's citizens have moved the state's politicians toward this concept and the result is that such glorious ribbons as the West Orange Trail or the Gainesville-Hawthorne Trail are available for those who want to get out and bike or hike or skate or even ride horses.

Rules of the trail are easy to follow: Be courteous, be aware of bends that may cause you to wander into the "oncoming lane," and—especially critical—if you're on a bike, yield the path to horses. Historically, horses and bicycles don't mix well and it is the cyclist's responsibility to exercise caution.

Often, a through-hiker can spend the night anywhere along the Florida Trail, free and without special permits, even if there is no designated primitive site nearby. Just move 200 feet off the trail and hang your hammock.

Outdoor Spoilers and Playing Smart

Your trip definitely could be ruined if you get bit, sick, or thirsty under the hot Florida sun. Be mindful of the following:

Water: Just because it looks clean doesn't mean you can drink it. Quite the opposite. You will sweat in Florida, so carry emergency water. Carry iodine tablets or a filtration system. You may never need a ceramic filter but if you are ever thirsty—ever really and seriously thirsty—you'll understand. I personally have given water to two hikers who offered me cash—all the cash they were carrying (I'm not making this up)—for my spare canteen of water.

Things that go bump in the night: Florida has its share of unnerving critters from the invisible chigger that will leave you itching for a week to the plentiful saltwater sharks that may leave you thinking (for a minute) that television is better than the outdoors. In between are alligators (truly dangerous), several varieties of poisonous snakes and spiders, numerous types of biting fly, and the mosquito. Sure, there are bears and panthers, but unfortunately the two most serious outdoor predators are the mosquito (no longer just annoying; they can carry a number of deadly and/or miserable diseases such as encephalitis and dengue fever) and other hominids of the fruit-and-nut persuasion—these, of course, may pop up anywhere. So, along with your insect repellent, I personally recommend carrying some variety of pepper spray on your belt, not in the bottom of your pack.

Getting lost: You perhaps believe that you couldn't get lost in Florida, "Oh, maybe the Everglades, but . . ." That's because you don't have sufficient experience in the outdoors. A person can become absolutely and undeniably dehydrated and die in a square mile a hundred yards from a McDonald's fast-food franchise. Florida has trackless swamps besides the Everglades: the appropriately named Tate's Hell and the Green Swamp and the Okefenokee, and even the lower reaches of the St. John's River. Map, compass, and signal mirror are the tried-and-true saviors, but if you don't know where you are, you won't know which direction you should head, and I have never heard of anyone who used a signal mirror to save their life. So to avoid getting lost, carry a map and a GPS with spare batteries. A whistle and fully-charged cellular phone also, of course. And let people know where you are going and when you will return.

Heat: In the summer—May through September—Florida is one hot and humid place. You gotta stay cool and hydrated: hat and water and rest, hat and water and rest.

Poison ivy/oak: You will come in contact with it in Florida. It's everywhere. Calamine lotion helps, and if you are especially allergic, bring your medicine. Avoiding thrashing about in the woods is a good idea, too, as that also stirs up the mosquitoes. There are plenty of bite salves and ointments on the market, so try them out.

Slithery, crawly things: Florida has rattlesnakes and coral snakes and water moccasins. Except for the very rare moccasin, these critters are not interested in wearing your hats or sleeping in your tent. Stay away from them when you see them and all will be well. Bites from poisonous snakes are so rare in Florida as to be almost unheard of. If you see one, leave it alone: Go the other way. If it takes up residence in your camping area, find a park ranger or manager to move it. Chances are that its GPS is low on batteries.

And related to snakes, the Big Daddy Reptile of Florida, faster than a racehorse in a short sprint: the alligator. It is true that in 2006, gators killed and ate—yes, ate—two people here. But there are a lot of people in Florida. So keep your distance. Do not feed them. In the highly unlikely case that you are bitten and being dragged underwater, the trick is to go for the eyes, or so I've heard.

Enjoying your stay: It may seem that I dwell on the worst-case scenario, but it is my responsibility to alert you to the possibilities. Probably 99.99 percent of the time, however, your camping visit in Florida will leave you with only pleasant memories.

Florida is an immensely diverse, crowded, and lonely place. Almost certainly, you will want to experience its different habitats, from oak hammock forests teeming with deer to beach campgrounds and country music, speeding personal watercraft and sunsets that take your breath away. This is the Sunshine State, after all, and every language is spoken here, so come down, have fun, make memories, and come back again or, as they say locally: "Y'all come back now ya hear."

Map Legend

Transportation

Interstate Highway

U.S. Highway

State Road

County/Forest Road

Hydrology

Body of Water

River/Creek

Marsh/Swamp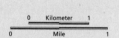

Symbols

Campground

Capital

City

State Line

GEORGIA
FLORIDA

Land Use

National Park/
Forest/Preserve

Reservation
Boundary

Scale

0 Kilometer 1
0 Mile 1

True North

N

The Panhandle Region

C ounties: Escambia, Santa Rosa, Okaloosa, Walton, Holmes, Washington, Jackson, Calhoun, Bay, Gulf, Gadsden, Liberty, Leon, Wakulla, Franklin, Jefferson

		Hookup Sites	Total Sites[1]	Max RV Length	Hookups	Toilets	Showers	Dump Station	Recreation	Fee	Can Reserve
1	Lake Stone Campground	77	77	-	WE	F	Yes	Yes	FBL	$$	Yes
2	Escambia River WMA	-	-	-	-	-	-	-	HFBL, hunting	-	No
3	Escambia County Equestrian Center	35	35	60	WE	F	Yes	Yes	R	$$$	Yes
4	Big Lagoon State Park	75	75	70	WE	F	Yes	Yes	HSFBLC	$$	Yes
5	Gulf Islands National Seashore	-	Group	-	-	F	Rinse only	No	HSFB, scuba, snorkeling	$	Yes
6	Blackwater River State Park	30	30	35	WE	F	Yes	Yes	HSFB tubing	$$	Yes
7	Blackwater River State Forest/WMA	-	-	-	WE	F	Yes	Yes	HSFBLRC, hunting	$-$$	Yes
8	Yellow River WMA	-	-	-	-	-	-	-	HFBL, hunting	-	No
9	Henderson Beach State Park	60	60	60	WE	F	Yes	Yes	HSFC	$$$	Yes
10	Eglin AFB WMA	-	-	-	-	-	-	-	HSFBLR, hunting	-	Yes/No
11	Fred Gannon Rocky Bayou State Park	42	42, T	50	WE	F	Yes	Yes	HSFBLC	$$	Yes
12	Topsail Hill Preserve State Park/ Gregory E. Moore RV Resort	156	156, C	45	WE	F	Yes	Yes	HSFBC	$$	Yes
13	Grayton Beach State Park	37	37, C	48	WE	F	Yes	Yes	HSFBLC	$$	Yes
14	Choctawhatchee River WMA	-	-	-	-	-	-	-	HFBLRC, hunting	-	No
15	Pine Log State Forest/WMA	-	20	-	WE	F	Yes	Yes	HSFBRC, hunting	$-$$	No
16	St. Andrews State Park	176	176, T	45	WE	F	Yes	Yes	HSFBLC, scuba, snorkeling, surfing	$$$	Yes
17	Falling Waters State Park	24	24, T	45	WE	F	Yes	Yes	HSFB	$$	Yes
18	Econfina Creek WMA	-	-	-	-	P	-	-	HSFBLR, hunting	-	No
19	Upper Chipola River WMA	-	-	-	-	-	-	-	HFBLR, hunting	$	No
20	Florida Caverns State Park	38	38, T	50: horse, 40: family WE	F	Yes	Yes		HSFBLRC	$$	Yes
21	Three Rivers State Park	30	30, T, C	50	WE	F	Yes	Yes	HFBLC	$$	Yes
22	Torreya State Park	30	30, T, Y	60	WE	F	Yes	Yes	HB	$$	Yes
23	Ocheesee Landing	-	-	-	-	-	-	-	FBL	-	No
24	Red's Landing	-	-	-	-	-	-	-	FBL	-	No
25	Gulf County Parks	10	20	-	WE	F	Yes	Yes	HFBL	$$	No
26	Apalachicola WMA	-	-	-	-	-	-	-	HFBLR, hunting	-	No
27	T. H. Stone Memorial St. Joseph Peninsula State Park	120	120, T, C	38	WE	F	Yes	Yes	HSFBLC, scuba, snorkeling	$$$	Yes
28	Apalachicola River WEA	-	-	-	-	-	-	-	HSFBLRC, hunting	-	No
29	Dr. Julian G. Bruce St. George Island State Park	60	60, T	43	WE	F	Yes	Yes	HSFBL	$$	Yes
30	Tate's Hell State Forest/WMA	-	-	-	-	-	-	-	HFBLO, hunting	$-$$	No
31	Lake Talquin State Forest	-	-	-	-	-	-	-	HFBLRC, hunting	$-$$	Yes

	Hookup Sites	Total Sites[1]	Max RV Length	Hookups	Toilets	Showers	Dump Station	Recreation	Fee	Can Reserve
32 Joe Budd WMA	-	34	-	-	-	-	-	HFBLC, hunting	-	No
33 Leon County Parks	-	-	-	WE	F	Yes	Yes	HFBLRC, hunting	$-$$	Yes
34 Ochlockonee River State Park	27	30, T	40	WE	F	Yes	Yes	HSFBLC	$$	Yes
35 Apalachicola National Forest	See individual listings for more detailed information. Sites vary from exceedingly primitive to well equipped.							HSFBLC, hunting	$	No
36 Newport Campground	13	34	-	WE	F	Yes	No	HFBL	$$-$$$	Yes
37 Aucilla WMA	-	-	-	-	-	-	-	HSFBLRC, hunting, snorkeling	$	No

Key:
Hookups: W = Water, E = Electricity, S = Sewer, C = Cable, P = Phone, I = Internet
Total Sites: T = Tents, C = Cabins, Y = Yurts
Maximum RV Length: Given in feet
Toilets: F = Flush, NF = No flush
Recreation: H = Hiking, S = Swimming, F = Fishing, B = Boating, L = Boat launch, O = Off-road driving, R = Horseback riding, C = Cycling

[1] T: Almost all Florida state parks have some prepared sites with water and electricity and a primitive camping (youth or group—tent-only) area with cold water available. Camping in the primitive area may be regulated by number of occupants, instead of specific sites. C: cabins are available. Y: This is a yurt, a 20-foot diameter temporary shelter with a wooden frame and canvas covering, heat, air-conditioning, and water. Camping in Florida's state forests, like the national forests, is regulated by area rather than site.

NOTE: The following state parks, state forests, and wildlife management areas in this region do not offer camping at present: Alfred B. Maclay Gardens, Apalachee WMA, Bald Point, Box-R WMA, Bluewater Creek WMA, Bradwell Unit—Apalachicola WMA, Camp Helen, Carr Unit—Blackwater WMA, Constitution Convention Museum, Deer Lake, Econfina River, Eden Gardens, Edward Ball Wakulla Springs (rustic lodge), Flint Rock WMA, John Gorrie Museum, Holmes Creek Water Management. Area, L. Kirk Edwards WEA, Lafayette Creek WMA, Little Jackson Mounds Archaeological, Lake Talquin, Letchworth-Love Mounds, Natural Bridge Battlefield Historic, Ochlockonee River WMA, Orman House, Perdido Key, Perdido River WMA, Point Washington State Park/WMA, Ponce de Leon Springs, Robert Brent WMA, San Marcos de Apalache Historic, Talquin WMA, Tarkiln Bayou Preserve, Wakulla State Forest, and Yellow River Marsh Preserve.

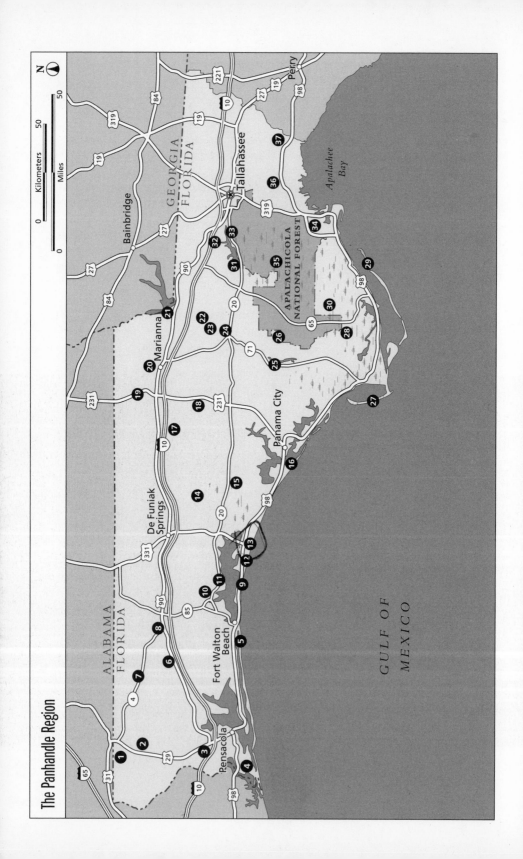

The Panhandle Region

1 Lake Stone Campground

Location: 801 W. SR 4, Century, FL, in Escambia County (30° 58' 13.9" N, 87° 17' 2.4" W)
Season: Year-round
Sites: 77 (Reservations can be made forty-five days in advance, but not for specific sites. Specific site assignment is first-come, first-served: lake_stone@co.escambia.fl.us.)
Maximum length: None
Facilities: Full-facility camping; water, electricity (20/30/50 amp), fire rings, nearby office with camp store and attendant. Escambia County has recently upgraded amenities to accommodate larger RVs and group camping. The campground also offers a boat ramp, public-use building, playground, hot showers, wheelchair-accessible restrooms, fishing pier, security lights, 2 sewage dump stations, and picnic areas.
Fee per night: $$
Management: Escambia County Parks & Recreation Department
Contact: (850) 256-5555, www.co.escambia.fl.us
Finding the campground: From I-10, turn north onto Pensacola Boulevard/CR95/US 29 at exit 10. Continue north almost to the state line to Century, and turn left (west) on CR 4/Bratt Road. Watch for signs and turn left (south) onto Lake Stone Road in about 2 miles.

While on the trail or looking for a primitive campsite, pay attention to trail and border signs, whose color-coded messages offer useful information.

About the campground: Beautiful cypress-ringed Lake Stone is the chief attraction at this quiet, family-friendly, one-hundred-acre campground that occasionally hosts local events: groups playing cards, small concerts, and even dances in the pavilion. You will find it comfortable, if not exciting. When the family is ready to escape your cooking, fast food is just a few miles away in the town of Century.

Every type of camper is accommodated here, from pup tents to expensive RVs, and leashed pets are welcomed too. Many sites are shaded and grassy; some are adjacent to the lake, so you could, in theory, fish right from your sleeping bag. It is the only Escambia County camping facility located on a freshwater lake. The period between 10:00 p.m. and 7:00 a.m. is designated as quiet time and, with an attendant on-site, this can be enforced. The boat ramp is well maintained, but gas-powered motors are not permitted on the lake. Boaters must break out the oars and trolling motor, or put their canoes and kayaks in this freshwater lake. A fish-cleaning stand is provided.

2 Escambia River Wildlife Management Area

Location: North of Pensacola and east of US 29 along the Escambia River in Escambia and Santa Rosa Counties (30° 26' 13" N, 87° 12' 33" W)
Season: Year-round
Sites: Except where prohibited, primitive camping is permitted throughout the area. You must take in everything you need, however, and take out everything you use. Campers are limited to tents, trailers, or self-propelled camping vehicles only.

One group campsite is available at Mystic Springs—limit 25 people—with a permit ($$$) from the Northwest Florida Water Management District, (850) 539-5999.
Facilities: The Mystic Spring campsite has picnic tables, fire rings, trails, charcoal grills, toilet, pavilion, and nearby boat ramp.
Fee per night: Call for current information
Management: Fish & Wildlife Conservation Commission (FWC) and Northwest Florida Water Management District (WMD)
Contact: (850) 539-5999, http://myfwc.com
Finding the campground: From I-10 in Pensacola, take exit 10 and drive north on US 29 about 25 miles. Mystic Springs Road is on your right between the crossroads of Bogia and the campground.
About the campground: At nearly 35,000 acres, this primitive area occupies both the east and west banks along 25 miles of the Escambia River, which separates Escambia and Santa Rosa Counties.

For recreational users, there are a dozen boat ramps in the WMA primarily for fishermen and for casual boaters. The Escambia River is a superior spot for a variety of freshwater fish available to anglers.

Most of the river in the WMA is bordered by floodplain forests or flatwoods, and heavy rains can cause the river to rise and the forests to flood quickly. Outdoor recreational users need to be aware of this tendency and that some of the diseases (encephalitis, for example) carried by a myriad of mosquitoes will almost certainly be encountered. Bug spray? Don't enter this WMA without it.

Hunting is permitted in season and is a primary recreational activity here. During any hunting season, be aware that thousands of people are in the woods with firearms or bows and arrows. The southern portion of the WMA is a dog hunt area, which means that hunters use trained hounds to flush game from deep cover.

3 Escambia County Equestrian Center

Location: 7750 Mobile Highway, Pensacola, in Escambia County (30° 30' 47.9" N, 87° 22' 11.5" W)
Season: During scheduled equestrian events
Sites: 35 RV sites only
Maximum length: 60 feet
Facilities: Full hookups
Fee per night: $$$
Management: Escambia County Parks & Recreation Department
Contact: (850) 941-6042, www.co.escambia.fl.us
Finding the campground: From I-10, take exit 5 and drive west on US 90/Nine Mile Road. Turn left (south) after about 3 miles on CR 99/Beulah Road. After 1.5 miles, turn left (southeast) on Mobile Highway/Business US 90. The Equestrian Center is less than 1 mile on the north side of the road.
About the campground: The Equestrian Center is a 178-acre equine park in Pensacola. Designed as a multifunction event facility, the center hosts numerous horse shows, rodeos, dog shows, and all types of private and public events. The site includes a 4,500-seat covered arena, three outdoor arenas, and thirty-five RV sites with full hookups, which can be reserved during equestrian events.

4 Big Lagoon State Park

Location: 10 miles southwest of Pensacola in Escambia County (30° 19' 12.5" N, 87° 24' 13.4" W)
Season: Year-round
Sites: 75
Maximum length: 70 feet
Facilities: Full-facility camping with water, electricity, and bathhouses
Fee per night: $$
Management: Florida Division of Recreation and Parks
Contact: (850) 492-1595, www.floridastateparks.org/biglagoon/default.cfm, www.reserve america.com
Finding the campground: Located at 12301 Gulf Beach Highway, approximately 10 miles southwest of Pensacola. From I-10, take exit 7 south on Pineforest Road/SR 297, for about 4 miles to the intersection with US 90. Continue south on US 90 and turn right (west) on SR 296/Saufley Field Road. In a little over 1 mile, turn left (south) on Blue Angel Parkway/SR 173 and continue south for about 10 miles. At this point, Blue Angel Parkway will continue forward into a military base and you will turn right onto SR 292A/Gulf Beach Hwy. The entrance will be on your left in a little over 4 miles.
About the campground: Big Lagoon is a coastal park that occupies the north shore of the Intracoastal Waterway, here named "Big Lagoon." Like so many others along Florida's coastline, the park caters to visitors who are interested in recreation in and on the water. Hence, there is swimming and a boat ramp, fishing, and plenty of paddle sports. Beaches here are not what one expects from those bordering the Gulf of Mexico, though, and are typically quite narrow. Be aware of boat traffic offshore.

At 712 acres, the site offers more than just lake sports; hiking the site's trails, picnicking, and group camping are popular. Several boardwalks and two fine wooden observation towers afford a wide view of the marsh and the Intracoastal. The park is part of the Great Florida Birding Trail, so kiosks with pictures and interpretive information are plentiful. Most campsites are quite private, screened by brush, palmetto, and trees.

5 Gulf Islands National Seashore

Location: The Seashore is in Florida, Alabama, and Mississippi, and all districts are south of I-10 on the Gulf of Mexico. In Alabama, take exit 57 or 50 to US 90 to Ocean Springs. In Florida, use exit 12 to I-110 or exit 22 to the Garcon Point Bridge to US 98 (30° 21' 52" N, 86° 58' 3" W).
Season: Year-round
Sites: Camping programs and facilities have been disrupted because of damage from hurricane activity in 2004 and 2005, and visitation has dropped from 5 million to 1.5 million per year, but restoration is in progress with facility repairs and some roads reopening.

Primitive camping is allowed on the eastern end of Perdido Key, beginning a half-mile east of the end of Johnson Beach Road. Campers need to avoid dunes and vegetated areas, and pack in and out all supplies (and trash). Fires are allowed on the beach below the extreme high tide. Most campers arrive by small boat, landing on the northern side of the island. For information about group and primitive camping here and at the wooded, 1,378-acre Naval Live Oaks Youth Camp-ground on US 98 east of Gulf Breeze, call (850) 492-0912/492-7278. (A day-use picnic area with comfort station and hiking trails along the beach and through the woods are also located there as are the sites of Native American campsites.) Some primitive camping is also allowed at Fort Pickens. Loops A, C, and E allow tent camping for "self-contained camping." One hundred fifty-eight sites are available on a first-come, first-served basis (without electricity or potable water). At this writing, repairs were scheduled to be completed in fall 2009.
Maximum length: Call for current information
Facilities: Primitive camping is allowed on Perdido Key on a pack-in, pack-out basis. Fort Pickens has portable toilets in the parking lot at Langdon Beach. An outdoor shower is available at Battery Worth. Some sites have picnic tables and are thinly shaded. Campers should take enough water for washing, drinking, and cleaning (usually 1 gallon per person per day).
Fee per night: $
Management: National Park Service
Contact: (850) 934-2600, www.nps.gov/guis/index.htm
Finding the seashore: The Perdido Key Area is off SR 292, southwest from Pensacola. Turn east on Johnson Beach Road. The Naval Live Oaks Area is on US 98 east of Gulf Breeze. The Okaloosa Day-Use Area is on US 98 east of Fort Walton Beach. To reach Fort Barrancas and the Advanced Redoubt Area on Pensacola Naval Air Station, use the Blue Angel Parkway (SR 173). The Fort Pickens Area is west of Pensacola Beach on Santa Rosa Island. (The damaged Fort Pickens Road has been closed to vehicles for several years, but visitors may use it for biking or hiking.) Water taxi service is available to the Fort Pickens Area. It is approximately a 2-mile, one-way hike to the fort from the drop off point. Contact Chulamar Charters, (850) 494-1099, for information and

reservations. The Santa Rosa Area is located east of Pensacola Beach. The J. Earle Bowden Way Area (SR 399) is intermittently closed to vehicles but visitors may walk or boat into the area.

About the seashore: Gulf Islands, America's largest National Seashore, consists of eleven separate units stretching along 150 miles from West Ship Island in Mississippi to the eastern tip of Santa Rosa Island in Florida. Visitors will experience sparkling unspoiled waters, beautiful snow-white beaches, and coastal marshes and maritime forests. There are prehistoric shell mounds and brick fortifications dating from the 1820s to as late as the 1940s, and yes, Civil War history runs deep here.

You can drive to some park areas, but others require a boat. Normally, four visitor centers in Florida and Mississippi offer help with visit planning. During years of high hurricane activity in the Gulf, these may not be open, however. Otherwise, Gulf Islands encourages bicycling, swimming, snorkeling, fishing, hiking, beach combing, bird watching, and boating. Pets are allowed in the park, but not on the beach. Insect repellent is absolutely necessary.

6 Blackwater River State Park

Location: 15 miles northeast of Milton off US 90 in Santa Rosa County (30° 42' 42.1" N, 86° 52' 44.6" W)

Season: Year-round

Sites: The park's 30 campsites have been renovated and are expected to re-open soon; call for current information.

Maximum length: 35 feet

Facilities: Full-facility camping with water, electric hookups, and bathhouses

Fee per night: $$

Management: Florida Division of Recreation and Parks

Contact: (850) 983-5363, www.floridastateparks.org/blackwaterriver/default.cfm, www .reserveamerica.com

Finding the campground: From I-10, take exit 31 in east Pensacola onto SR 87 and head north. After 0.5 mile, turn right (east) on US 90. It is 7 miles to the left turn (north) onto Deaton Bridge Road and 3 miles to the main gate.

About the campground: Blackwater River is only 590 acres, but it encompasses a fine section of the Blackwater River. The river itself has a pure sand bottom, and its banks and the many sandbars are excellent for swimming, tubing, splashing, fishing, and generally having a great time. Although the water—which averages only 2.5 feet in depth—is a deep golden brown, stained with leeched tannin from tree roots, the river's environment contrasts remarkably with the often muddy and smelly swamp rivers of the region.

While Blackwater is a destination for canoeists and kayakers, its shallow depth and multitude of other users may make a paddle frustrating, depending upon a person's sense of humor. Canoe and tube rentals are available from outfitters in the area. The park's shaded and recently renovated campsites are a short walk from the river. Several trails offer excursions to the interior of the park.

7 Blackwater River State Forest and Blackwater Wildlife Management Areas

Location: Forest headquarters is located 20 miles north of Milton on SR 191/Munson Highway in the community of Munson/Belandville. The forest covers parts of both Santa Rosa and Okaloosa Counties (30° 51' 27" N, 86° 52' 22" W)

Season: Year-round

Sites/Facilities: The following recreation areas offer campsites (except noted) in Blackwater River State Forest/WMA:

Bear Lake: 107 acres, electricity, restrooms, showers; boat ramps, pier, hiking trails; fishing, hunting, hiking, mountain-biking, canoeing

Camp Paquette: youth groups only; restrooms, showers, trail; hiking, fishing, canoeing, swimming

Coldwater: electricity, restrooms, showers, equestrian trails, horse stalls (reservations required; call (850) 957-6161 weekdays between 7:00 a.m. and 3:30 p.m. CST)

Hurricane Lake (318 acres):

- North Area—electricity, restrooms, showers, single-lane boat ramp, unimproved parking lot for twenty-five vehicles; canoeing, hiking (reservations required for primitive camping with restrooms nearby)

- South Area—primitive camping with restrooms, picnic facilities, limited number of water faucets, boat launch; canoeing, fishing, boating

Karick Lake (65 acres):

- North Area—electricity, water, restrooms, showers, boat ramp, pier; hiking, fishing, canoeing (reservations required for primitive camping in youth area with restrooms nearby)

- South Area—water, electricity, restrooms, showers, boat ramp; fishing, canoeing, boating

Krul: electricity, restrooms, showers, hiking trails; campsites are beside a five-acre lake; swimming, fishing, hiking

Maximum length: Call for current information

Fee per night: $ (seniors and primitive sites); $$ (sites with electricity and/or water)

Management: Division of Forestry and Fish & Wildlife Conservation Commission

Contact: (850) 957-6140, www.fl-dof.com/state_forests/blackwater_river.html, http://myfwc .com and www.floridatrail.org

Finding the forest: The forest and the contiguous, overlapping management area are located northeast of Pensacola. The area borders Conecuh National Forest and extends southward toward Eglin Air Force Base. Headquarters are 20 miles north of Milton on SR 191 in the community of Munson/Belandville.

About the forest: The gently rolling longleaf pine and wiregrass ecosystem of this 206,350-acre area once covered sixty million acres in the southeastern U.S. With the Conecuh National Forest to the north and Eglin Air Force Base to the south, it is the largest contiguous ecological community of this type in the world. Thus camping here is a privilege, because longleaf pine communities are rich in established plant and animal life, including many species classified for protection.

This is not flatwoods and swamp, though there are isolated areas inside the WMA and forest. This is well-drained sandy upland and your camping and nature experience will reflect that. Many lovely streams cut through the area as does the Florida Scenic Trail, and the area is part of the Great Florida Birding Trail also. Visitors need to be aware that prescribed burning, timber harvesting, and hunting are part of WMA-managed activites.

8 Yellow River Wildlife Management Area

Location: In Santa Rosa and Okaloosa Counties this WMA parallels I-10 between Milton (30° 37' 49" N, 87° 02' 47" W) and Crestview (30° 45' 15" N, 86° 34' 22" W)
Season: Year-round
Sites: Camping in tents, trailers, and self-propelled vehicles is permitted throughout, except at Grassy Point, where camping is restricted and authorized by permit only from the Northwest Florida Water Management District.
Maximum length: Call for current information
Facilities: Call for current information
Management: Fish & Wildlife Conservation Commission (FWC) and Northwest Florida Water Management District (WMD)
Fee per night: Free except for special occasions at Grassy Point
Contact: FWC, (850) 265-3676; NFWMD, (850) 539-5999, www.floridatrail.org, http://myfwc .com, www.nwfwmd.state.fl.us
Finding the campground: From I-10, take exit 56 and drive north on SR 85 to Crestview. Turn left (west) on US 90 and drive about 3 miles to the Yellow River. Or from I-10, take exit 31, which is east of Milton, and drive south on SR 87 for 3.5 miles to the Yellow River.
About the campground: Three attractions highlight this lightly visited but beautiful 18,555-acre area: the canoe/kayak trail along the Yellow River, habitat for carnivorous plants at Garcon Point Peninsula (between Escambia and Blackwater Bays), and an abundance of birds.

The state has purchased land along 20 miles of the Yellow River. From its banks you can hike, fish, hunt, camp, and bird-watch. You also might see black bear, jumping Gulf sturgeon, plenty of mayflies, and common plants such as mountain laurel and spider lilies. The outlook is less certain for the small and endangered Okaloosa darter.

If you're interested in carnivorous plants, the diverse habitats (tidal marsh, wet prairie, and flatwoods) of Garcon Point Peninsula may offer you a look at carnivorous sundews, butterwort, and bladderworts. These areas also brim with wild flowers including orchids.

Campers should bring DEET and also watch the weather: Heavy rainfall on the Yellow River frequently results in flooding.

9 Henderson Beach State Park

Location: East of the city of Destin on US 98 in Okaloosa County (30° 23' 11.8" N, 86° 26' 51.1" W)
Season: Year-round
Sites: 60
Maximum length: 60 feet

Florida boasts an award-winning system of state parks. Most require reservations, but the atmosphere and, usually, the amenities are wonderful.

Facilities: Water and electricity; bathhouses (heated and air-conditioned); coin-operated washers, dryers, vending machines; boardwalk with cold showers and beach access; covered pavilions for picnicking and grilling; playground; nature trail; paved bike road; back-in and pull-through sites for RVs; available beach wheelchairs. Pets allowed under owner-control and off campsite with leash.
Fee per night: $$$
Management: Florida Division of Recreation and Parks
Contact: (850) 837-7550, www.floridastateparks.org; (800) 326-3521, www.reserveamerica.com
Finding the campground: From I-10 in the west Florida Panhandle, take any exit south to US 98. The park is located east on Eglin AFB and Ft. Walton, next to Destin and immediately adjacent to the highway.
About the campground: Florida is known for nicely situated and well-maintained state parks, and this is one of the best. Though only 208 acres, Henderson Beach occupies more than 1 mile of shoreline. Its white-sand beaches are scenic and ideal for sunbathing and swimming, and fishing is fine in the clean, clear waters of the Gulf of Mexico.

Endangered sea turtles nest along this beach in May and June. Hatchlings fight their way out of the eggs and sand in late summer and early fall, so there may be occasional restrictions about use of the beach and lights along the shoreline as stray lights may confuse helpless baby turtles.

10 Eglin Air Force Base Wildlife Management Area

Location: In Santa Rosa, Okaloosa, and Walton Counties. The Jackson Guard, which issues permits, is located in Niceville on US 85 North (30° 30' 58" N, 86° 28' 18" W)
Season: Year-round
Sites: The Anderson Pond Recreation Area just north of Niceville offers camping. In addition, sections of the Florida National Scenic Trail cross the Eglin WMA (http://westgate.floridatrail.org/EglinTrailSketches.html), and each section of the trail—Weaver Creek, Titi Creek, Catface, and Alaqua—has designated primitive trailhead campsites (two other sections are under development).
Maximum length: Call for current information
Facilities: Anderson Pond Recreation Area—elevated boardwalk, picnic shelter, pier, and camping area with wheelchair-accessible facilities
Management: Fish & Wildlife Conservation Commission and U.S. Air Force
Contact: (850) 882-4164, http://myfwc.com, www.floridatrail.org, http://floridabirdingtrail.com (for information on Eglin's outdoor recreation, camping, hunting, and fishing permits, call The Jackson Guard permit sales lobby at (850) 882-4165/882-4166)
Finding the campground: To reach the Niceville-area campsites, drive south from I-10 either at exit 56, SR 85, or at exit 70, SR 285. The Jackson Guard, or Eglin Natural Resources Branch, is located on US 85 just north of SR 20.
About the campground: Eglin AFB covers nearly half a million acres. There are bombing and gun ranges with unexploded ordnance, secret installations, and army rangers in training, so it is not a place you want to lose your way in or casually discover that you do not have the correct permits.

An Eglin permit is required to access 280,000 acres of this military reservation that is conditionally open for recreation: public use is of secondary importance to military needs. Recreation permits and a comprehensive map and regulation summary are available from the Natural Resources Branch office (commonly referred to as The Jackson Guard) at 107 US 85 North, in Niceville.

Eglin WMA nevertheless has a great deal to recommend it. It is a beautiful area of mostly open pine and palmetto uplands. Recreational opportunities are outstanding: hunting, fishing twenty-one ponds, canoeing/kayaking, mountain biking, and hiking the Florida National Scenic Trail.

More than ninety-three rare or listed plant and animal species are found on this WMA, sixty-three of which are considered "globally rare." The area is a site on the Great Florida Birding Trail, too.

11 Fred Gannon Rocky Bayou State Park

Location: East of Niceville-Valparaiso on the south side of Rocky Bayou, an arm of Choctawatchee Bay, and surrounded by Eglin Air Force Base in Okaloosa County (30° 29' 46.8" N, 86° 25' 57.1" W)
Season: Year-round
Sites: 42, plus primitive camping (including youth groups; pets welcome on leashes)
Maximum length: 50 feet
Facilities: Full-facility camping. Four wheelchair-accessible sites are situated next to a heated, air-conditioned shower facility; emergency telephone, vending machines, coin-operated laundry facilities; canoe rental available at the park office.
Fee per night: $$

Management: Florida Division of Recreation and Parks

Contact: (850) 833-9144, www.floridastateparks.org/rockybayou/default.cfm; (800) 326-3521, www.reserveamerica.com

Finding the campground: From the west, take I-10 to SR 85, exit 56, and drive south through Eglin AFB to SR 20. (From the east, turn south on SR 285, exit 70.) Turn left (east) on SR 20. The park entrance is approximately 5 miles on the left (north) side of the highway.

About the campground: Rocky Bayou Aquatic Preserve is this park's main feature. The trailing arm of Choctawhatchee Bay, the Preserve is excellent for both freshwater and saltwater fishing, boating, and kayaking or canoeing. The park says its double-lane boat ramp is "one of the best launches on the bay."

Rocky Bayou also preserves towering old-growth longleaf pines, several of which are more than three hundred years old. These great pines once dominated north and central Florida. They were extensively harvested for ship masts and "farmed" by the naval stores/turpentine industry. Their restoration is a principal objective of many Florida naturalists.

Although the park is only 357 acres in extent, it offers several hiking trails and freshwater fishing and canoeing on the oddly named Puddin' Head Lake.

12 Topsail Hill Preserve State Park/ Gregory E. Moore RV Resort

Location: In Santa Rosa Beach east of Destin in Walton County (30° 22' 31.2" N, 86° 17' 58.4" W)

Season: Year-round

Sites: 154, plus 16 cabins

Maximum length: 45 feet

Facilities: Full-facility camping, swimming pool, tennis and shuffleboard courts, furnished bungalows for weeklong visits, camp store

Fee per night: $$

Management: Florida Division of Recreation and Parks

Contact: (850) 833-9144, www.floridastateparks.org/rockybayou/default.cfm; (800) 326-3521, www.reserveamerica.com

Finding the campground: Located in Santa Rosa Beach 10 miles east of Destin. Take I-10 to exit 85 (DeFuniak Springs) and follow US 331 south for about 27 miles to US 98. Turn right (west) for approximately 5 miles. Watch for the signs and turn left (south) on SR 30A. The park entrance is in about 1 mile.

About the campground: As this guide is written, Topsail is upgrading many of its facilities including camping and accessibility features within the 1,643-acre park. When completed—and consistent with the recovery of Florida's economy—this should be a wonderful place to pitch a tent or park an RV.

Plenty of activities—swimming, sunbathing, cycling, and hiking the nature trail—are available behind the 3.2 miles of white-sand beach and the exquisite dunes, some of which reach 25 feet in height. Rare "coastal dune lakes" provide excellent freshwater fishing for bass, bream, and catfish, and, properly licensed, you can also fish the Gulf shore. Unfortunately or fortunately, depending upon your point of view, boats are not allowed in the park, and there is no launching facility. A tram is available to shuttle visitors from the day parking area to the beach.

13 Grayton Beach State Park

Location: Near the town of Grayton Beach on CR 30A south of US 98 in Walton County (30° 19' 58.36" N, 86° 9' 27.06" W)
Season: Year-round
Sites: 37 campsites in a wooded area near or next to Western Lake and 30 two-bedroom, one-bath cabins on the western end of the park
Maximum length: 48 feet
Facilities: Sites have picnic tables, grills, water, and electricity. Ice and firewood are sold at the park entrance. A private boardwalk leads to the Gulf beaches.
Fee per night: $$
Management: Florida Division of Recreation and Parks
Contact: (850) 833-9144, www.floridastateparks.org/rockybayou/default.cfm; (800) 326-3521, www.reserveamerica.com
Finding the campground: This state park is south of US 98 approximately halfway between Panama City Beach and Destin. Take CR 283 south from US 98 and turn left (east) at the stop sign on CR 30A. The entrance is about 0.5 mile east of the intersection of CR 30A and CR 283.
About the campground: When snow falls and wind blows, many a northerner dreams of a sunny Florida white-sand beach with a gentle breeze and a magnificent sunset. Grayton Beach is the place they are dreaming about even if they do not know its name.

At only 2,200 acres, Grayton Beach may be overshadowed by such internationally recognized places as Daytona, Ft. Lauderdale, and Miami, all of which are wonderful if you like crowds and souvenir stands and fast-food establishments. If you are looking for a true beach getaway, however, and a relaxed camping experience, Florida's Gulf Coast beaches are hard to beat.

This mile-long, sugar-sand beach allows visitors to swim and sunbathe and even try their hand at ocean kayaking and surf fishing. One can rent a canoe and paddle the park's Western Lake for a close look at a salt marsh ecosystem. A boat ramp on the lake allows both freshwater and saltwater fishing.

Several trails for hikers and bikers wind through a coastal forest of scrub oaks and magnolias, trees bent and twisted by salt winds, which have an eerie "Middle Earth" look, much like the landscape described in books by author J.R.R. Tolkien. Park rangers provide programs seasonally.

14 Choctawhatchee River Wildlife Management Area

Location: In Bay, Holmes, Walton, and Washington Counties. The Tilley Landing camping area is not far from Redbay, an unincorporated hamlet in Walton County (30° 35' 31" N, 85° 56' 42" W)
Season: Year-round
Sites: According to the Fish & Wildlife Conservation Commission, primitive camping is permitted throughout the area, but limited to tents, trailers, and self-propelled camping vehicles. The WMD, however, provides a specific open camping location at Tilley Landing Recreational Area on Lost Lake.
Maximum length: Call for current information
Facilities: At Tilley Landing, covered picnic pavilion with tables and grills, parking, and a stabilized (unpaved) boat ramp

Management: Fish & Wildlife Conservation Commission (FWC) and Northwest Florida Water Management District (WMD)

Contact: FWC, (850) 265-3676, or WMD, (850) 539-5999, http://myfwc.com, www.nwfwmd .state.fl.us

Finding the campground: From I-10, take exit 96 and drive south about 10 miles on SR 81—past the unincorporated hamlet of Redbay—and then watch for signs on the left (east) side of the road.

About the campground: This is the kind of flatwoods and swampy region where interesting things might happen, if you were lucky. There is a chance that in the old growth bottomland hardwood forests you might hear or see a bird long thought to be extinct, the ivory-billed woodpecker. There have been documented incidents where biologists recorded its call. Wouldn't that be worth a week in the swamp.

This 57,000-acre WMA is strung along more than 30 miles of the Choctawhatchee through less than well-heeled or well-populated counties.

Because most of the area is prone to flooding, access is primarily by boat, and there are numerous boat landings along the Choctawhatchee and Holmes Creek. By last count, 31 boat ramps are maintained between the Alabama border and the Bay. Vehicle access is limited.

Hunting and fishing are the primary recreational activities here, but campers and other visitors enjoy recreational boating, hiking, horseback riding, and bird-watching.

15 Pine Log State Forest and Pine Log Wildlife Management Area

Location: South of Ebro in northwestern Bay and southwestern Washington Counties, 14 miles north of Panama City Beach on SR 79 (30° 26' 35" N, 85° 52' 51" W)

Season: Year-round

Sites: 20 in the recreation area, plus specific primitive youth/group areas. The WMA is inside the boundaries of the state forest, near Ebro. Camping is permitted at 3 designated primitive campsites and at the Sand Pine Campground. First-come, first served camping is allowed only at designated primitive campsites and the Sand Pond campground; daily fee required.

Maximum length: Call for current information

Facilities: Full-facility camping

Fee per night: $ (seniors and primitive sites); $$ (sites with electricity and/or water). Fees are due after site selection. A self-service pay station is located at the campground entrance.

Management: Division of Forestry and Fish & Wildlife Conservation Commission

Contact: (850) 535-2888/872-4175, www.fl-dof.com, http://myfwc.com/recreation/cooperative/ pine_log.asp

Finding the forest: From I-10, take SR 81 south at exit 96. After about 22 miles, turn left (east) on SR 20. It is a little more than 5 miles to the community of Ebro and the intersection with SR 79. The forest is south and east of Ebro, and access is available from SR 79 or on marked forest roads. The campground is about 1 mile south of Ebro and west of SR 79 off Crews Lake Road.

About the forest: Like many remote areas in Florida's Panhandle, this 6,911-acre forest and WMA is managed for multiple uses, from commercial forestry to recreation. Purchased nearly seventy years ago, Pine Log was Florida's first state forest and more than a million dollars of timber is still harvested here each year.

Campers routinely see white-tailed deer, and the sighting of a black bear is not impossible. There are tortoises and an abundance of bird species. In addition, the forest offers maintained trials that offer opportunities to hike, cycle (single-track trails only), and ride horses. Cyclists should beware of startling horses and give plenty of leeway to riders. Swimming (in East Lake beside the camping area), fishing, and hunting are permitted activities. Pets on leashes are allowed.

16 St. Andrews State Park/State Recreation Area

Location: Southwest of Panama City and east of CR 3031 in Bay County (30° 8' 4.7" N, 85° 44' 38.3" W)
Season: Year-round
Sites: 176
Maximum length: 45 feet
Facilities: Full-facility camping plus primitive youth group camping; two piers, jetty, boat ramp, fenced playground, covered beachside pavilions
Fee per night: $$$
Management: Florida Division of Recreation and Parks
Contact: (850) 833-9144, www.floridastateparks.org/rockybayou/default.cfm; (800) 326-3521, www.reserveamerica.com
Finding the campground: From US 98, which parallels Florida's Gulf Coast, turn south on CR 3031 (Thomas Drive) just west of Panama City. Follow Thomas Drive to CR 392 and turn left (southeast) to enter the park.
About the campground: St. Andrews occupies most of the tip of a peninsula south of Panama City, an area popularly called America's "Redneck Riviera," because its beaches and multiple touristy attractions are easily available to residents not only of Florida, but Georgia and Alabama as well.

A former military installation, St. Andrews has miles of "sugar-white sand" beaches and, beyond them, the clear, emerald green waters of the Gulf of Mexico and, to a lesser extent, the Grand Lagoon. Water-related activities are available here in abundance: swimming, sunbathing, snorkeling, scuba diving, surfing, kayaking and canoeing, and fishing.

Two nature trails offer opportunities to spot deer and alligators. Bird-watching opportunities are spectacular too: look for eagles, herons, osprey, pelicans, and dozens of other species. Tours to offshore Shell Island are available spring and summer.

17 Falling Waters State Park

Location: 3 miles south of Chipley off SR 77A in Washington County (30° 43' 52.8" N, 85° 31' 44.3" W)
Season: Year-round
Sites: 24, plus primitive and youth group camping
Maximum length: 45 feet

Facilities: Full-facility camping with 24 shaded campsites, picnic tables, ground grills, clotheslines plus access to water and electricity, restrooms, a dump station for RVs, nearby showers with hot water

Fee per night: $$

Management: Florida Division of Recreation and Parks

Contact: (850) 638-6130, www.floridastateparks.org/fallingwaters/default.cfm, www.reserve america.com

Finding the campground: From I-10, take exit 120 and drive south on SR 77A approximately 1 mile. Turn left (east) onto State Park Road and follow it to the park entrance.

About the campground: This fine 171-acre park is built around Florida's highest waterfall. Dropping 73 feet, water from a small stream falls into a 100-foot-deep, 20-foot-wide cylindrical pit and disappears into the aquifer. Large trees and fern-covered sinks line Sink Hole Trail, the boardwalk that leads to the waterfall.

Falling Waters Park has a two-acre lake where visitors can swim, sunbathe, and fish; a butterfly garden; playground; and nature trails. Ranger-led campfire circles and interpretive programs round out park activities.

A portion of the campsite is one of Florida's highest hills, 324 feet above sea level. (Britton Hill in Walton County is Florida's highest point at 345 feet.)

18 Econfina Creek Wildlife Management Area

Location: In Washington, Jackson, and Bay Counties west of US 231 roughly between Alford (30° 41' 41" N, 85° 23' 35" W) and Fountain (30° 28' 44" N, 85° 25' 11" W)

Season: Year-round

Sites: Camping is allowed only at designated sites, but reservations are not needed for primitive camping. Primitive campsites are available first-come, first-served and have been established at a number of places along Econfina Creek, at Porter Lake (Tom Johns and White Oak boat landings), and at the Pine Ridge Equestrian Trail Campground. The Crooms Branch Mobility Impaired Campground is open during hunting season only.

Group Camping is available at Blue Spring, Rattlesnake Lake North and South, and Sparkleberry Pond. There is no charge, but group camping does require a reservation; an application is on line on the WMD site.

Maximum length: Call for current information

Facilities: Covered pavilions, picnic tables, fire rings, grills, and portable toilets are provided.

Management: Fish & Wildlife Conservation Commission (FWC) and Northwest Florida Water Management District (WMD)

Contact: FWC, (850) 265-3676, or WMD, (850) 539-5999, www.floridatrail.org, http://myfwc .com, www.nwfwmd.state.fl.us

Finding the WMA: Take exit 130 south from I-10 onto US 231. This WMA sits to the west of 231, roughly between Alford and Fountain. Most of the campsites are in Washington County; the wheelchair-accessible campground is in Bay.

About the WMA: This 41,159-acre management area runs for 14 miles along the course of Econfina Creek. It encompasses miles of sandhill uplands with dozens of shallow, clear, sand-bottomed lakes. These uplands are now being restored to longleaf pine and wiregrass habitat.

Along the heavily shaded creek, hardwood forests and hammocks grow above fern-covered limestone bluffs and outcrops. In spring, visitors may see blossoming dogwoods and other flowering plants, including redbuds, mountain laurel, and wild azaleas.

Recreational activities include hunting, fishing, hiking (on a 14-mile segment of the Florida National Scenic Trail), horseback riding, swimming, bird-watching, and paddling. The Econfina is a fine canoe trail and a site on the Great Florida Birding Trail.

19 Upper Chipola River Wildlife Management Area

Location: In Jackson County north of Florida Caverns State Park (30° 48' 50" N, 85° 13' 59" W) and Marianna, the county seat of Jackson County
Season: Year-round
Sites: Camping is allowed at designated sites. A primitive campsite is located immediately west of the Christoff boat landing.
Maximum length: Call for current information
Facilities: Call for current information
Fee per night: Call for current information
Management: Fish & Wildlife Conservation Commission (FWC) and Northwest Florida Water Management District (WMD)
Contact: FWC, (850) 265-3676, or WMD, (850) 539-5999, www.floridatrail.org, www.fnai.org, http://myfwc.com, www.nwfwmd.state.fl.us/recreation/chipolariver.html
Finding the campground: From I-10, take exits 136 (CR 276/176) or 142 (SR 71) and drive north into downtown Marianna. Turn north onto CR 167 and drive north about 7 miles to SR 162. Turn left (west) for the short drive to the Chipola River; 0.5 mile past the river turn left (south) on White Pond Road, which angles into Bumpnose Road in 1.0 mile. Continue left on Bumpnose for almost 1 mile, watching for signs on the left (east side of the road) to the public boat ramp and the Christoff Landing primitive camping area.
About the campground: The Upper Chipola River WMA is unusual among Florida wildlife areas in that its 7,377 acres are contiguous, though very irregular in dimension. The WMA is designed to protect the upper watershed of the Chipola River, which is fed by numerous freshwater springs and creeks.

Abundant bird life will wake you early, and because fishing for bass, bream, and catfish is a way of life in the Panhandle, your chance to sleep in will also be rare except on weekdays. Although you must know where to look for the rare species, you will commonly spot alligators, turtles, and white-tailed deer. Many rare and some endangered species are found in small areas of the Apalachicola and Chipola River watersheds.

Access to this WMA is almost exclusively by small boat. In the fall, deer hunting is an area tradition. Depending upon rainfall, the multiuse trail in the WMA is used by hikers, cyclists, and horseback riders.

⅃∪ Florida Caverns State Park

Location: 3 miles north of Marianna, off US 90 on SR 166 in Jackson County (30° 48' 30.7" N, 85° 12' 46.5" W)

Season: Year-round

Sites: 38, with a primitive youth group camping area; 3 RV sites next to the stables for campers bringing horses. Reservations are recommended, but the park holds 10 percent of its campsites for first-come, first-served walk-in patrons.

Maximum length: 50 feet in horse sites, 40 feet otherwise

Facilities: Full-facility camping

Fee per night: $$

Management: Florida Division of Recreation and Parks

Contact: (850) 482-9598, www.floridastateparks.org/floridacaverns/default.cfm; (800) 326-3521, www.reserveamerica.com

Finding the campground: Florida Caverns State Park is located 3 miles north of Marianna, off US 90 on SR 166. From Tallahassee, take I-10 west to exit 142, turn right (north) on SR 71 to US 90, and turn left (west). Turn right on SR 167 in Marianna and follow the brown park signs.

About the campground: This lovely state park offers visitors views of some of the most magnificent of the dry caves and caverns of Florida. Forty-five-minute tours give visitors views of stalactites, stalagmites, draperies, flowstone, soda straws, columns, and rim-stone pools that developed in a slow process over millions of years.

The 1,319-acre Florida Caverns also offers two networks of nature trails. The short Visitor Center Trail winds through hardwood forests and limestone bluffs above the river floodplain. The 6 miles of Upper Chipola multiuse trails offer hikers, bicyclists, and horseback riders many hours of enjoyment in the woodlands along the Chipola River.

This park is also popular for swimming, fishing, picnicking, canoeing, boating, hiking, bicycling, and horseback riding. Stables are available for equestrian campers (a current Coggin's test certificate is required for each horse).

An equestrian facility is located in the multiuse trail system. Riders can use the stables and wash rack to clean and cool the horses after a day on the trail. Restrooms and picnic shelters are also nearby.

21 Three Rivers State Park

Location: 2 miles north of Sneads between CR 271 and the Seminole Reservoir in Jackson County (30° 44' 21.1" N, 84° 56' 11.2" W)

Season: Year-round

Sites: 30

Maximum length: 50 feet

Facilities: Full-facility camping plus primitive youth and group camping and one cabin (pets allowed in the campground, not in cabin), picnic area with tables and grills, 60-person rental pavilion for large gatherings

Fee per night: $$ camping; $$$ cabin

Management: Florida Division of Recreation and Parks

Contact: (850) 482-9006, www.floridastateparks.org/threerivers/default.cfm; (800) 326-3521, www.reserveamerica.com

Finding the campground: The park address is 7908 Three Rivers Park Rd. in Sneads. Turn off I-10 at exit 158 and travel north on SR 286 to the town of Sneads. Turn left (west) onto US 90 and then turn right (north) onto CR 271/River Road at the flashing yellow light. The park is 2 miles north of Sneads on the east side of the road.

About the campground: Three Rivers was established on 2.5 miles of Lake Seminole shoreline where Florida meets the southwest corner of Georgia. The lake and park are the result of the Jim Woodruff Dam, which creates a reservoir from waters of the south-flowing Chattahoochee and Flint Rivers and Spring Creek.

This park especially appeals to anglers and boaters and a fishing pier is available.

After an hour of fishing, hike through the rolling hills of pine and hardwoods. Watch for fox and gray squirrels, white-tailed deer, gray fox and the abundant bird life for here you can regularly see raptors such as hawks and eagles, songbirds, migratory waterfowl, and the ever-present freshwater shore and wading birds. At night you will hear owls, nighthawks (regionally called bull bats), and perhaps the lonesome call of a whippoorwill.

22 Torreya State Park

Location: Off SR 12 on CR 1641, 13 miles north of Bristol in Liberty County (30° 33' 2.4" N, 84° 56' 38.2" W)

Season: Year-round

Sites: 30

Maximum length: 60 feet

Facilities: Full-facility camping plus primitive and youth/group camping and one YURT (Year-round Universal Recreational Tent)

Fee per night: $$

Management: Florida Division of Recreation and Parks

Contact: (850) 643-2674, www.floridastateparks.org/torreya/default.cfm; (800) 326-3521, www.reserveamerica.com

Finding the campground: Turn off I-10 west of Quincy at exit 174 onto SR 12. Drive south toward Bristol, following SR 12. Turn right onto CR 271 and follow it to the park.

About the campground: This park is named after a small conifer, the endangered Florida torreya tree that is found only within this 13,000-acre park and on the east bank of the Apalachicola River.

Torreya is one of Florida's most scenic but under-visited parks. It is easy to visit for camping, hiking, bird-watching, and picnicking. The high bluffs overlooking the Apalachicola are rugged, and the section of the Florida Trail that circles inside the park is not an easy stroll.

Torreya was developed by the Civilian Conservation Corps in the 1930s, and this gives buildings a rustic touch. You can see about one hundred species of birds in the park, and during the fall, enjoy the fine display of color put on by this northerly park's hardwoods. Another sight worth seeing: the Gregory House, a fully furnished plantation home built in 1849. Guided tours are given at 10:00 a.m. on weekdays and 10:00 a.m. and 2:00 and 4:00 p.m. on weekends and holidays.

Primitive campsites abound on the 1,400-mile Florida Trail. It is one of only eight National Scenic Trails in the U.S.

23 Ocheesee Landing [Boat Launch]

Location: This ramp is in northeast Calhoun County on the Apalachicola River (30° 34' 55" N, 84° 57' 58" W)

Season: Year-round

Sites: Primitive camping is first-come, first-served

Maximum length: Call for current information

Fee per night: None

Management: Fish & Wildlife Conservation Commission (FWC)

Contact: (850) 488-4676, www.floridaconservation.org/Recreation/boat_nwramps.htm#calhoun

Finding the campground: At I-10, exit 152, drive south on SR 69 to the Ocheesee crossroads in Calhoun County. Turn left (east) on CR 286 and go 3.6 miles. Turn right on the dirt road, which may be marked "Land Store Road," and drive 2.5 miles to the ramp.

About the campground: Here, on the western bank of the Apalachicola River, FWC owns a single-lane ramp and an associated unimproved parking lot. Torreya State Park can be reached by boat traveling 1 mile upstream or downstream. The lot accommodates ten vehicles, if drivers park carefully, especially when boat trailers are attached.

The shaded grounds are available for overnight stays only. There are no improvements such as restrooms or potable water spigots, however, and there is no attendant or security. Technically, this is not a "campground," so much as a site where one may pitch a tent. Campers are advised to carry bug repellent, make sure their flashlights or lanterns are in good working order, and to maintain "situational awareness."

24 Red's Landing [Boat Launch]

Location: Northeast Calhoun County on the Apalachicola River
Season: Year-round
Sites: Primitive camping is first-come, first-served.
Maximum length: Call for current information
Facilities: Call for current information
Fee per night: None
Management: Fish & Wildlife Conservation Commission (FWC)
Contact: (850) 488-4676, www.floridaconservation.org/Recreation/boat_nwramps.htm
Finding the campground: Take exit 152 on I-10 and drive south on SR 69 toward Blountstown. About 6 miles from Blountstown watch for John Redd Road or Red's Landing Road (dirt) on the left (east) side and follow it 2.2 miles to the ramp and the unimproved overnight camping area.
About the campground: For many years FWC worked almost exclusively for the hunters and anglers of the state. Consequently, it owns hundreds of boat ramps like the single-lane ramp and associated unimproved parking lot capable of accommodating 20 vehicles. These days FWC's mandate has evolved and includes cooperative efforts to preserve the wildlife and habitat; and yet, one of its driving principles is to get the public outside to understand and enjoy nature.

The overnight camping option at this boat ramp is unusual among FWC ramp sites. Still, no restrooms, potable water, or hookups of any sort are provided and neither is there any security. Enjoy the shaded sites, the wide and rapidly flowing river, and be aware of your neighbors and your surroundings.

25 Gulf County Parks

Location: North of Wewahitchka (30° 8' 21.8" N, 85° 2' 1.8" W)
Season: Year-round
Sites: 20 campsites, 10 with electricity and 4 for RVs
Maximum length: Call for current information

Facilities: Picnic tables, bathhouse, dump station

Fee per night: Call for current information

Management: The Dead Lakes County Park is occasionally referred to as a State Recreation Area, but it is under the jurisdiction of Gulf County.

Contact: The mailing address is Dead Lakes Park, P.O. Box 989, Wewahitchka, FL 32465, (850) 639-2702, www.gulfcounty-fl.gov/countyparks.cfm

Finding the campground: North of Wewahitchka—local folks refer to it simply as "Wewa"—on SR 71, turn right (east) on Gary Rowell Road and drive to the park.

About the campground: Gulf County is still part of the nineteenth century. Gulf has a population of only 24 persons per square mile over 559 miles, but this is misleading, because much of the county is flatwoods (poorly drained and subject to flooding) and wet swamp. This concentrates the population along the "high ground," which may only be a few feet above sea level. In some years, this causes a series of evacuations during hurricane season.

If you enjoy fishing, most of the Panhandle's county parks will be of special interest. Some have boat rentals and it may be a universal rule that a bait and tackle shop will be located not far from the entrance. There you will be able to buy worms and crickets or, if the waterway offers access to salt water, live shrimp.

Gulf County's Dead Lakes falls well within this mode and activities are structured around a boat ramp: fishing, boating, hiking, and nature viewing. Standing skeletons of dead trees scattered across the margins of the lake provide excellent fish habitat.

26 Apalachicola Wildlife Management Area– Florida River Island

Location: West of CR 379 in Liberty County

Season: Year-round

Sites: Camping is permitted at designated primitive campsites year-round (including during the general firearms hunting season) and at the Northwest Florida Water Management District campground at Florida River Island

Maximum length: Call for current information

Facilities: Florida River Island has spaces for RVs, but no hookups

Fee per night: Call for information

Management: Fish & Wildlife Conservation Commission, U.S. Forest Service, and Northwest Florida Water Management District (WMD)

Contact: Call the WMD Lands Division for available recreational brochures, (850) 539-5999, http://myfwc.com, www.nwfwmd.state.fl.us/recreation/apalachicolariver.html

Finding the campground: From I-10 west of Quincy, take exit 174 south on SR 12 through Bristol for about 12 miles to the intersection with SR 379. Watch for FR 188 and turn right (west) to a network of dirt roads and the camping areas.

About the campground: The half-million-acre Apalachicola WMA is part of the Apalachicola National Forest. The protected river basin here is a biodiverse and economically important aquatic area. It has, for instance, the highest density of amphibians and reptiles.

The Florida River Island Campground offers a 2.6-mile interpretive trail, and the Florida National Scenic Trail crosses here.

This vast area provides an endless variety of outdoor activities: canoeing, boating, hunting, fishing, horseback riding, hiking, bird-watching, and, not least, just kicking back for a day with a picnic basket, family, and friends.

27 T. H. Stone Memorial St. Joseph Peninsula State Park

Location: South of Port St. Joe on Cape San Blas in Gulf County (29° 45' 28.6" N, 85° 23' 48.1" W)
Season: Year-round
Sites: 120
Maximum length: 38 feet
Facilities: Full-facility camping plus primitive youth-group tent camping and eight modern cabins (no pets in cabins)
Fee per night: $$$
Management: Florida Division of Recreation and Parks
Contact: (850) 227-1327, www.floridastateparks.org/stjoseph/default.cfm; (800) 326-3521, www.reserveamerica.com
Finding the campground: From I-10 turn south at exit 142 southeast of Marianna onto SR 71. It is about 75 miles to the intersection with US 98 in Port St. Joe. Turn left (south) on US 98 and, in a couple of miles, veer right (south) onto CR 30A. Travel about 7 miles and turn right onto 30E/Cape San Blas Road. Follow this road through a section of Eglin Air Force Base to the park entrance.
About the campground: This is one of the finest parks in America. Its 9 miles of white sugar sand backed by high dunes and strung along a thin peninsula are unbeatable. In summer, days become so hot your tent may take time to cool before you are able to stretch out for sleep. The hours of early morning and evening, however, are pleasant, and the sky is colorful and exciting.

On the west side of the park is the Gulf of Mexico and on the east side, St. Joseph Bay, and everywhere a wide variety of beach activities: sunbathing (sunscreen recommended), snorkeling, scuba diving, fishing, and swimming. Plenty of shoreline is available to launch canoes and kayaks, and the park offers a modern boat ramp at Eagle Harbor on the bay side.

Hundreds of species of birds, from pelicans to osprey, are routinely sighted in the park. An insect repellent that includes DEET is recommended for mosquitoes and a biting midge known as a no-see-um, which can make your evenings unpleasant.

The picturesque campground is a short walk from the beach and the primitive group camp-sites near the wilderness preserve. Bayside cabins offer alternative accommodations.

Campsites numbered 53 to 58 and 98 to 103 are now developed to ADA standards; it's recommended that these 20-by-40-foot concrete pads be used for pop-ups, trailers, and RVs only.

28 Apalachicola River Wildlife & Environmental Area

Location: In Franklin and Gulf Counties north of the town of Apalachicola (29° 43' 31" N, 84° 59' 33" W)

Season: Year-round

Sites: Camping is permitted throughout the 86,617-acre area, except where NO CAMPING signs are posted. Camping is limited to tents, trailers, and self-propelled camping vehicles. No permit is required.

Maximum length: Contact for current information

Facilities: Contact for current information

Fee per night: Contact for current information

Management: Fish & Wildlife Conservation Commission (FWC)

Contact: http://myfwc.com

Finding the WEA: The Apalachicola River WEA stretches north to south along the Apalachicola and Chipola Rivers for dozens of miles. It can be accessed at any number of points, but the closest town of any size is Apalachicola. To reach Apalachicola from I-10 in Tallahassee, take exit 203 and drive south through the state capital on US 319/SR 61. Follow US 319 to its juncture with US 98 on the Gulf Coast and swing right (west). Follow this coastal highway to Apalachicola.

About the WEA: One of the best ways to explore this 86,617-acre area is by canoe or kayak. Fishing, hunting, and boating are the recreational passions of most visitors.

The WEA not only encompasses the Apalachicola and Chipola Rivers, but as it nears the town of Apalachicola, hundreds of small streams and creeks wend their way to East Bay. A map or GPS unit is recommended, because with nearly a hundred miles of waterway, it is easy to become disoriented.

This area, which ends at the picturesque town of Apalachicola, has a diversity of environments and bird-watching opportunities. Eagles soar above pine and palmetto uplands where you hear whippoorwills at night, and these lands ease into freshwater cypress marshes or oak hammock lowlands close to the rivers where pileated woodpeckers and owls are common. There are swamps and, as one nears East Bay, marshes with wading birds and osprey.

29 Dr. Julian G. Bruce St. George Island State Park

Location: On the east end of St. George Island south of Eastpoint in Franklin County (29° 41' 3" N, 84° 47' 48" W)

Season: Year-round

Sites: 60, plus pet camping and tents-only group camping

Maximum length: 43 feet

Facilities: Full-facility camping with water, electricity, and bathhouses, plus a primitive campsite with restrooms, cold water showers, picnic tables, and a campfire circle that can be accessed by trail or by private boat; alcohol prohibited

Fee per night: $$

Management: Florida Division of Recreation and Parks

Contact: (850) 927-2111, www.floridastateparks.org/stgeorgeisland/default.cfm; (800) 326-3521, www.reserveamerica.com

Finding the campground: From I-10, take exit 174 south on SR 12/Greensboro Hwy. Follow SR 12 as it turns and zigzags through Greensboro and Bristol until it intersects with SR 65 in the hamlet of Wilma. Turn right onto SR 65 and continue to the intersection with US 98/319, then turn right (west) to Eastpoint. Turn left (south) at Patton or Island Drives and cross the 4-mile Bryant Grady Patton Bridge to St. George Island. Turn left on Gulf Beach Drive and continue to the park entrance on the east end of St. George Island.

About the campground: This long, narrow barrier island features 9 miles of undeveloped beaches and dunes, and it is all open to the public. The 1,962-acre St. George Island park is rare for Florida where developers, the wealthy, and their political hires have too often bulldozed sand dunes, roped off beach for private use, killed wildlife, and built cheap high-rise condominiums.

The beach is sparkling white and ideal for swimming, sunbathing, ocean kayaking, and fishing, and offers up particularly nice specimens if you like to search for shells to take back home.

The northern side of the island borders St. George/Apalachicola Bay. Two boat ramps allow anglers to fish for saltwater species such as flounder and Spanish mackerel, and recreational boaters to sightsee the inlets and waterways. Boats up to 24 feet can be accommodated although the bay is shallow in many areas. Both sides of the island offer canoes and kayaks for adventuresome days on the water and they can be rented in the park.

Hikers can use two trails, one to the primitive camping area at Gap Point and the other to East End through an environmentally sensitive zone. For day visitors, the park has six large picnic shelters equipped with grills, tables, and restrooms.

30 Tate's Hell State Forest/Wildlife Management Area

Location: Tate's Hell is located primarily in Franklin County, between the Apalachicola and Ochlockonee Rivers. The forest and management area extend into the southeast corner of Liberty County, south of the Apalachicola National Forest and 1.5 miles northwest of the town of Carrabelle (29° 51' 14" N, 84° 39' 57" W). Access to Tate's Hell is from US 98, CR 67, or SR 65.

Season: Year-round

Sites: Primitive camping is allowed at several dozen areas throughout Tate's Hell. In addition, sites are designated for youth groups and seasonal hunt camps. (Womack Creek Recreation Area just north of Carrabelle has a primitive campground with a picnic pavilion, bathhouse, and boat ramp; the ramp offers access to the Ochlockonee River. Tent camping only is allowed, and a self-serve pay station is located at the entrance. All stays are restricted to 14 consecutive days in any 30-day period. The Ochlockonee River, the Crooked River, and CR 67 border the Womack Creek Recreation Area.)

Maximum length: Call for current information

Facilities: None

Fee per night: $-$$

Management: Division of Forestry and Fish & Wildlife Conservation Commission

Contact: (850) 697-3734, www.fl-dof.com, http://myfwc.com/recreation/cooperative/tates _hell.asp

Finding the forest: From I-10, take exit 181 and drive south on Cr 267/Lake Talquin Highway. After about 12 miles, turn left (east) at the intersection with SR 20. After about 3 miles, turn right (south) on CR 375/Smith Creek Road and follow it to Sopchoppy. Turn right (south) on US 319 and follow it until it merges with US 98. Take the right fork west and continue to Carrabelle.

About the forest: Tate's Hell State Forest is both wonderful and primitive. During any season, insect repellent with DEET, map and GPS, snakebite kit, and spare water are highly recommended on this tract of 202,414 acres in Franklin and Liberty Counties.

Did we mention that the area was primitive? Of course this is a wonderful reason to explore its many camping areas, some of which are exceedingly remote and rarely visited.

Florida began purchasing this region from timber companies in 1994. Its most dominant feature is wet swamp interspersed with hammocks and uplands, most of which has recovered from years of clear-cutting by the timber interests. During a rainy spell, the water can rise quickly and one must stay aware of weather conditions.

Tate's Hell offers a variety of recreation activities. There are 35 miles of rivers, streams, and creeks available for canoeing, boating, and fishing. A concrete boat launch site is located at Cash Creek, with additional launch sites available at locations throughout the forest. A portion of the forest borders the Gulf of Mexico, so both fresh- and saltwater fishing are popular.

Picnicking at one of the many day-use areas is popular and hiking is always fun and challenging. Bird-watchers will normally be rewarded with sightings of bald eagles, osprey, and a variety of forest birds such as red-cockaded woodpeckers.

31 Lake Talquin State Forest

Location: This forest is located just west of Tallahassee (30° 27' 6.48" N, 84° 16' 21.97" W). It lies north of SR 20 and south of I-10 and US 90 along the Ochlockonee River in Gadsden, Leon, and Liberty Counties.

Season: Year-round

Sites:

Bear Creek Educational Forest: A primitive group campsite in this 492-acre subforest area is available for a small fee and requires a state forest use authorization. Visitors can hike multiple trails and experience an audio enhanced "Living Forest trail."
Directions: From I-10, take exit 181 onto SR 267. Go south for 4.8 miles; the entrance is on the left.

Fort Braden: This 1,242-acre tract features three moderately strenuous hiking trails and two horse trails. Primitive campsites are available for individuals and for groups. Campers must first obtain a state forest use authorization from the headquarters on Geddie Road.
Directions: From Tallahassee, drive west 8.7 miles on SR 20 from Capital Circle. The tract entrance road is on the right.

High Bluff: High Bluff has 34 primitive sites for tent campers or RVs with ground grills and picnic tables; toilet facilities are also available. First-come, first-served; no reservations. A boat launch is nearby. Camping fees ($) are deposited in an honor box at the campground and any open campsite may be selected. The maximum stay is two weeks. RVs and tent campers are welcome. For information, call (850) 488-1871.
Directions: From I-10, take exit 192 and drive north on US 90 toward Quincy/Midway for 2.4 miles. Turn left on CR 268/Martin Luther King Boulevard and drive 2.5 miles. Turn left on Peters Road and drive 1 mile. Stay left at the fork where the road becomes High Bluff Landing Road. The campground is at the end of the road.

The monument to Our Fallen Heroes, Confederate veterans of the Civil War, stands in front of the county courthouse in Quincy, Gadsden County.

Line's Track Off-Road Bicycle Trail: Line's Tract features a 10-mile off-road trail that is rated beginner to intermediate. One group campsite is located on the trail, off the Talquin Loop. Obtain a forest use permit from the Lake Talquin headquarters on Geddie Road.

Directions: Take exit 181 from I-10 and drive south on SR 267 for 7 miles. Turn left onto Cook's Landing Road. The entrance is 1.5 miles on the right.

Maximum length: Call for current information

Facilities: Call for current information

Fee per night: $–$$

Management: Division of Forestry

Contact: (850) 488-1871, www.fl-dof.com/state_forests/lake_talquin.html

Finding the forest: From Tallahassee, take SR 20 west into the forest.

About the forest: Lake Talquin, west of Tallahassee, is composed of ten primary tracts of pine and oak, and many smaller ones. Not all areas are contiguous. Most of the forest adjoins Lake Talquin and the north-south flow of the Ochlockonee River. Since 1977, Florida's Division of Forestry has managed this area for multiple consumer uses that balance environmental learning and recreational opportunities. Much emphasis is placed on reforestation and ecosystem restoration of commercially cut-over areas.

32 Joe Budd Wildlife Management Area

Location: South of I-10, but north of Lake Talquin in Gadsden County

Season: Year-round

Sites: 34 open and shaded primitive sites for tent campers or RVs. Required permits available at self-service pay or honor station at campground. First-come, first-served; no reservations taken. Two week maximum stay. RVs and tent campers welcome.

Maximum length: Call for current information

Facilities: Ground grills, picnic tables; available toilet facilities

Fee per night: Call for current information

Management: Fish & Wildlife Conservation Commission and Division of Forestry

Contact: (850) 488-1871, http://myfwc.com

Finding the campground: From I-10 west of Tallahassee, take exit 192 to US 90. Drive east a few blocks to CR 268. Turn right (west) and the Joe Budd WMA will stretch along to your left (south of the road) for miles. In about 3.5 miles, watch for Peters Road and turn left, following it 1.2 miles to High Bluff Road. Turn left on High Bluff Road and follow it to the lake and the campground.

About the campground: Along the north shore of Lake Talquin, Joe Budd WMA overlaps Lake Talquin State Forest, and the whole area is just a few miles west of Tallahassee.

There is plenty to do around Lake Talquin and a highlight of the 11,039-acre Joe Budd year is its primitive weapons hunting opportunities. Only bows and muzzleloaders are permitted: no modern shotguns or rifles. The area is closed to hunting for more than 300 days each year. Thus, most days, you can hike, bike, or horseback ride on Joe Budd's roads and through its regrown forests. A boat launch near the campground gives easy access to the lake.

33 Leon County Parks

Location: Each Leon County Parks campground is on the south side of Lake Talquin, west of Tallahassee and north of SR 20.
Season: Year-round
Sites:
>   **Coe's Landing:** Full-service RV center, electricity, water, hot showers, restrooms, dump station, fishing pier, picnic shelter.
>   *Directions:* The campground is approximately 7.4 miles west of Tallahassee. Turn north on Coe's Landing Road, which dead-ends at the landing.
>   **Hall's Landing:** Tent camping only; potable water, hot showers, restroom, boardwalk, fishing pier, picnic shelter.
>   *Directions:* Hall's is approximately 12 miles west of Tallahassee. Turn north on Luther Hall Landing Road 1 mile west of the Harvey Creek Bridge. Luther Hall Road will dead-end at the landing.
>   **Williams Landing:** Tent or RV camping only with covered shelters, picnic areas, barbecue grills, fishing pier.
>   *Directions:* Williams is approximately 10 miles west of Tallahassee. Turn north on William's Landing Road, which dead-ends at the landing.

Maximum length: Call for current information
Facilities: Boat ramp or launching site
Fee per night: $$
Management: Leon County Division of Parks and Recreation
Contact: Leon County Division of Parks and Recreation, 2280 Miccosukee Road, Tallahassee, FL 32308, (850) 606-1470, www.leoncountyfl.gov/parks/; for reservations, call (850) 350-9560 or (866) 350-9560

34 Ochlockonee River State Park

Location: 4 miles south of the town of Sopchoppy on US 319 in Wakulla County (29° 59' 56" N, 84° 29' 8" W)
Season: Year-round
Sites: 30
Maximum length: 40 feet
Facilities: Full-facility camping
Fee per night: $$
Management: Florida Division of Recreation and Parks
Contact: (850) 962-2771, www.floridastateparks.org/ochlockoneeriver/; (800) 326-3521, www.reserveamerica.com
Finding the campground: From I-10 and Tallahassee, drive south on US 319. Approximately 4 miles south of Sopchoppy, turn left (east) into the park.
About the campground: If you want a quiet campground, make reservations at Ochlockonee River. Here, where the Dead River merges with the Ochlockonee, you can find a peaceful setting in a

Florida's national forests—Apalachicola, Ocala, Osceola—have wonderful campsites. Ranging from highly developed to primitive, they have many uses and users.

shaded environment. It is sufficiently distant from the state capital—40 miles—to be too far for an easy overnight and yet close enough to be accessible for the weekend.

Ochlockonee's 392 acres offer groomed hiking trails, access to the rivers for canoes and kayaks, a launch for power boats, covered picnic pavilion, an archeological site, and a scenic overlook where the rivers meet.

Anglers can toss a worm from the shoreline or take their boat upstream for freshwater or downstream for saltwater fishing. Bass, bream, catfish, and speckled perch are plentiful.

35 Apalachicola National Forest

Location: Most of the Apalachicola National Forest's more than half-million acres are in Liberty County
Season: Year-round
Sites: Primitive camping anywhere in the forest; developed campsites, hunt camps. Maximum of 14-day stays in a 30-day period, except during hunting season. Campsites are first-come, first-served. Detailed list below.
Maximum length: Call for current information
Facilities: Developed campgrounds do not provide hookups, and generators not allowed after 10:00 p.m. Campfires may be prohibited in dry seasons. Pets allowed, restrained or on leash. Alcohol prohibited throughout the forest.
Fee per night: $

Apalachicola National Forest

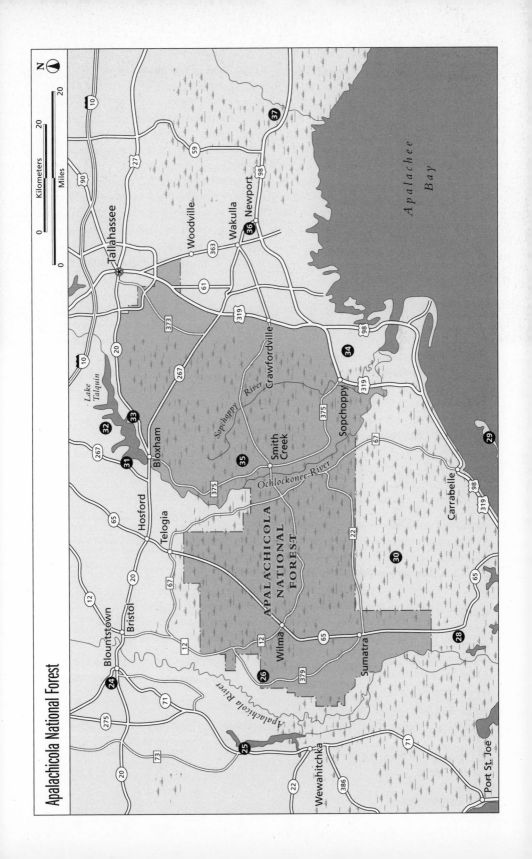

Management: USDA Forest Service

Contact: Apalachicola Ranger District, 11152 NW State Rd. 20, Revell Building, Bristol, FL 32321, (850) 643-2282; Wakulla Ranger District, 57 Taff Dr., Crawfordville, FL 32327, (850) 926-561, www.fs.fed.us

About the forest: This vast national forest, much of it swamps and hammocks virtually untouched by man, offers every possible outdoor challenge with the possible exception of rock climbing. Fishing and hunting are especially valued and attract hundreds of thousands of visitors during the year. Many numbered dirt roads bisect the forest and this makes access easy.

Bicycling is popular, especially on the designated mountain bike trail at Munson Hills in Leon County, which consists of an 8-mile and a 5-mile loop on a sandy trail traveling through narrow pine trees. Hikers enjoy the approximately 85 miles of designated hiking trails—and of course the rest of the forest, where they are always welcome. About 64 miles of the statewide Florida National Scenic Trail (FNST) wind through the diverse ecosystems of the forest. The 18 miles through the Bradwell Bay Wilderness Area (a wet swamp) are considered the most challenging because the trail may be under water.

The forest affords opportunities for riding too, although horses are not allowed on the Florida National Scenic Trail or in developed recreation areas. Most riders park alongside a forest road near where they want to ride. As long as vehicles do not obstruct traffic or destroy natural resources, this is permitted. Camping with horses in the general forest area is allowed; see the detailed list below. Horses are also allowed in the primitive (no amenities) hunt camps, although cleaning up after your horses is expected and appreciated. The Vinzant Horse Trail in Leon County, with an 11-mile and a 23-mile loop, is the only designated horse trail in the forest. The trailhead (a mowed field with no amenities) is located near the intersection of FR 342 and SR 267.

Developed Campgrounds

Camel Lake Recreation Area

Location: Forest Site 11, Liberty County (30° 16' 33" N, 84° 59' 27" W)

Sites: 10 sites for tent camping with views of Camel Lake, 5 with electricity and water

Facilities: Picnic table, grill, fire ring; bathhouse with hot showers, drinking water, flush toilets

Finding the campground: Take SR 12 south from Bristol for 12 miles; turn left (east) on FR 105 for 2 miles

About the campground: This fine and level camping facility is located on a 37-acre natural lake with a small, white-sand beach along the Florida Trail. In the midst of pines and scrub oak and with palmetto and wiregrass ground cover, it is nevertheless ADA-accessible. It is a great place for picnicking, swimming, boating from the launch, canoeing/kayaking, fishing, and hiking along the Florida Trail. Paddleboats or electric boat motors are allowed. A volunteer host is usually available on site.

Hickory Landing

Location: Forest Site 3, Franklin County (29° 59' 20" N, 85° 0' 47" W)

Sites: 12 sites in a thick stand of pines

Facilities: Picnic table, grill or fire ring; nearby drinking water, vault toilets, concrete boat ramp

Finding the campground: Take SR 65 south from Sumatra for 2 miles, then turn right (west) on FR 101 for 1.5 miles. Turn left on FR 101-B for 1 mile.

About the campground: There is good fishing for bass, bream, and catfish among beautiful cypress stands; picnicking, and canoeing along Owl Creek with access to the Apalachicola River. A volunteer host lives on site. It is also an easy day trip to historic Fort Gadsden (29° 56' 29" N, 85° 0' 45" W) to learn about the War of 1812 through the Civil War.

Mack Landing

Location: Forest Site 14, Wakulla County (30° 5' 35" N, 84° 38' 42" W)
Sites: 10 sites for tents or self-contained RVs available on a first-come, first-served basis
Facilities: Picnic table, grill or fire ring, drinking water from a communal spigot, vault toilets, boat ramp, and no electricity
Finding the campground: Follow US 319 south from Tallahassee to the small town of Sopchoppy. When US 319 turns left in Sopchoppy, continue straight ahead on CR 375. Follow CR 375 through the hamlet of Sanborn (road curves north) and a sign for Mack Landing will be on your left in about 2 miles.
About the campground: The concrete boat ramp at Mack Landing is steep and leads to a stream that empties into the Ochlockonee River. It is easy to launch canoes and kayaks for fishing or paddling.

Wright Lake

Location: Forest Site 4, Franklin County (30° 00' 07" N, 85° 00' 10" W)
Sites: 18 spacious and relatively level sites; first-come, first-served
Facilities: Picnic table, grill, tent pad, light post, fire ring, drinking water, bathhouse with hot showers, flush toilets (wheelchair-accessible), nearby dump station for RVs
Finding the campground: From Tallahassee, follow SR 20/Blountstown Highway west to the intersection with SR 65. Turn left (south) and follow SR 65 through the forest, and once past the hamlet of Sumatra, turn right (west) at the signs for FR 101, which you will take to the campsite.
About the campground: This quiet, scenic campground set in a pine grove next to spring-fed Wright Lake offers picnicking, fishing, canoeing and kayaking (electric motors are allowed), swimming, and hiking around the lake. A volunteer host lives on site.

FOREST HUNT CAMPS

During general gun hunting season (usually mid-November through mid-February), camping is allowed only at designated hunt camps and, unless otherwise noted, the above listed developed campgrounds. These woodsy getaways attract thousands of men and women each year. Portable restrooms and trashcans are provided at most sites and campers may stay the entire season in a single camp, from 14 days prior to opening day to the last day of general gun hunting season (usually encompassing the Thanksgiving weekend, and usually stretching through January). In areas open to using dogs when hunting, individual permits for dog pens may be purchased from a local Forest Service office. There are no fees for hunt camps, but they do have to be reserved well in advance of the deadline and often are, in a sense, passed down through family connections from generation to generation.

Big Gully Landing: Forest Site 10, Liberty County: primitive camping. Boat launching and parking facilities along Big Gully Creek allow visitors to fish for bass, catfish, and bream on Equaloxic Creek with access to the Apalachicola River 6 miles downstream.

Directions: Take SR 12 south from Bristol for 12.8 miles; veer right on CR 379 at Orange for 1.0 mile. Turn right (west) on FR 133 for 1.0 mile.

Brown House Hunt Camp: Forest Site 21, Leon County: Primitive forest camping virtually within sight of the capitol.

Directions: From Tallahassee, take SR 20/Blountstown Highway west to the hamlet of Holland and turn left (south) on Joe Thomas Rd. In about 1 mile, the road intersects FR 301/Backwoods Jackson Bluff Road. Turn left (east), travel 0.75 mile and turn right (south) onto FR 360. Follow FR 360 for about 2 miles across CR 267, and after about 2 miles watch for signs on the right.

Buckhorn Hunt Camp: Forest Site 22, Leon County: Another primitive campsite in the woods just west of Tallahassee.

Directions: From Tallahassee, take SR 20/Blountstown Highway west to the hamlet of Holland and turn left (south) on Joe Thomas Rd. In about 1 mile, the road intersects with FR 301/Backwoods Jackson Bluff Road. Turn left (east), travel 0.75 mile, and turn right (south) onto FR 360. Follow FR 360 for about 2 miles across SR 267, and after about 1 mile watch for signs on the right.

Cliff Lake Hunt Camp: Forest Site 9, Liberty County: A primitive campsite.

Directions: From Tallahassee, take SR 20/Blountstown Highway west to SR 65 and turn left (south). At about 17 miles, watch for FR 13 (these dirt roads are sometimes called "highways," but that should be irrelevant for directions) on your left and turn left (east). After 1 mile, begin watching for signs. The camp should be on the left.

Cotton Landing Hunt Camp: Forest Site 5, Liberty County: There are 4 primitive campsites along Kennedy Creek, with picnicking, sanitary facilities, drinking water, and a boat ramp. Fishing has a reputation for excellence here, and launching kayaks or canoes is easy.

Directions: Take CR 379 northwest from Sumatra for 3.2 miles and turn left (west) on FR 123 for 2.8 miles. Then turn left on FR 123-B for 0.7 mile.

Hitchcock Lake Hunt Camp: Forest Site 13, Liberty County: 10 primitive campsites with picnicking and sanitary facilities, but no drinking water. This site offers fishing and boating, plus boat launching facilities on the Ochlockonee River.

Directions: Take CR 67 south from Telogia for 22.8 miles, then turn left (east) on FR 184 for 1.5 miles.

Magnolia Hunt Camp: Forest Site 7, Liberty County: Primitive camping and an excellent and scenic spot to launch a paddleboat. The camp is on the north edge of the 8,090-acre Mud Swamp/New River Wilderness area. This boggy wilderness is one of the most remote areas in Florida, thick with mosquitoes and home to black bears and alligators.

Directions: From Tallahassee, take SR 20/Blountstown Highway west to SR 65 and turn left (south). At about 17 miles, watch for FR 13 on your left and turn east. After about 2 miles, turn right (south) on FR 114. In 0.75 mile, it takes a 90-degree turn left; follow it for 2 miles to FR 182 and turn left. Watch for signs on your right after about 1 mile.

Otter Hunt Camp: Forest Site 19, Leon County: Some hunt camps are little more than a sign in the woods denoting primitive camping. Such is the case at this site, which may or may not, depending upon Florida's fiscal situation, have portable toilets.

Directions: From Tallahassee, take SR 20/Blountstown Highway west to FR 344 and turn left (south). The camp will be on your left in about 3.5 miles. Watch for a parking area and a sign.

Pine Creek Landing Hunt Camp: Forest Site 18, Wakulla County: Primitive camping with a boat launch on the Ochlockonee River.

Directions: From Tallahassee, take SR 20/Blountstown Highway west to the hamlet of Bloxham, just prior to crossing the Ochlockonee River, and turn left (south) on CR 375. Take CR 375 for about 7 miles to FR 335. Turn right and take the short drive to the camp, about 0.5 mile.

Pope Still Hunt Camp: Forest Site 20, Wakulla County: Fully primitive camping near Lost Creek and a few miles northeast of the Sopchoppy River and the 24,602-acre Bradwell Bay Wilderness. Should you hike and wander into this area, expect waist-deep water over trails and thickets of titi trees.

Directions: From Tallahassee, take US 319 south to Crawfordville and turn right (west) on Bay Avenue/Arran Highway. Follow Arran Highway/Arran Road as it winds through the forest to FR 13 and turn right (northwest). It is about 2 miles to the intersection with FR 350; turn right (north) and watch for a sign on the left.

Porter Lake Hunt Camp: Forest Site 17, Liberty County: Primitive camping (6 sites) along the Florida Trail and the Ochlockonee River, plus picnicking, sanitary facilities, drinking water and hiking on the Florida Trail. Expect excellent fishing and canoeing on the Ochlockonee River.

Directions: Take CR 67 south from Telogia for 16.9 miles. Turn left on FR 13 for 2.9 miles.

Revell Landing Hunt Camp: Forest Site 15, Liberty County: Primitive camping with boat launch and fishing on the Ochlockonee River west of the Bradwell Bay Wilderness.

Directions: From Tallahassee, take SR 20/Blountstown Highway west to the hamlet of Hosford, and turn right (south) on SR 65. After about 2 miles, turn left (east) on CR 67. Follow CR 67 for about 15 miles and you should see a sign for Revell Landing on your left. (Watch for FR 119 on your right and you will be in the vicinity.)

Smith Creek Hunt Camp: Forest Site 1, Franklin County: Primitive camping along the Apalachicola River north of historic Fort Gadsden.

Directions: From Tallahassee, take SR 20/Blountstown Highway west to SR 65 and turn left (south). Once past the hamlet of Sumatra, signs should appear on your right.

Twin Poles Hunt Camp: Forest Site 8, Liberty County: Primitive camping virtually in the center of the forest.

Directions: From Tallahassee, take SR 20/Blountstown Highway west to SR 65 and turn left (south). Follow SR 65 about 10 miles and turn left (east) onto FR 120. Twin Poles will be about 6.5 miles south on the east side of FR 120.

White Oak Landing Hunt Camp: Forest Site 6, Liberty County: Primitive camping, with portable toilets, but no drinking water; boat launch facilities on River Styx with access to the Apalachicola River and superb fishing. With a name like River Styx, it ought to be very good or very bad.

Directions: Take SR 12 south from Bristol for 12.8 miles and veer right on CR 379 at Orange. Drive 9 miles and turn right (west) on FR 115 for 3 miles.

Wood Lake Hunt Camp: Forest Site 12, Wakulla County: Primitive camping with a boat launch and fishing, just across the Ochlockonee River from Tate's Hell State Forest.

Directions: Follow US 319 south from Tallahassee to the small town of Sopchoppy. When US 319 turns left, continue straight on CR 375 and turn left (south) at the intersection with CR 299. Watch for signs on the right (west) along either FR 340 or FR 338.

36 Newport Campground

Location: South of Tallahassee in Wakulla County in the hamlet of Newport (30° 11' 56" N, 84° 10' 52" W)
Season: Year-round
Sites: 13 full hookups, 21 primitive campsites
Maximum length: Call for current information
Facilities: Sewage hookup, bathhouse/restroom, boat ramp, potable water, picnicking, a playground, river observation area
Fee per night: Full hookup $$$; primitive camping $$
Management: County Parks & Recreation Department
Contact: Wakulla County Parks & Recreation Department, 79 Recreation Dr., Crawfordville, FL 32327, (850) 925-4530/926-7227, or email at info@wcprd.com (to reserve a site or discuss availability)
Finding the campground: Off US 98 in the unincorporated hamlet of Newport.
About the campground: A surprisingly inviting site on the St. Marks River with mixed sun and shade, this facility is a popular manatee-spotting area, and the occasional alligator wanders through as well. Canoes and kayaks can be rented at the nearby Lighthouse Center (beside the bridge on US 98 over the St. Marks River).

37 Aucilla Wildlife Management Area

Location: Southern Jefferson and Taylor Counties, near the hamlet of Wacissa (30° 21' 30" N, 83° 59' 14" W)
Season: Year-round
Sites: Camping up to 10 days is allowed along the Wacissa River at the 1,060-acre Goose Pasture Campground except during the general gun season. Primitive camping (tents only) is also allowed at designated sites along the Florida Trail. All camping is first-come, first served. For information contact the Suwannee River Water Management District (WMD) at (386) 362-1001 or in Florida at (800) 226-1066. Camping permits can be obtained at the Goose Pasture kiosk or, for primitive camping, from the WMD.
Maximum length: Call for current information
Facilities: Goose pasture, boat ramp, picnic area, toilet facilities
Fee per night: Call for current information
Management: Fish & Wildlife Conservation Commission (FWC) and Suwannee River Water Management District (WMD)
Contact: http://myfwc.com, http://www.srwmd.state.fl.us/index.asp?nid=183
Finding the campground: From Perry, travel 22 miles west on US 98 to Powell Hammock Road and turn right (north). Drive 4 miles and turn left (west) on Goose Pasture Road. Travel 2.75 miles and the tract are on both sides of the road. Continue for 1 mile and the road ends at Goose Pasture Campground.
About the campground: Goose Pasture in Jefferson County is an intertwined area of pine plantation and hardwoods. The developed park is on the west or Wacissa side of the WMA. Two rivers

running generally north-to-south define the Aucilla WMA: the Wacissa (the larger western section) and the Aucilla (the smaller eastern section). Within the area's 47,532 acres there are plenty of ways to have fun.

The Wacissa is not a swamp river. Spring-fed and beautiful, it is ideal for canoeing, fishing, swimming, and snorkeling. (In the river one must be extremely cautious to avoid speeding motorboats and airboats, however; in the freshwater springs there's a possibility of meeting gators or moccasins.) A boat ramp, picnic area, and toilet facilities are located at the river's headwaters.

The Aucilla River is narrower; its dark gold, but clear waters flow between high limestone banks and dense hardwood forests. In other sections, kayakers experience muddy swamp with cypress and gum (cypress "knees" are protected). Downstream, there is a stretch of rocky shoals.

In the Aucilla section one can hike the Aucilla Sinks Trail, which passes sinkholes and caves created in the underlying limestone when the river, its waters laced with tannic acid, rises and falls. (Tannic acid leeched from sources such as oak tree roots gives the water its golden-brown hue. Harmless to humans, because its concentration is low, the acid-laced water over thousands of years has dissolved holes in the stone.)

The North Central Region

Counties: Madison, Taylor, Hamilton, Suwannee, Lafayette, Dixie, Columbia, Gilchrist, Baker, Union, Bradford, Alachua, Levy, Nassau, Duval, Clay, Putnam, Marion Citrus

The North Central Region

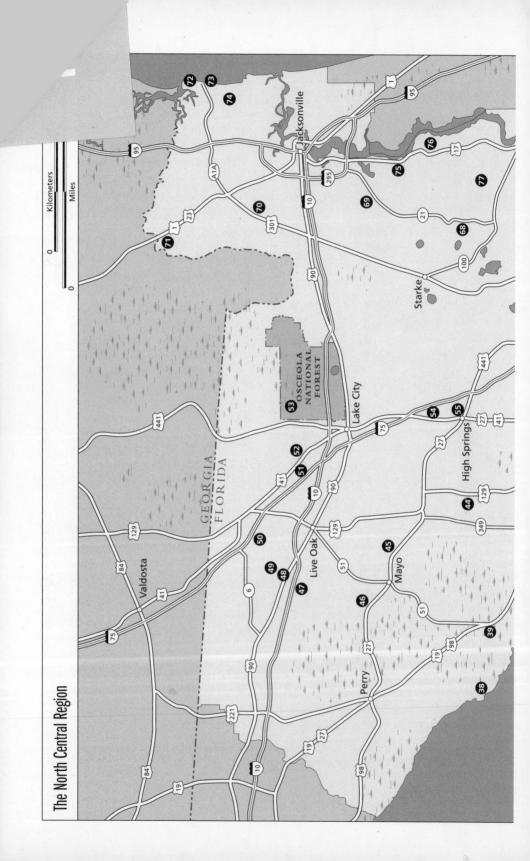

GEORGIA

FLORIDA

OSCEOLA NATIONAL FOREST

Jacksonville

Starke

Lake City

High Springs

Live Oak

Mayo

Perry

Valdosta

Kilometers

Miles

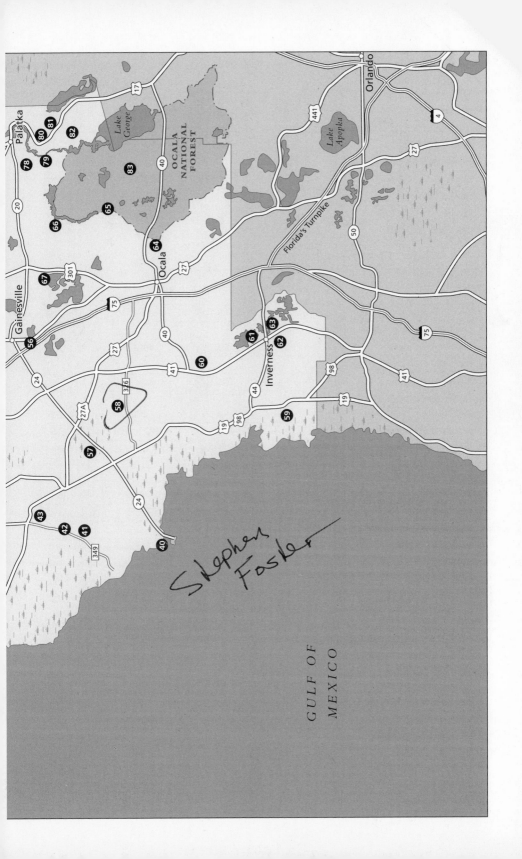

#	Name	Hookup Sites	Total Sites[1]	Max RV Length	Hookups	Toilets	Showers	Dump Station	Recreation	Fee	Can Reserve
38	Big Bend WMA	-	-	-	-	-	-	-	HSFBL, hunting	-	Yes
39	Steinhatchee Springs WMA	-	-	-	-	-	-	-	HFBR, hunting	-	No
40	Shell Mound Levy County Park	20	30	-	WE	F/NF	Yes	No	HSFBLC	$	No
41	New Pine Landing	-	-	-	-	-	-	-	FBL	-	No
42	Manatee Springs State Park	92	92, T	35	WE	F	Yes	Yes	HSFBC, scuba	$$	Yes
43	Dixie County Public Parks	See individual listings for more detailed information. Sites vary from primitive to well equipped.							SFBL	$$	No
44	Rock Bluff Ferry	-	-	-	-	-	-	-	FBL	-	No
45	Troy Springs WMA	-	-	-	-	-	-	-	HFBLRC, hunting	-	No
46	Lafayette Blue Springs State Park	-	16, T, C	-	WE	NF	-	-	HSFBL, scuba	$	Yes
47	Twin Rivers State Forest/WMA	-	-	-	-	-	-	-	HSFBR, hunting	$	No
48	Suwannee River State Park	30	30, T, C	94	WE	F	Yes	Yes	HFBLC	$$	Yes
49	Nobles Ferry	-	-	-	-	-	-	-	FBL	-	No
50	Hamilton County Parks	-	-	-	E	F	No	No	SHFBL	-	No
51	Stephen Foster Folk Culture Center State Park	45	45, T, C	100	WE	F	Yes	Yes	HFBRC	$$	Yes
52	Suwannee River Wilderness Trail	-	-	-	-	F	Yes	-	HFBLRC, hunting	-	Yes
53	Osceola National Forest	See individual listings for more detailed information. Sites vary from exceedingly primitive to well equipped.							HSFBLC, hunting	$–$$	No
54	O'Leno State Park	55	61, T, C	61	WE	F	Yes	Yes	HSFBRC	$$	Yes
55	River Rise Preserve State Park	-	T	0	WE	F/NF	Yes	No	HSFBLRC	$	Yes
56	Payne's Prairie Preserve State Park[3]	35	50, T	53	WE	F	Yes	Yes	HFBL2RC	$$	Yes
57	Devil's Hammock WMA	-	-	-	-	-	-	-	HSFBLR, hunting	$	Yes
58	Goethe WMA	-	-	-	-	-	-	-	HFBR, hunting	-	Yes
59	Citrus County Parks	36	52, T	-	WES	F	Yes	Yes	HFBL	$$	Yes
60	Rainbow Springs State Park	53	60	56	WES	F	Yes	Yes	HSBC, snorkeling	$$	Yes
61	Potts WMA	-	-	-	-	-	-	-	HFBLRC, hunting	-	No
62	Flying Eagle WMA	-	-	-	-	-	-	-	HFBLR, hunting	-	Yes
63	Fort Cooper State Park	-	4, T	-	-	NF	-	-	HSFBC	$	Yes
64	Silver River State Park	69	69, T, C	100	WE	F	Yes	Yes	HSBRC, snorkel	$$	Yes
65	Gore's Landing County Park	-	-	-	-	-	-	-	HFBL	$	No
66	Horseshoe Lake Park & Retreat	-	C	-	-	F	Yes	No	HFB	$$$	Yes
67	Lochloosa WMA	-	-	-	-	-	-	-	HFBL (nearby), hunting	-	No
68	Mike Roess Gold Head Branch State Park[2]	84	89, T, C	45	WE	F	Yes	Yes	HS1FBRC	$$	Yes
69	Jennings Forest WMA	-	-	-	-	-	-	-	HFBLRC, hunting	-	No

	Hookup Sites	Total Sites[1]	Max RV Length	Hookups	Toilets	Showers	Dump Station			
70 Cary State Forest	-	-	-	-	F	Yes	No	HR, huntin.,		
71 Ralph E. Simmons Memorial State Forest/WMA	-	-	-	-	-	-	-	HRC, hunting	-	No
72 Fort Clinch State Park	62	66, T	-	WE	F	Yes	Yes	HSFC	$$$	Yes
73 Little Talbot Island State Park	12	40, T	30	WE	F	Yes	Yes	HSFBLC	$$	Yes
74 Huguenot Memorial Park	-	71	40	-	F	Yes	Yes	HSFBL, surfing	$	Yes
75 Camp Chowenwaw	-	15, T, C	-	-	F	Yes	No	HSFBLC	$$-$$$	Yes
76 Bayard WMA	-	-	-	-	-	-	-	HSFBLRC, hunting	-	Yes
77 Etoniah Creek State Forest and WMA	-	-	-	-	-	-	-	HFBR, hunting	$-$$	No
78 Marjorie Harris Carr Cross Florida Greenway	82	108	-	WE	F	Yes	Yes	HRC	$-$$	Yes
79 Caravelle Ranch WMA	-	-	-	-	-	-	-	HFBLR, hunting	$	No
80 Murphy Creek Conservation Area	-	-	-	-	-	-	-	HFB	-	-
81 Dunn's Creek WMA	-	-	-	-	-	-	-	HFBRC, hunting	-	No
82 Welaka State Forest	-	-	-	-	-	-	-	HR	$-$$	No
83 Ocala National Forest	See individual listings for more detailed information. Sites vary from exceedingly primitive to well equipped.							HSBLRC, snorkel	$-$$	Yes

Key:
Hookups: W = Water, E = Electricity, S = Sewer, C = Cable, P = Phone, I = Internet
Total Sites: T = Tents, C = Cabins, Y = Yurts
Maximum RV Length: Given in feet
Toilets: F = Flush, NF = No flush
Recreation: H = Hiking, S = Swimming, F = Fishing, B = Boating, L = Boat launch, O = Off-road driving, R = Horseback riding, C = Cycling

[1] T: Almost all Florida state parks have some prepared sites with water and electricity and a primitive camping (youth or group—tent-only) area with cold water available. Camping in the primitive area may be regulated by number of occupants, instead of specific sites. C: cabins are available. Y: This is a yurt, a 20-foot diameter temporary shelter with a wooden frame and canvas covering, heat, air-conditioning, and water. Camping in Florida's state forests, like the national forests, is regulated by area rather than site.

[2] At the time of this writing in 2009, Mike Roess Gold Head Branch State Park manager Warren Poplin said that due to drought conditions and low water levels the primary lake (Little Lake Johnson) was temporarily closed to swimming. If conditions improve, the lake will reopen for swimming.

[3] Gasoline-powered boats are not permitted on Lake Wauburg, and no rentals are available.

[4] Reservations are not required but can be made since camping is generally first-come, first-served.

e following state and national parks, state forests, and wildlife manage-
eas in this region do not offer camping at present: Amelia Island, Big Shoals
· Park WMA/State Forest, Big Talbot Island, Camp Blanding WMA, Castillo de
san Marcos National Monument, Cedar Key Museum, Cedar Key Scrub WMA,
Crystal River Archeological/Preserve, Cypress Creek WMA, Devil's Millhopper
Geological, Dudley Farm Historic, Fanning Springs (cabins), Fernandina Plaza,
Forest Capital Museum, Fort George Island Cultural, Fort Matanzas National
Monument, Gainesville-Hawthorne State Trail, George Crady Bridge Fishing Pier,
Grove Park WMA, Gulf Hammock WMA, Homosassa Springs, Homosassa WMA,
Ichetucknee Springs, John M. Bethea State Forest, Little River WMA, Madison
Blue Springs, Marjorie Kinnan Rawlings Historic, Middle Aucilla River WMA,
Nassau WMA, Olustee Battlefield Historic, Peacock Springs, Pumpkin Hill Creek
Preserve, Raiford WMA, San Felasco Hammock Preserve, San Pedro Bay WMA,
Santa Fe Swamp WEA, Troy Springs, Waccasassa Bay Preserve, Yellow Bluff Fort
Historic, and Yulee Sugar Mill Ruins Historic.

38 Big Bend Wildlife Management Area

Location: On the Gulf of Mexico coast in Dixie and Taylor Counties
Season: September 1 to June 30
Sites: Camping is prohibited in this WMA with the exception of 7 island sites on the Big Bend
Saltwater Paddling Trail
Maximum length: Call for current information
Facilities: Call for current information
Fee per night: No charge for camping on these sites, but they are reserved for sea kayakers
with permits
Management: Fish & Wildlife Conservation Commission (FWC)
Contact: (850) 488-4676/5520 for camping permit information or visit http://myfwc.com/
recreation/big_bend/default.asp, or www.floridapaddlingtrails.com for a description of campsites
and trip options beyond the scope of this guide. Also see www.purewaterwilderness.com and www
.steinhatcheetoperry.com for lists of outfitters, guides, shuttles, and secure parking. The concessionaire at Econfina River State Park, (850) 584-2135, will also have information about secure parking.
Finding the WMA: Perhaps the best spot from which to find each of the five WMA units—Hickory
Mound, Spring Creek, Tide Swamp, Jena, and Snipe Island—is Perry (30° 6' 52" N, 83° 34' 57" W)
in Taylor County. Otherwise, your outfitter for the paddling trail will direct you to a meeting location.
About the WMA: Big Bend Wildlife Management Area consists of five units. From a paddler's—
and hence a camper's—point of view, all are the same and yet all are slightly different. On Jena,
you can drive, bike, or horseback ride up and down ancient sand dunes to a panoramic view of
exposed limestone, salt marsh, and the Gulf. At Hagen's Cove on Tide Swamp, you can scallop, gig
flounder at night, picnic, and barbeque. On Spring Creek and at Tide Swamp, you'll find the only
remaining coastal scrub in the Big Bend, and at the Hickory Mound Impoundment, you can crab,
hunt waterfowl in season, and observe a diverse abundance of birds year-round.

The 105-mile Big Bend Saltwater Paddling Trail offers an excellent chance for paddling campers to explore the area. This is a physically demanding paddle; campsites are 10 to 15 miles apart and your kayak will be filled with gear, food, and water.

Site 1: A free, first-come, first-served primitive campsite on the west bank of the Econfina River 0.4 mile downstream from the public boat ramp. If the site is occupied, check with the Econfina River State Park concessionaire, (850) 584-2135. Park camping is nearby as well as showers and bathrooms; there is a small fee.

Site 2: Rock Island is remote and scenic. The campsite, partially shaded by live oaks, is on the west side of the 20-acre island and has a fire ring. Expect bugs.

Site 3: Spring Warrior Creek is beside a creek 1 mile north of the hamlet of Spring Warrior. Great views of the night sky.

Site 4: Just past Keaton Beach, Sponge Point is an island-like hardwood hammock connected to the mainland by salt marsh. The campsite is shaded by live oaks. Watch for prickly pear cactus.

Site 5: To reach this remote hammock at the mouth of Dallus Creek, you must hike a cleared trail to reach the grassy, shaded campsite. Watch for rattlesnakes.

Site 6: At the town of Steinhatchee, you must arrange for camping or lodging separately. See www.steinhatcheetoperry.com or www.purewaterwilderness.com for more information.

Site 7: The campsite is in a hardwood hammock along Sink Creek. FWC calls this area "remote and wild."

Site 8: At Butler Island, you camp beneath cedars, live oaks, and palms near huge piles of oyster and clam shells (called "middens") left by Native Americans. Watch for poison ivy.

39 Steinhatchee Springs Wildlife Management Area

Location: North from Tenille (29° 46' 36" N, 83° 19' 30" W) in Lafayette, Dixie, and Taylor Counties
Season: Year-round
Sites: Truly primitive camping is prohibited during periods open to hunting and otherwise only by permit.
Maximum length: Call for current information
Facilities: Call for current information
Fee per night: Call for current information
Management: Fish & Wildlife Conservation Commission and Suwannee River Water Management District (WMD)
Contact: (386) 362-1001 for permits, www.srwmd.state.fl.us/index.asp?nid=185, http://myfwc.com
Finding the campground: From I-10, take exit 283 south on US 129/SR 51 into Live Oak, the county seat of Suwannee County. Continue on SR 51 to Mayo, the county seat of Lafayette County. The WMA is 16 miles south of Mayo.
About the campground: This enormous, 20,909-acre WMA surrounds the Steinhatchee River and helps keep developers away from beautiful natural lands and waters. The Steinhatchee River begins in the Mallory Swamp in Lafayette County and runs to the Gulf of Mexico. It goes underground north of the hamlet of Tennille and rises again about 0.5 mile south.

The area is open to the public year-round for hunting, fishing, wildlife viewing, horseback riding (three trails are available in the R.O. Ranch segment), hiking, and biking. Paddling the

Boardwalks over wetlands give visitors an opportunity to get closer to the exotic birds, reptiles, mammals, and plants that thrive in the Sunshine State.

Steinhatchee River is a wonderful experience because the area can be almost totally silent, and the scenery is very tropical.

Access is limited because of the swampy nature of this WMA and the lack of roads into the interior. Entrances and river access points are open for fishing and nature study every day and are located off SR 51 and the graded roads adjacent to the river. Look for the brown public river access signs. Motorized vehicles may be operated only on named or numbered roads. The use of tracked vehicles, airboats, motorcycles, or all terrain vehicles (ATVs) is prohibited. Horses are prohibited during periods open to hunting and are otherwise restricted to marked roads and trails.

40 Shell Mound Levy County Park

Location: Just north of Cedar Key (29° 12' 27" N, 83° 3' 56.3" W), Levy County
Season: Year-round
Sites: 20 campsites with water and electric hookups, and 10 primitive camping sites
Maximum length: Call for current information
Facilities: Restroom, shower facilities, RV dump station, boat ramp, fish cleaning area; volleyball and basketball nets
Fee per night: Call for current information
Management: Levy County Commission
Contact: (352) 221-4466/543-6153 for information on availability

Finding the campground: From exit 384 on I-75 in Gainesville, take SR 24 an hour southwest until the town of Cedar Key on the Gulf Coast is within sight. Turn right (north) on CR 347 and, in a little more than 2 miles, turn left on CR 326. Follow it past the end of the pavement to the park.

About the campground: This "pile of shells" is an ancient feature that was created by Indians over thousands of years. Apparently, eating at this site was very good. The physical height of the mound was achieved as Indians discarded the shells of oysters, clams, and mollusks and the bones of animals plus assorted camp trash. This process took as much as six thousand years. At one time the county mined the mound for materials for road construction; the mound is now protected from all but foot traffic. Perhaps the Indians also enjoyed the amazing sunsets over the Gulf.

As a special note for kayakers—and we might customarily say canoers and kayakers, but the percentage of kayaks has zoomed far beyond that of canoes—wilderness camping on Clark Island (352-543-6463: 29° 14' 29" N, 83° 3' 41" W) is only an hour paddle north of Shell Mound.

41 New Pine Landing

Location: On the west bank of the Suwannee River in Dixie County south of US 19/98/27A (29° 31' 48" N, 82° 58' 42" W).

Season: Year-round

Sites: First-come, first-served primitive camping

Facilities: Restroom, boat ramp with unimproved parking (accommodates 12 vehicles); no drinking water

Maximum length: Call for current information

Facilities: Call for current information

Fee per night: None

Management: Fish & Wildlife Conservation Commission

Contact: (850) 488-4676, http://myfwc.com

Finding the campground: From Cross City, the county seat in the center of Dixie County, drive east on US 19/98/27A to CR 349 in Old Town. Turn right (south) on 349 for 5.1 miles to New Pine Landing Boulevard. Turn left (east) for 1.2 miles to the ramp and camping.

About the campground: Expect a great view of the tannin-laden Suwannee River, the sound of wind whispering through the pines and palmettos.

42 Manatee Springs State Park

Location: 6 miles west of Chiefland in Levy County and on the Suwannee River (29° 29' 21" N, 82° 58' 37" W).

Season: Year-round

Sites: 92, all with water and electricity. Sites 26–39 and 48, located in the Magnolia 1 area, are tent only. Organized groups of six or more can camp in the primitive youth camp area reserved for non-profit, organized groups.

Maximum length: 35 feet

Facilities: Centrally located, full-service comfort stations; drinking water; outdoor shower; park concession offering food, drinks, gifts, camper supplies; canoe/kayak rentals, toilets, showers, drinking water, fire rings, picnic tables
Fee per night: $$
Management: Florida Division of Recreation and Parks
Contact: (352) 493-6072 (park office), www.floridastateparks.org/manateesprings/default.cfm
Finding the campground: Manatee Springs is approximately 7 miles west of Chiefland in Levy County. From the US Highway 19/27A intersection with CR 320 in Chiefland, drive west approximately 5.2 miles on CR 320 to the entrance of the park.
About the campground: The heart of this park is a crystal-clear first-magnitude spring that maintains a steady 72 degrees year-round. On a hot Florida day, a swim begins by checking for manatees and then a quick plunge into water so cold you will expect ice cubes to float past.

The manatee is a herbivore related to the hippo. In winter, manatees swim from the river into the spring. They are protected, although in select places you can join a guided group to feed them and stroke their backs. Gentle giants, their encounters with motorboat propellers cause them grievous injuries.

Scuba diving is also popular in the central spring pool and along the spring's 0.25-mile run to the Suwannee.

43 Dixie County Public Parks

Location: Dixie is a big county (864 square miles). The county seat is Cross City (29° 38' 7" N, 83° 7' 29" W) on US 19/98/27A. The eastern boundary is formed by the Suwannee River; the western boundary by the Steinhatchee River; and the southern boundary by the Gulf of Mexico.
Sites:

Gornto Springs: 24 shaded sites, 10 with electricity; boat ramp at the Suwannee River, 20-vehicle parking lot, RV hookups; showers (but no potable water); picnic area; no reservations accepted: first-come, first-served; swimming, fishing ($$)
Directions: Take CR 351 north from Cross City to CR 349 and turn left (north). Turn right on Rock Springs Church Road/NE 816 Avenue and follow it to the camping area. (Gornto, variously spelled Guaranto, is at 29° 46' 47.2" N, 82° 56' 23.8" W).

Hinton Landing/John O. Green: Tent camping and RV hookups at this site on the Suwannee River (29° 33' 30" N, 82° 56' 54" W); boat ramp (but no swimming), parking area for up to 20 vehicles, restrooms, picnic area ($$)
Directions: Take US 19/98/27A east from Cross City. With the Suwannee River on the left (north), turn right (south) on CR 317 (Google Maps calls it "SE 317 Hwy") and watch for the sign.

Horseshoe Beach: 14 RV sites, 5 tent sites at this little area; water and electric hookups, restrooms with showers, a few picnic tables, open-air pavilion. Swimming here is terrific as are views of the setting sun. ($$)
Directions: Take CR 351 south from Cross City to the hamlet of Horseshoe Beach (29° 26' 24" N, 83° 17' 36" W) on the Gulf of Mexico. Turn right on Eighth Avenue and drive the few blocks to the park. (It is also called Butler Douglas Memorial Park.)

Shired Island: 17 RV sites and 5 tent sites; electricity, picnic tables, grills, 6 covered pavilions, wheelchair-accessible restrooms with cement floors, no showers, ramp for boaters and anglers on Shired Creek. Mosquitoes, sand flies, and other biting insects can be a huge problem depending upon the time of year. Swimming in the Gulf is wonderful, but don't expect white sand at these Big Bend beaches, which are brown, coarse and sometimes muddy. Sunsets, though, can be magnificent.

Directions: Take CR 351 south from Cross City to CR 357 and into the Lower Suwannee National Wildlife Refuge. The campground, which is on the Gulf of Mexico, is on the right just past Shired Creek (29° 23' 54" N, 83° 12' 36" W).

Fee per night: $$ per day—no credit cards—at Gornto Beach, Horseshoe Springs, and Shired Island. An off-site attendant visits once a day to collect fee.

Management: Dixie County Board of County Commissioners

Contact: (352) 498-1239, http://dixie.fl.gov/public_works_parks_and_recreation.html

About Dixie County: This lightly populated (about 15,000) county is known for its flatwoods, oak, cypress, and pine thickets, all of which are prone to flooding, plus some old-fashioned country-side, and miles of pine plantations. The Gulf coastal area of the Big Bend region was formerly known as the "Mud Coast," but has recently been dubbed Florida's "Nature Coast."

Quickly filleted, lightly breaded, and browned in a skillet with butter, speckled trout from the Gulf of Mexico are delicious.

44 Rock Bluff Ferry

Location: The junction of SR 340 on the west bank of the Suwannee River in Gilchrist County (29° 47' 56.7" N, 82° 55' 07" W)
Season: Year-round
Sites: Primitive camping only; first-come, first-served
Maximum length: Call for current information
Facilities: Picnic facilities, but do not expect water or restroom facilities. Single-lane ramp with an unimproved parking lot capable of accommodating 20 vehicles. Note: Your cell phone coverage may not reach here.
Fee per night: None
Management: Fish & Wildlife Conservation Commission
Contact: (850) 488-4676, http://myfwc.com/
Finding the campground: From I-75, take exit 404 and drive west on CR 236 to High Springs. Drive straight through the town of High Springs and turn right (west) on CR 340. Follow this road west to the Suwannee River and the boat ramp.
About the campground: It is beautiful here on the banks of the Suwannee, but there are no amenities. Bank fishing is allowed on the site and fishing is fine in the river.

45 Troy Springs Wildlife Management Area

Location: In Lafayette County on the Suwannee River (camping at the northernmost Adams Tract, 30 2' 6" N, 83 1' 12" W)
Season: Year-round
Sites: By permit at designated sites only
Maximum length: Call for current information
Facilities: Call for current information
Fee per night: Call for current information
Management: Fish & Wildlife Conservation Commission and Suwannee River Water Management District
Contact: (386) 362-1001 for permits or visit http://myfwc.com
Finding the campground: From I-10, take exit 283 south on SR 51 to Mayo and turn left (southeast) on US 27. The Troy Springs complex is 8.5 miles on the left.
About the campground: Troy Springs is a 1,080-acre, three-parcel WMA that lies along more than 4 miles of the Middle Suwannee River in east Lafayette County. Troy Springs State Park and a county park are between the WMA tracts.

The springs at Troy Springs pump 65 million gallons of water into the Suwannee each day. The WMA is a small game-hunting area that permits hiking, off-road biking, wildlife viewing, and horseback riding on its trails. Fishing, canoeing, and boating opportunities are available on the Suwannee, and two canoe launches and a boat ramp are adjacent to the WMA.

46 Lafayette Blue Springs State Park

Location: 7 miles northwest of Mayo on the west side of the Suwannee River in Lafayette County (30° 7' 35" N, 83° 13' 34" W)

Season: Year-round

Sites: 11 tent sites and 5 fully-furnished cabins

Maximum length: RVs are not allowed overnight

Facilities: Non-flush toilets, drinking water, fire rings, picnic tables. The park has 5 full service cabins that sleep 6 and include a dishwasher, fireplace, and large screened porch; no pets. Cabin reservations can be made up to 11 months in advance through Reserve America online or calling 1-866 I CAMP FL (1-866-422-6735) or 1-800-326-3521.

Fee per night: $

Management: Florida Division of Recreation and Parks

Contact: (386) 294-3667, www.floridastateparks.org/lafayettebluesprings/default.cfm

Finding the campground: From Mayo, the county seat of Lafayette County, drive northwest on US 27 for 4.3 miles. Turn right (north) on CR 292 and continue for 2.1 miles. Turn right (east) on Blue Springs Road and drive 0.2 mile to the park entrance.

About the campground: The Suwannee is a river of great contrasts. Upstream, flowing out of the Okefenokee Swamp, the golden flow rushes between white sand and limestone bluffs topped with pine and hardwood forests. Downstream, the river gradually widens as it makes its way to the Gulf of Mexico, and the banks gradually diminish in height as palm, cedar, and cypress become the dominant trees.

You may enter Blue Springs by car or by boat from the Suwannee. Situated next to the camping area, the springs pump 168 million gallons of cold, clear water into the Suwannee each day. Swimming and snorkeling in the spring are as popular as is fishing in the river. Scuba diving is permitted (with proof of appropriate cave-diving certification) through Blue Springs into the Green Sink Cave System and the 12,000 feet of surveyed cavern passageways. During rainy seasons the river water may back up into the springs, and when this occurs, swimming and diving are prohibited.

47 Twin Rivers State Forest & Wildlife Management Area

Location: Twin Rivers State Forest and WMA is located along the banks of the Withlacoochee and Suwannee Rivers. The forest encompasses eastern Madison, western Hamilton, and northwestern Suwannee Counties. The Twin Rivers State Forest office is located on US 90, about 2 miles west of the town of Live Oak (30° 17' 41" N, 82° 59' 09" W). The hamlet of Ellaville (30° 22' 52" N, 83° 10' 22" W) is situated at the intersection of US 90, the Suwannee River, and the northern forest units.

Season: Year-round

Sites: Full-facility camping is not available, but a few primitive camp areas are located along multiple-use trails. Permits are required for special or group recreational activities, and can be obtained from the forest office at no charge. On the Blue Springs Unit of the WMA, camping is prohibited during bird-dog training, but is allowed by landowner permit during other periods.

Call for current information

current information

-$$

ivision of Forestry and Fish and Wildlife Conservation Commission

208-1460, www.fl-dof.com/state_forests/twin_rivers.html, http://myfwc.com,

www.nor._ .org, http://floridabirdingtrail.com

Finding the forest: Take exit 275 on I-10 in Suwannee County and drive west on US 90. It is about a dozen miles to the hamlet of Ellaville and the Suwannee River. Various units of the state forest are to the north and south of this location.

About the forest/WMA: Twin Rivers State Forest comprises fourteen noncontiguous tracts, which makes planning a visit all the more necessary. Multiple use of the forest includes forest management for timbering, ecosystem restoration, recreation, wildlife management, watershed protection, and environmental education.

Camping is primitive. Plan to take out whatever you take in, but remember that there is no water, that cellular telephone coverage may be non-existent, and that it could take rescue crews days to locate you. So make sure your camping plan includes directions and locations, contact information (if possible). This is not a rugged forest, but sections can be difficult and swampy at times, so bug dope is recommended at all times of the year.

48 Suwannee River State Park

Location: West of Live Oak, off US 90 in Suwannee County (30° 22' 44" N, 83° 9' 57" W)

Season: Year-round

Sites: 30 partially shaded sites with electricity and water, plus state-of-the-art bathhouses; primitive youth group site; 5 fully equipped, air-conditioned, riverside, 2-bedroom cabins (accommodating 6 people each); pets welcome, except in cabins

Maximum length: Unlimited in the pull-through sites

Facilities: Full-facility camping with water, electric hookups, bathhouses

Fee per night: $$

Management: Florida Division of Recreation and Parks

Contact: (386) 362-2746, www.floridastateparks.org/suwanneeriver/default.cfm, www
.reserveamerica.com

Finding the campground: From I-10, take exit 275 onto US 90 and drive west. The entrance to the park is approximately 6 miles west on the north side of the road.

About the campground: Here you'll find high scenic bluffs and sandy ridges, second-growth scrub oak and white sandbars in the glowing golden-brown flow of water.

Here one still finds earthworks built during the Civil War to guard against the union navy, which did steam up the river, although the shifting sand, the high bluffs, and the narrow riverbed made navigation exceptionally hazardous. Other remnants of history include one of the state's oldest cemeteries and a paddle-wheel shaft said to be from a nineteenth-century steamboat.

There are five active trails, ranging from 0.25 mile to 18 miles. These loop through surrounding woodlands and provide panoramic views of the rivers. Paddling is a great way to spend a day as the river is incredibly scenic and both the Withlacoochee and Suwannee River Trails have trailheads at the park.

49 Nobles Ferry

Location: In southwest Hamilton County on the Suwannee River (30° 26' 18" N, 83° 5' 36" W)
Season: Year-round
Sites: First-come, first-served primitive camping
Facilities: Single-lane boat ramp and parking lot for 25 vehicles; no restrooms, electricity, or potable water
Maximum length: Call for current information
Facilities: Call for current information
Fee per night: None
Management: Fish & Wildlife Conservation Commission
Contact: (850) 488-4676, http://myfwc.com/
Finding the campground: From exit 460, the intersection of SR 6 and I-75, go west on SR 6 for 3.3 miles. Turn left (south) on CR 751 and drive 3.5 miles. The ramp is on the right side of the road before River Bridge Park.
About the campground: Noble's Ferry allows overnight camping, but it is usually only frequented by fishermen or young people escaping briefly from the bonds of parental authority. If you find yourself in the neighborhood and cannot find accommodations elsewhere, this is a reasonable but distant back-up.

50 Hamilton County Parks

Location: Gibson Park is at 6884 SW County Rd.751, Jasper, FL 32052 (30° 26' 12" N, 83° 5' 36" W)
Season: Year-round
Sites: First-come, first-served rustic camping; maximum stay 10 days
Maximum length: Call for current information
Facilities: Water, electricity, flush toilets, RV hookups, screened pavilions with cement picnic tables and brick grills, boat ramp
Fee per night: Primitive tent camping, $; RV hookup with electricity and water, $$
Management: Call for current information
Contact: (386) 792-1631, http://hcrecreation.com/gibsonpark.aspx
Finding the campground: From I-75, take SR 6 west 3 miles to CR 751. Turn left (south) and drive 4 miles to the Suwannee River. The campground is on the right just before crossing the river.
About the campground: On the north bank of the Suwannee River, county-operated Gibson Park is sandy, but shady, and while there is some road noise, CR 751 is rarely busy. Recreationally, the well-appointed boat ramp allows easy access to the Suwannee River for fishing and boating, and this is an especially fine place to launch a canoe or kayak. Campers are asked to register at the Florida Agricultural Inspection Station—manned 24/7 so there is security and a telephone—directly across the road. There is a large conservation area within a short bike ride and hiking opportunities in the area are plentiful.

51 Stephen Foster Folk Culture Center State Park

Location: In White Springs, Columbia County (30° 20' 9.0" N, 82° 46' 11.6" W)
Season: Year-round
Sites: Newly renovated campground with 45 oak-shaded sites; primitive youth group camping site; 5 fully equipped, riverside, 2-bedroom cabins accommodating up to 6 people; pets welcome on leash, except in cabins
Maximum length: Unlimited in drive-through sites
Facilities: Full-facility camping with water, electricity, and bathhouses
Fee per night: $$
Management: Florida Division of Recreation and Parks
Contact: (386) 397-2733, www.floridastateparks.org/stephenfoster/default.cfm; (866) 422-6735/(800) 326-3521, www.reserveamerica.com
Finding the campground: From I-75 to SR 136 (exit 439), travel east on SR 136 for 3 miles. Turn left on US 41. The park entrance is on the left. From I-10 to US 41 north (exit 301), travel 9 miles to White Springs. The park entrance is on the left.
About the campground: Located on the north bank of the Suwannee River, the park is named after, and the museum or exposition center honors, composer Stephen Foster, who wrote "Old

Wildflowers carpet Florida's roadsides in the early summer.

Folks at Home." Although its lyrics are reminiscent of the pre–Civil War era, it is still the Florida state song—and the song that made the river famous.

The park's museum features nineteenth-century-era exhibits, and small dioramas built in the 1950s when the park was private, which relate to Foster's most famous songs. His music can be heard from the park's ninety-seven-bell carillon, which plays throughout the day. Craft Square offers demonstrations of blacksmithing, quilting, stained-glass making, and other crafts, and often has re-enactors who re-create nineteenth-century life.

Hiking, bicycling, canoeing, and wildlife viewing are popular activities. Miles of trails wind through scenic areas. Cabins can be reserved as can the sites in the park's full-facility campground.

Every Memorial Day weekend, the park hosts the Florida Folk Festival, which has become a crowded and joyous event for thousands of attendees. Other events include concerts, weekend retreats, a monthly coffeehouse, a regional quilt show, and an antique tractor show.

52 Suwannee River Wilderness Trail

Location: On the Suwannee River beginning in White Springs, Columbia County (30° 19' 54" N, 82° 45' 22" W)

Season: Year-round

Sites:

Woods Ferry River Camp: Campsite 1: 1,094 acres in Suwannee County on the south bank of the Suwannee River; 5 sleeping platforms, picnic pavilion, restrooms with hot showers, tent camping area. Jerry Branch (519 acres), a primitive recreation area, occupies the north bank of the river.

Holton Creek River Camp: Campsite 2: 2,536 acres in Hamilton County on the north side of the Suwannee River (the second river camp between White Springs and Branford); 5 screened shelters, picnic pavilion, restrooms with hot showers, tent-camping area. Across the river is the 60-acre Trillium Slopes primitive recreation tract.

Peacock Slough River Camp: Campsite 3: 1,174 acres in Suwannee County, on the north side of the river. Sleeping platforms, hot showers, restrooms. Spend the night in comfort while you enjoy paddling the Suwannee.

Adams Tract River Camp: Campsite 4: 983 acres in Lafayette County on the south side of the river, adjacent to Owens Springs (474 acres) and Walker Springs (983 acres) and across the river from Little River (2,202 acres), which is in Suwannee County and provides 5 sleeping platforms, picnic pavilion, restrooms with hot showers, group camping area.

Maximum length: Call for current information

Fee per night: None

Management: The Suwannee River Wilderness Trail is a cooperative effort of the Florida Department of Environmental Protection and the Suwannee River Water Management District, which provides management services.

Contact: Call (800) 868-9914 for reservations, www.srwmd.state.fl.us, www.floridastateparks.org/wilderness/default.cfm

Finding the campgrounds: Campgrounds can be accessed from land, but they are meant to be used by paddlers on the Suwannee River.

About the campgrounds: Natural Florida is defined by the Suwannee, identified forever with the Old South by Stephen Foster's song of that era, "Old Folks at Home." The 170-mile Suwannee River Wilderness Trail begins in White Springs where the upper Suwannee is narrow, flowing through towering pines and stately cypress along the riverbanks and high bluffs. The current is typically slow and lazy.

The middle stretch from Suwannee River State Park to the town of Branford is cold, freshwater-spring country. The river begins to widen here, with numerous clear springs and shifting sandbars. On hot summer days, spring hopping or lounging on the sandbars is popular.

The lower Suwannee, south of the town of Branford, runs wide and deep. It is a favorite area for powerboats and anglers as well as paddlers. The sandy banks become lower, sloping gently toward the river. Anglers on the lower Suwannee have their choice of saltwater or freshwater catches with manatees and jumping sturgeon to watch for. A Special Use Authorization is required before camping along the river. Paddlers should contact the Suwannee River Water Management District, (386) 362-1001, for restrictions, access, or special conditions.

53 Osceola National Forest

Location: Straddling I-10 just west of Jacksonville, just south of Okefenokee Swamp in Columbia County. The Ocean Pond Campground is at 30° 14' 24" N, 82° 26' 0" W. Mailing address is Osceola Ranger District Office, P.O. Box 70, Olustee, FL 32072, (386) 752-2577. The Olustee Depot visitor center is on East Highway 90, Olustee, FL 32072. The Ocean Pond Campground is in Columbia.
Season: Year-round. General gun season for deer (or feral hogs) runs from mid-Nov into Jan (dates vary by year), and during that time all camping is restricted to designated hunt camps and to Ocean Pond Campground.
Sites: Ocean Pond Campground has 67 sites for tents, trailers, or RVs, some at lakeside; there are also 9 hunt camps in the forest, 1 with permanent toilet and potable water, others only during hunting season; some primitive and group camping also (list below).
Maximum length: Call for current information
Facilities: Ocean Pond has beach area for swimming, sunbathing; boat ramp, drinking water, hot showers, flush toilets. No sewer hookups, but a dump station is situated near the campground entrance; electrical hookups are available at 19 of the sites.
Fee per night: From $ to $$, depending on site
Management: USDA Forest Service, Florida's Division of Forestry, Florida Fish & Wildlife Conservation Commission, two water management districts (Suwannee River and St. John's)
Contact: (386) 752-0147, www.fs.fed.us
Finding Ocean Pond Campground: From I-10 west of Jacksonville, take exit 324 and turn west on US 90. It is about 7 miles to CR 250A, which turns right (north) into the forest. As this road bends left (west) at about 4 miles, look for the signs and the forest road that leads immediately to the campground on the north side of Ocean Pond.

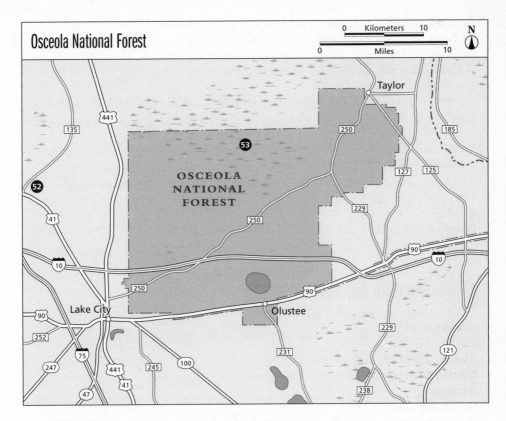

Osceola National Forest

OSCEOLA NATIONAL FOREST

About the campground: Sites are located on the north side of Ocean Pond, a 1,760-acre lake that is the only significant body of water in the national forest other than thousands of small streams and rivulets. Although the lake is relatively small, power boating, fishing, and even water-skiing are allowed. A section of the Florida Trail runs through the forest. It links to the campground by a 0.5-mile trail spur.

About the forest: At 194,803 acres, the Osceola is the smallest of Florida's three national forests. Unlike the Ocala or the Apalachicola, which draw hundreds of thousands, perhaps millions of visitors a year, the Osceola is, on any given day, a quiet place that seems more remote than its location. The two notable exceptions are the opening of hunting season in November and the reenactment, in February, of the Civil War battle of Olustee, the hamlet in the southern end of the forest.

The forest lies south of the Okefenokee Swamp, the "land of trembling earth," now the Okefenokee National Wildlife Refuge. Thus, the forest is primarily swamp and low uplands or "flatwoods," a mixed area of low pine ridges separated by runnels of water with cypress, magnolia, and bay. It is filled with deer, feral hogs, black bears, and alligators; snakes and raptors are also abundant.

The park offers more than 50 miles of trails for riders. Consisting of four interconnected loops, these trails pass through quiet, open pine flatwoods and wet, scenic bays. Trails begin at West Tower where there is an area for horse camping, horse stalls, drinking water, and a flush toilet.

FOREST RECREATION AREAS/CAMPGROUNDS

Primitive and Group Campsites

No-fee primitive camping is allowed everywhere in the forest except at Olustee Beach. A primitive camp shelter is located along the Florida National Scenic Trail and can be used on a first-come, first-served basis. All directions from I-10, exit 324.

Sandhill: Forest Site 1, Columbia County

Directions: Drive west on US 90 past the Olustee Battlefield and turn right (north) on CR 250A. Follow CR 250A about 5 miles to CR 250 and turn right (north). In 0.5 mile, turn left (north) onto FR 233 and follow it around several miles to FR 234. Turn right (north) and drive 2-plus miles to FR 272 on the right. It is about 1.0 mile to the camp on the right along FR 272.

Big Camp: Forest Site 2, Baker County

Directions: From Olustee Battlefield, drive north on Seventeen Mile Camp Road (FR 207) about 10 miles to Old Sand Road and turn left (west). Drive about 1.0 mile and turn right on FR 212 to the campsite.

East Tower: Forest Site 4, Baker County; restrooms, drinking water

Directions: From Olustee Battlefield, drive north on Seventeen Mile Camp Road (FR 207) and turn right (east) after about 5 miles on CR 250. After 2.50 miles, turn left (north) on CR 229. The campsite is about 2 miles on the right.

Seventeen Mile: Forest Site 5, Baker County

Directions: From Olustee Battlefield, drive north about 6 miles on Seventeen Mile Camp Road (FR 207) to the intersection with CR 250. Turn right (east), and in about 0.25 mile, begin watching for signs.

West Tower: Forest Site 6, Columbia County; restrooms, drinking water, horse trail

Directions: From Olustee Battlefield, drive 8 miles west on US 90 to Still Road and turn right. Still Road becomes FR 236. At the intersection with CR 250, turn right and almost immediately FR 236 branches off to the left (north). Follow 236 to the intersection with Greenfield Tower Road and turn right. The camp is about 0.50 mile on the right.

Wiggins: Forest Site 7, Columbia County

Directions: From Olustee Battlefield, drive west on US 90 for about 5 miles and turn right (north) on FR 215. The camp is located just before the intersection with CR 250 on the west side of the road.

Hog Pen Landing: Forest Site 8, Baker County; restrooms, boat launch, fishing; $

Spanish moss draped along the long limbs of live oak trees is a hallmark of Florida camping. It gives a soft Southern feel to an Alachua County historic site, Boulware Springs.

Directions: From Olustee Battlefield, drive west on US 90 for about 4 miles and turn right on FR 241. In about 2 miles, watch for signs on the right.

Cobb: Forest Site 10, Baker County; primitive, restrooms

Directions: From Olustee Battlefield, drive north on Seventeen Mile Camp Road (FR 207) about 2 miles and turn left (west) on FR 235. In about 1.0 mile, watch for signs on the right.

Landing Group Area: Near the Ocean Pond Campground, the Landing offers a secluded group campsite available by reservation only (Osceola Ranger District Office, 386-752-2577); maximum of 50 persons allowed; swimming, boating, camping, picnicking. Facilities include a sand beach, a boat launch for small boats, picnic shelter, large group grill, and restrooms with showers. $$$

54 O'Leno State Park

Location: Beside US 441 6 miles north of High Springs in Alachua County (29° 55' 01" N, 82° 35' 02" W)

Season: Year-round

Sites: 61 family sites (55 accommodate RVs), 3 primitive areas, 17 cabins (in-season, rented as a group but from September 1 to May 1 available for individual rental), dining hall with its own kitchen facility, recreation hall, and centrally located bathhouses. Cabins complex can be reserved up to 1 year in advance.

Maximum length: 61 feet

Facilities: Tables, in-ground grills, fire rings, pavilion, and complete bathhouses. The Smokehouse campsite and the cabin area have complete shower/restroom facilities. In addition, three other restroom facilities are located in the park. Primitive camping areas have pavilions, campfire circles, and, except for Sweetwater Lake, cold showers.

Fee per night: $$ full-facility; $ primitive

Management: Florida Division of Recreation and Parks

Contact: (386) 454-1853, http://www.floridastateparks.org/oleno/default.cfm

Finding the campground: O'Leno is located just west of I-75 in the southern end of Columbia County in north Florida. It can be reached from the north by taking the 414 exit south on US 441 for about 6 miles. From the south, take the 404 exit and travel southwest on CR 236 about 4 miles to High Springs and then turn north on US 441 for 6 miles. The state park is situated on the east side of US 441.

About the campground: If you are an equestrian, horse camping is available. The horse barn has 20 stalls and there are plenty of trails to give your steed a workout. For the wilderness-minded camper, the Sweetwater Lake primitive area requires a 6.5-mile hike in to sites with a privy, but no water or electricity.

O'Leno is excellent for hiking, wildlife viewing (you may see deer on the entrance road), and especially paddling the quiet and practically unspoiled Santa Fe River. The Santa Fe is known as a brownish-gold tannin-laced river, and in the park, it disappears underground into a sink, reemerging in adjacent River Rise State Preserve more than 3 miles away.

55 River Rise Preserve State Park

Location: 2 miles west of High Springs on US 27 in Alachua and Columbia Counties (29° 54' 10.3" N, 82° 35' 17.3" W)

Season: Year-round

Sites: Primitive camping with fire rings and water; camping with pets is available; equestrian camping

Maximum length: Call for current information

Facilities: Tables, in-ground grills, fire rings, pavilion

Fee per night: $

Management: Florida Division of Recreation and Parks

Contact: (386) 454-1853, www.floridastateparks.org/riverrise/default.cfm

Hundreds of wonderful opportunities to ride and even camp with your horse await you in Florida's state and national park and forest system.

Finding the campground: From I-75, take exit 404 and travel west on SR 236 to the intersection with US 441 in High Springs, about 4.5 miles. River Rise Preserve State Park is actually located beside O'Leno State Park, which is located directly adjacent to US 441, 6 miles north of High Springs.

About the campground: The Santa Fe River may go underground in O'Leno State Park, but it reemerges 3 miles away in River Rise as a circular pool. From this point, it heads toward the Suwannee River and from there to the Gulf of Mexico. Canoeing, kayaking, hiking, and wildlife viewing are favorite activities here. Few amenities are on site but many are nearby.

estrians can explore 20 miles of trails and camp overnight with their horses. Located near
[en]rance to the park, the horse camp has primitive campsites, restrooms, and a 20-stall horse
barn available on a first-come, first-served basis.

56 Payne's Prairie Preserve State Park

Location: 10 miles south of Gainesville on the east side of US 441 in Alachua County (29° 30'
01" N, 82° 22' 52" W)
Season: Year-round
Sites: 50 sites, 15 tent-only, 35 for RVs

*Florida's network of multipurpose trails is strengthened by thousands of volunteers. This kiosk is
on the north rim of Payne's Prairie Preserve State Park south of Gainesville.*

Maximum length: 53 feet
Facilities: Tables, in-ground grills, fire rings, pavilion, water, electricity, and complete bathhouses
Fee per night: $$
Management: Florida Division of Recreation and Parks
Contact: (352) 466-3397, http://www.floridastateparks.org/paynesprairie/default.cfm
Finding the campground: Take exit 374, the Micanopy exit, from I-75 and turn east onto CR 234. Stay on this road 1.4 miles until it intersects with US 441. Turn left onto US 441 and go 0.6 mile to Paynes Prairie Preserve State Park (on the right).
About the campground: On the edge of the vast basin that has periodically become a lake, complete with steamboats, this 21,000-acre state park is now a National Natural Landmark. People have been camping here for 10,000 years, when they could still hunt mammoths and prehistoric bison.

You can expect magnificent birding on the trails—the park is a site on the Great Florida Birding Trail—and along the edges of the occasionally flooded prairie. A 50-foot tower lets you spot deer, wild horses, alligators, and perhaps one of the wild bison.

The local flora thrives in the park's sandy soils with tall pines, spreading oaks, and thick palmetto hummocks.

57 Devil's Hammock Wildlife Management Area

Location: In north central Levy County southwest of the town of Bronson (29° 26' 56" N, 82° 38' 11" W)
Season: Year-round
Sites: Primitive camping is restricted to specific sites by permit only issued by the Levy County Commission during periods closed to hunting, and prohibited during hunting seasons
Management: Fish & Freshwater Game Commission, Suwannee River Water Management District and Levy County
Contact: (352) 486-5218, http://myfwc.com
Finding the campground: From I-75, take exit 384 and drive southwest on SR 24 to Bronson. Continue 6.5 miles on SR 24 to Long Branch Road on the right.
About the campground: You must be persistent to explore many of Florida's WMAs, and the 7,635-acre Devil's Hammock takes a special breed—to get the permit and then to enjoy camping in this wild area. It is wild because Levy County is one of Florida's poorest, most rural, and most thinly populated areas and the land is hardly higher than sea level; flooding is a continuing fact of life.

Devil's Hammock grows hardwoods such as oak, hickory, and cypress, plus pine trees and alligators. Cypress forests line the Waccasassa River and Otter Creek and there are two canoe launches north of US 19. Other recreation includes hiking, wildlife viewing, fishing, and hunting.

You can enjoy a practically solitary experience in Devil's Hammock and, indeed, in many of Florida's under-publicized WMAs. It is important however to exercise good judgment in making safety and contact arrangements. In these remote areas, you will be able to experience starry nights, and you should prepare for every imaginable emergency.

58 Goethe Wildlife Management Area

Location: This WMA runs north-south in southeastern Levy County, and begins 5 miles south of Bronson (29° 26' 56" N, 82° 38' 11" W)
Season: Year-round
Sites: Primitive camping is allowed by permit from the Division of Forestry
Maximum length: Call for current information
Facilities: Call for current information
Fee per night: Call for current information
Management: Fish & Wildlife Conservation Commission and Division of Forestry
Contact: (352) 465-8585, http://myfwc.com
Finding the campground: From I-75, take exit 384 and drive southwest on SR 24 to Bronson, and then about 5 miles south on CR 337. The WMA roughly parallels CR 337.
About the campground: At 48,442 acres, Goethe is a substantial WMA. Its large tract of old-growth longleaf pines is home to several species you don't see every day: the rare red-cockaded woodpecker, gopher tortoise, Sherman's fox squirrel, and the bald eagle.

Within Goethe an extensive trail system may be accessed at three separate trailheads, and recreational activities include hunting, fishing, wildlife viewing, bicycling, hiking, horseback riding, and picnicking.

59 Citrus County Parks 352 382-2200

Location: Chassahowitzka River Campground, 8600 W. Miss Maggie Dr., Homosassa, FL 34448 (28° 42' 48" N, 82° 34' 36" W)
Season: Year-round
Sites: 52 developed sites; 36 have water, electricity, picnic tables, and sewer hookups; others are primitive tent sites (no water at site, but at strategically placed spigots) *yes no?*
Maximum length: Call for current information
Facilities: Modern bathhouse with flush toilets and hot showers; horseshoe pit, coin-operated laundry, shuffleboard, country store, streetlights, dump station, fish-cleaning station, boat ramp; nearby boat, canoe, and kayak rentals (The Nature Coast Outpost Kayak Adventures, 352-382-0800)
Fee per night: $$ for camping (primitive to full hookup); $ for use of the dump station
Management: Call for current information *$38/night*
Contact: www.bocc.citrus.fl.us, www.swfwmd.state.fl.us
Finding the campground: From I-75, take exit 329 onto SR 44, heading west. Just past Lecanto, turn left (southwest) onto Homosassa Trail to Homosassa Springs and turn left (south) onto US 19/98. In 7.5 miles or so, turn right (southwest) onto Miss Maggie Drive and proceed to the campground.
About the campground: Chassahowitzka is a quiet 40-acre park with hard-packed dirt roads. The numbered campsites here are shaded and usually have palmettos, trees (oaks and palms), and brush that give campers privacy. The campground is within walking or boating distance (or a short drive) of numerous wild areas, both state parks and national wildlife refuges.

The Chasshowitzka River is spring-fed and lined with beautiful cypress trees and the curious and protected cypress knees. The boat ramp at the park offers plenty of chances for fishing (fresh-and saltwater) and recreational boating, and it is a short run to the Gulf of Mexico for manatees here.

60 Rainbow Springs State Park /-352-465.8555

Location: 2.5 miles north of Dunnellon in western Marion County (29° 6' 12.7" N, 82° 26' 20.9" W). This park is unusual in Florida in that it is separated into two parts and has three entrances.
Season: Year-round
Sites: 60 total sites. Recently renovated campground has 10 new sites: 3 for pull-through RVs and 7 for tents only. Remaining 50 sites are RV or tent, 8 sites paved and enhanced for visitors with mobility challenges.
Maximum length: 56 feet
Facilities: Full-facility family campground; 3 new restrooms, new pavilion by the playground, remodeled dump station, remodeled camp store. All sites have 20/30/50 amp electrical service, and all RV sites have sewer connections at the site. Campground roads are paved. Common parking area at new sites.
Fee per night: $$
Management: Florida Division of Recreation and Parks
Contact: (352) 465-8555, http://www.floridastateparks.org/rainbowsprings/default.cfm; (800) 326-3521, www.reserveamerica.com
Finding the campground: From I-75 in Ocala, exit onto SR 40 and drive west until it dead-ends at US 41. Turn left. The park entrance is on the left side of the road. From Tampa, drive north on US 41 through Dunnellon. The park is on the right side of the road about 2.5 miles north of Dunnellon.
About the campground: Rainbow Springs is one of those places a chamber of commerce likes to call a "treasure." In the case of these first magnitude freshwater springs, however, that is an understatement. The Rainbow pumps an astonishing 500 million gallons of cold, fresh water each day.

Naturally, there is an abundance of recreational opportunity from swimming, snorkeling, hiking, birding, canoeing to just relaxing in a truly beautiful natural area. When you are tired of swimming, go for a hike in the park's hand-planted gardens, which date from the years the area was a private resort. You will see carefully cultivated native plants and manmade waterfalls. Rental canoes are available, and both scuba and tubing are available just outside the park.

61 Potts Wildlife Management Area

Location: In northeast Citrus County near Inverness (28° 50' 21" N, 82° 20' 25" W)
Season: Year-round
Sites: 5 campsites by permit from the Water Management District. Group camping in Oak Hammock, equestrian camping at individual sites located near the intersection in the WMA with Dee River (Ranch) Road. Three primitive tent sites are located on the Withlacoochee River (River and Far Point) and on Tsala Apopka Lake (Holly Tree).
Maximum length: Call for current information
Facilities: Call for current information

Fee per night: Call for current information

Management: Fish & Wildlife Conservation Commission and Southwest Florida Water Management District (WMD)

Contact: (800) 423-1476, http://myfwc.com/recreation/cooperative/potts.asp, http://florida birdingtrail.com/

Finding the campground: From I-75, take exit 329 west on SR 44 to Inverness. Turn right on US 41 and it is less than 1 mile to the right turn (north) onto Ella Avenue. Swing right onto East Turner Camp Road/CR 581, which twists and turns quite a bit, but turn left (north) onto Dee River (Ranch) Road and watch for signs.

About the campground: Florida's system of wildlife management areas are designed to protect the ecosystem of plants and animals from development, and to provide recreational opportunities to Floridians. In their earliest manifestations, they were places people could go to hunt and fish, but as the state has grown, their importance has become magnified, and they are now thought of primarily as zones that protect the state's precious water resources.

Potts's 7,408 acres was purchased to protect the Withlacoochee River, and the many streams flowing into it, and the Tsala Apopka Chain of Lakes. A casual look at any Florida map will show an intricately mixed area of water and land: marsh, swamp, flatwoods, oak hammocks, and high pine ridges.

Hunting, fishing, paddling, wildlife viewing (watch for the threatened Florida scrub jay), and frogging are some of the recreational opportunities available in the area. You can also hike on nearly 30 miles of marked and mapped paths, with two loop trails. Roads in the WMA are often hard-packed and excellent for biking; and there are 12 miles of marked woods trails for horses. Look for white-tailed deer, gopher, tortoise, alligators, river otters, and wild turkey.

You can paddle the area free, but need a permit (it's free) from the WMD to use a vehicle to transport your boat to the closest water entry. This area is a site on the Great Florida Birding Trail.

62 Flying Eagle Wildlife Management Area

Location: In southeastern Citrus County on the west side of the Withlacoochee River and south of SR 44. The entrance on East Moccasin Slough Road is at 28° 49' 17.9" N, 82° 15' 9" W.

Season: Year-round

Sites: Separate, primitive camping is available for individuals, groups (in Moccasin Slough), and equestrians (in Pole Barn), but prohibited during fall big game hunting seasons. A permit is required to camp, and camping is not permitted during hunts. Several campsites are available for paddlers.

Maximum length: Call for current information

Facilities: Portable toilets are available at the entrance, but no potable water is available.

Fee per night: Call for current information

Management: Fish & Wildlife Conservation Commission and Southwest Florida Water Management District (WMD)

Contact: (800) 423-1476, http://myfwc.com, www.swfwmd.state.fl.us/recreation/areas/flying eagle.html

Finding the campground: From exit 329 on I-75, drive west on SR 44 for 5.5 miles to the Withlacoochee River. The WMA begins 0.5 mile past this river on the south side of the road; watch for signs.

About the campground: Flying Eagle WMA is a great mosaic of lakes, marshes, and swamps along 5 miles of the Withlacoochee River. Some maps identify the area as the Tsala Apopka Chain of lakes. Its 10,247 acres provide hunting, fishing, wildlife viewing, and primitive camping. There are 13 miles of trails for bicycling, 9 miles for horseback riding, and 16 miles of wooded trails for hiking. Paddling is permitted in the creeks and marshes but you need a WMD permit to use a vehicle to transport a boat to the closest water entry.

This area is part of the Great Florida Birding Trail. Its roads are scenic, passing through either dry, sandy, wooded hammocks or pasture. Camping is on grassy areas with shade provided by spreading live oaks draped with Spanish moss.

63 Fort Cooper State Park

Location: 2 miles south of Inverness in Citrus County (28° 48' 59.2" N, 82° 18' 13.8" W)
Season: Year-round
Sites: 4 group or individual tent sites; primitive camping, no hookups; no pets in campground
Facilities: Non-flush toilets, drinking water, grills, fire rings, picnic tables
Fee per night: $
Management: Florida Division of Recreation and Parks
Contact: (904) 277-7274, www.floridastateparks.org/fortcooper/default.cfm; (352) 726-0315 for reservations
Finding the campground: From the extended junction of SR 44 (east-west) and US 41 (north-south) in Inverness, turn south on US 41 and continue about 1 mile. Turn left (east) at the traffic light on Eden Drive. Make an immediate right (south) at the four-way stop onto Old Floral City Road. Follow its turns about 1.0 mile to the park entrance on the right.
About the campground: This quiet, semi-primitive campground is nestled in a shady oak hammock. Two sites back up to Lake Holathlikaha, but are separated from it by a marsh.

One mile from the campground is a central area with a playground. Here visitors enjoy swimming (when water levels are high enough) or fishing in the 160-acre lake. The park rents canoes and paddleboats; private boats are not permitted. Occasional reenactments of 1836 Seminole War–era life are educational and superbly researched. There are 5 miles of self-guided hiking trails and the trailhead for the 46-mile Withlacoochee Trail, the longest paved rails-to-trails path in Florida.

64 Silver River State Park

Location: East of Ocala, 1.0 mile south of SR 40 on SR 35 in Marion County (29° 12' 3.7" N, 82° 3' 10.1" W)
Season: Year-round
Sites: 59, primitive group camping site, 10 cabins (sleeping six)
Maximum length: None
Facilities: Full-facility camping, water and electrical (30 amp) hookups (6 with 50 amp), luxury cabins, playground, picnic area with 3 pavilions with grills that may be rented for group outings;

sites and cabins have fire ring, grill, and picnic table. Firewood (available at ranger station), dump station for RVs.

Fee per night: $$$

Management: Florida Division of Recreation and Parks

Contact: (352) 236-7148, www.floridastateparks.org/silverriver/default.cfm; (800) 326-3521, www.reserveamerica.com

Finding the campground: Silver River State Park is east of Ocala, 1.0 mile south of SR 40 on SR 35. From I-75, take exit 352 onto SR 40 east, and continue 9 miles to SR 35. From I-95, take exit 268 to SR 40 west; it's about 60 miles to SR 35.

About the campground: This park has dozens of springs, acres of wide-spreading oaks hung with Spanish moss, miles of beautiful trails, and of course, the Silver River, said to be one of the best in Florida for kayaking.

The park is also home to a pioneer "cracker" village and the Silver River Museum and Environmental Education Center. Operated by the Marion County School District in cooperation with the park, the center is open on weekends and holidays from 9:00 a.m. to 5:00 p.m. (www.marion.k12 .fl.us/district/srm/index.cfm).

Campers can hike, canoe the clear river (rentals available in the park), bike along miles of nature trails, or enjoy the variety of birds. Mornings, park rangers often lead guided bird hikes. An equestrian trail is planned.

65 Gore's Landing County Park

Location: In Marion County at 13750 NE 98th St., Ft. McCoy, FL 32134 (29° 17' 21" N, 81° 55' 34" W)

Season: Year-round

Sites: Semi-primitive camping

Maximum length: Unlimited

Facilities: Picnic table, potable water from spigots scattered through the campgrounds, bathrooms (outside cold showers), above-ground grill; no electricity, boat ramp

Fee per night: $

Management: Marion County Board of County Commissioners and Fish & Wildlife Conservation Commission

Contact: (352) 671-8560

Finding the campground: From I-75, take exit 352 east through the city of Ocala on SR 40, past Silver Springs, and turn left (north) on CR 315. Turn right (east) on NE 105th Street, then right again (south) on NE 130th Avenue and finally left (east) on 98th Street to the boat landing/campsite on the Oklawaha River.

About the campground: The boat ramp at Gore's Landing is open 24/7 and there is a fee of $ per car for parking if you are kayaking the Oklawaha. All of the campsites are pleasantly situated beneath large trees giving tents plenty of shade. The boat ramp is on your left about 150 feet after you pass the self-service pay area.

The Ocklawaha River is about 100 miles long and flows from Lake Apopka to the St. Johns River. You may see alligators, turtles, deer, black bear, and river otters, plus herons, osprey, and about two hundred additional species of birds.

66 Horseshoe Lake Park & Retreat

Location: 10800 E. Hwy 318, Orange Springs, FL 32682 (29° 29' 30" N, 81° 57' 30" W)
Season: Year-round
Sites: Rustic-style cabins
Maximum length: None
Facilities: Rustic cabins, playground
Fee per night: $$$. Cabin reservations are taken no more than 1 year in advance. 2-night minimum, 6-month maximum.
Management: Marion County Board of County Commissioners
Contact: (352) 671-8560, www.marioncountyfl.org/parks/pr_parks/PR_Horseshoe_Lake_Main.htm
Finding the campground: From I-75, take exit 368 and drive east on CR 318 approximately 25 miles to the park. Follow the signs into park, which is on the south side of CR 318.
About the campground: Just north of the Ocala National Forest, Horseshoe Lake Park & Retreat offers a variety of outdoor activities, including canoeing and kayaking (no boat motors are allowed), fishing, hiking, picnicking, and swimming. The lake wraps around the park, making it a small peninsula. Fish caught must be released or consumed on site.

The park is covered with large live oaks and, typical of central Florida lakes, the quiet shoreline is a thin strand of white sand.

67 Lochloosa Wildlife Management Area

Location: Southeastern Alachua County, north of the unincorporated hamlet of Citra (29° 24' 42" N, 82° 06' 36" W)
Season: Year-round
Sites: Primitive camping (with permit—outside of hunting season)
Maximum length: Call for current information
Facilities: Call for current information
Fee per night: Call for current information
Management: Fish & Wildlife Conservation Commission and St. Johns River Water Management District
Contact: (386) 329-4404, http://myfwc.com, http://floridabirdingtrail.com
Finding the campground: From I-75, take exit 368 east on CR 318 to the hamlet of Citra. Turn left (north) on US 301, and about 2 miles past the intersection with CR 325 and the hamlet of Island Grove, turn left (west) on Burnt Island Road. Bear right for about 2 miles and watch for signs.
About the campground: Here is a wild and primitive area that deserves a week of exploration, but bring your insect repellent for as wonderful as camping under the spreading and moss-hung oaks can be—especially in cool weather, although that is typically the time of most intense hunting—there are bugs galore. Expect everything from mosquitoes to ticks and several species of biting fly. And watch for alligators and moccasins, for every body of water is thick with these native reptiles.

Pine plantations and oak ridges in this 11,149-acre WMA provide habitat for populatons of sandhill cranes, which migrate here in the winter. Their chuckling flights overhead and curious dances on the prairies where they mate and feel safe are wonderful Florida sights. Recreational

…es include hunting, fishing, wildlife viewing, hiking, bicycling, horseback riding, canoe-
…oating.

68 Mike Roess Gold Head Branch State Park

Location: Midway between Jacksonville and Gainesville, 6 miles northeast of Keystone Heights in Clay County on SR 21 (29° 49' 55" N, 81° 57' 11" W)
Season: Year-round
Sites: 89 including 2 primitive campgrounds without water or electricity; 3 group campsites with access to water, outside cold shower, and flush toilets; 74 family campsites with water, picnic tables, fire rings, and access to flush toilets and showers, all but 11 with electrical hookups; 16 cabins on Little Lake Johnson, 9 rustic, 5 block, and 2 wheelchair-accessible
Maximum length: 45 feet
Facilities: Toilets, showers, drinking water, fire rings, and picnic tables
Fee per night: $$ family; $ primitive
Management: Florida Division of Recreation and Parks

Professionals help make great camping experiences happen. Here a park ranger teaches a young camper to throw the atlatl, a spear-throwing device.

Contact: (352) 473-4701, www.floridastateparks.org/goldhead/default.cfm, www.reserve america.com

Finding the campground: Gold Head Branch State Park is approximately 6 miles northeast of Keystone Heights in Clay County on the south side of CR 21. It is due west of St. Augine, mid-way between I-95 and I-75.

About the campground: This park began as a Civilian Conservation Corps project during the 1930s and several of the visitor cabins are original, although they have been updated significantly. In years with good rainfall (or perhaps several hurricanes), the lakes will be "up" and swimming, canoeing, and fishing will be popular. Canoe rentals are available. Florida has suffered from recurrent drought, however, and lakes in the central, sandy ridge such as those in Gold Head Branch are very low and often closed to recreation. This is a very interesting and popular park, so if you want to camp here, book a spot early—and then do not miss hiking around the canyon and along the clear, cold streams that flow out of it. Like riding? The park has equestrian trails too.

69 Jennings Forest Wildlife Management Area

Location: Primarily in Clay County, northwest of the town of Middleburg (30° 03' 03" N, 81° 54' 07" W)

Season: Year-round

Sites: Primitive camping by permit (no charge) from the Division of Forestry, (904) 291-5530

Maximum length: Call for current information

Fee per night: None

Management: Fish & Wildlife Conservation Commission, St. Johns River Water Management District and Division of Forestry

Contact: (904) 291-5530 for permit, http://myfwc.com, http://sjr.state.fl.us (the recreational guide), www.fl-dof.com/state_forests/jennings.html

Finding the campground: From Jacksonville, drive west on I-10 to I-295 and turn south. At exit 12, turn south onto SR 21, and at Middleburg, take SR 218. Five different entrances have signs posted. Canoe launch areas are reached from Nolan Road and Hattie Nolan Road.

About the campground: The Division of Forestry says you may encounter green tree frogs in this park, and, if that were not exciting enough, you will almost certainly see cottontail rabbits. Of course, spotting alligators will become de rigeur, but one may also see a rare river otter here.

Foresters claim the forest and WMA also contain wild coveys of bobwhite quail. A covey of wild quail would be worth seeing because habitat for quail has become very rare, and our children will never see coveys of truly wild birds.

At 23,995 acres, the Jennings area protects the headwaters of Black Creek. On its pine and palmetto uplands and oak and magnolia wetlands, there are opportunities for hunting, fishing, wildlife viewing, primitive camping, hiking, horseback riding, bicycling, and canoeing. There are four designated canoe/kayak launch sites. This forest is also a site on the Great Florida Birding Trail.

70 Cary State Forest

Location: In northeastern Florida in Nassau and Duval Counties; look for the hamlet of Bryceville (30° 23' 04" N, 81° 56' 20" W) on US 301

Season: Year-round

Sites: 3 first-come, first-served primitive camping areas

Maximum length: Call for current information

Facilities: 1 restroom facility with showers for campers and day-use visitors

Fee per night: Call for current information

Management: Division of Forestry

Contact: (904) 266-5021 for required state forest use permit (reservations recommended), www.fl-dof.com/state_forests/cary.html

Finding the forest: Take I-10 to Baldwin, exit 343, and turn north on US 301 for 7 miles. Watch for the two 90-degree turns in Baldwin, because the signs are small. The forest is on the right, 0.5 mile past the fire station in Bryceville.

About the forest: Near Jacksonville, Cary State is a popular destination for people who enjoy the outdoors. At 13,045 acres, it is one of Florida's smaller state forests, but has fine hiking and horseback riding. The nature trail winds through a cypress swamp and includes a boardwalk across the wetlands. Horseback riding is allowed on all forest roads and the 8-mile Red Root Trail.

In addition to recreation and camping, Florida's state forests are managed for multiple purposes, principally timber and wildlife.

The ecology here varies between pine and palmetto uplands and swampy lowlands filled with cypress ponds. An observation tower and a field planted with high-protein grasses help visitors watch the forest's abundant birds and wildlife, especially very early and late in the day. It is only a short distance off the nature trail.

71 Ralph E. Simmons Memorial State Forest (and Wildlife Management Area)

Location: Near Boulogne in Nassau County (30° 46' 17" N, 81° 58' 34" W)
Season: Year-round
Sites: 2 primitive campsites along the St. Mary's River, available first-come, first-served. These sites can only be accessed from the river, but you do not need a permit to camp, although there is no camping during hunting seasons. Organized group camping is available with a forest use authorization from the Division of Forestry in Hilliard. During hunting seasons, camping is reserved for hunters. Regulations and hunting season dates can be obtained at http://myfwc.com/hunting/.
Maximum length: Call for current information
Facilities: Call for current information
Fee per night: Call for current information
Management: Division of Forestry and the Fish & Wildlife Conservation Commission
Contact: (904) 845-4848/3597, www.fl-dof.com, http://myfwc.com
Finding the forest: If traveling from the town of Hilliard, go north on US 1 for 7 miles to the hamlet of Boulogne. From Boulogne, go east on SR 121/Lake Hampton Road to the forest.
About the forest: Prior to 1996, this 3,638-acre forest area was known as St. Mary's State Forest. It is primarily pine and wiregrass uplands, with interspersed bogs and ravines. Quite a few rare and endangered plants are found here: Florida toothache grass, purple balduina, many-flowered grasspink, and hooded pitcher plant.

The forest borders the St. Mary's River. The view across the river into Georgia alternates from low sandy beaches to high limestone bluffs reminiscent of the Suwannee River, for the two rivers are the principal drainages for the Okefenokee Swamp. The Suwannee winds its way southeast to the Gulf of Mexico and the St. Mary's in a convoluted manner makes its way to Nassau Sound and the Atlantic Ocean.

A variety of activities is available in and on the borders of the Simmons forest: hiking, biking, paddling, horseback riding, boating and fishing in the river, and, of course, hunting.

72 Fort Clinch State Park

Location: In Fernandina Beach on Amelia Island, Nassau County (30° 40' 9.5" N, 81° 26' 4.1" W)
Season: Year-round
Sites:
    Atlantic Beach Campground: 21 sites here, each with 20- and 30-amp hookups. This wide-open campground is next to the beach, and there is no shade, but there is potable water. Sites

have in-ground fire rings and picnic tables. Bathrooms with hot showers are centrally located; coin-operated washing machines are available. Back-in gravel sites accommodate RVs of any size. A dump station is near the entrance. Simply walk up the beach to the old fort. $$$

Amelia River Campground: 41 sites situated in a shady oak hammock near the river. All sites are back-in and have 20- and 30-amp hookups, potable water, in-ground fire rings, and picnic tables. 2 full-service bath facilities, each with hot showers and laundry, and dump station near the campground entrance. $$$

Youth Group Campground: A maximum of 100 occupants may occupy these 4 shaded sites. There are bathrooms with hot water, and facilities are ADA-accessible. $

Maximum length: Call for current information

Management: Division of Recreation and Parks

Contact: (904) 277-7274, www.floridastateparks.org/fortclinch/default.cfm; reservations available through www.reserveamerica.com

Finding the campground: Located at 2601 Atlantic Ave. (SR A1A) in Fernandina Beach. Exit I-95 at milepost 373/exit 129 (Callahan/Fernandina); proceed east 15–16 miles on SR A1A/8th Street into town. Turn right on Atlantic Avenue. The entrance is about 2 miles on the left (north).

About the campground: This park is centered around a pre–Civil War brick fortress designed to protect Fernandina's harbor. Fully dressed and well-rehearsed reenactors are often at the fort for demonstrations and tours.

The three Fort Clinch campgrounds have distinct personalities. The beach campground is just a hundred yards from the ocean, depending upon the tide. A dangerous undertow discourages swimming here, but you can walk the white sand beach, fish, and go shelling for miles. Hot in the summer, it can be blustery and cold in the fall and winter. The river campground is shady and cool.

The Atlantic Beach Campground at Fort Clinch State Park on Amelia Island north of Jacksonville lacks shade but is only a two-minute walk from the beach.

Not far from the brick fortress, it offers access to hiking trails and the narrow paved park roads for biking. Fish from the shore or from the park's long pier. The youth/group campground is tucked deep into an oak hammock in the middle of the park. Pets are welcome but must be on a 6-foot leash and may not be left unattended.

73 Little Talbot Island State Park

Location: 17 miles east of I-95, on the beach in Jacksonville, Duval County (30° 27' 30" N, 81° 25' 00" W)
Season: Year-round
Sites: 40
Maximum length: 30 feet
Facilities: 2 fully equipped bath and toilet facilities, drinking water, fire rings, and picnic tables
Fee per night: $$
Management: Florida Division of Recreation and Parks
Contact: (904) 251-2320; www.floridastateparks.org/littletalbotisland/default.cfm
Finding the campground: From I-95 in Jacksonville, take the Heckscher Drive (SR 105) exit 358 east for 17 miles. Heckscher Drive merges with SR A1A at the St. John's River ferry (and becomes Buccaneer Trail north onto Amelia Island). Continue east and north on A1A to the park entrance on the right.
About the campground: The Talbots are virtually unspoiled islands. Here, 5 miles of wide white beach and sand dunes are covered with picturesque sea oats.

Little Talbot is ideally positioned so that campers can enjoy a day on the beach and an evening in Jacksonville or can simply sit by the beach and listen to the rumble of the surf. With a little bug spray and a couple lawn chairs, stars overhead, and a ship or two headed into port, you may feel your life is complete.

The Little Talbot campground is situated on the west side of SR A1A—here called the Buccaneer Trail—and borders the Myrtle Creek tidal marsh. It is mostly shaded from the hot Florida sunshine by spreading live oaks draped with Spanish moss. Thick clumps of palmetto give recently renovated campsites some privacy.

Facilities are wheelchair-accessible, and beach wheelchairs are available. If you have never ridden a Segway, a quiet, two-wheeled, battery-operated device that responds to the way you lean, a park concessionaire gives introductory classes and 5-mile tours. Canoes and kayaks can be rented and guides are available for tours.

74 Huguenot Memorial Park

Location: 10980 Hecksher Drive, Jacksonville, FL 32226 in Duval County (30° 24' 49.6" N, 81° 36' 21.1" W)
Season: Year-round
Sites: 71
Maximum length: 40 feet

Facilities: Beach access, benches, boat ramp, 91 car parking sites, concession stand, 5 grills, 4 picnic shelters, 78 picnic tables, 2 sets of playground equipment, 11 restrooms, shower facilities, visitor/interpretative center, camp store, drinking fountains

Fee per night: $

Management: City of Jacksonville

Contact: (904) 251-3335, www.coj.net/Departments/Recreation+and+Community+Services/Water front+Management+and+Programming/Preservation+Project/Huguenot+Memorial+Park.htm

Finding the campground: From I-95 in Jacksonville, take exit 358A to merge onto Heckscher Drive/SR 105 E/Zoo Parkway. Follow Heckscher Drive to the entrance on the right. It is 17 miles.

About the campground: Not only is the park itself strikingly beautiful, but it offers swimming, shelling, sunbathing, fishing, and surfing. Some of the campsites in the 295-acre park are right on the water; however, campsites are not shaded, and they are close together; so privacy is minimal. Additionally, because the hot summer sun heats up tents, an over-tent tarp is needed for comfort—as is bug spray or netting.

Huguenot has great birding opportunities and fine views of natural areas. It isn't all that far from the Mayport naval base, either, and on occasion some of the navy's finest are available for tours. Plus, it is only 1 mile from the entrance south along Heckscher Drive to the ferry across the St. Johns. A round-trip ride with your car or motorcycle or as a pedestrian is only $.

Huguenot Park is a designated site on the Great Florida Birding Trail. Expect to see an abundance of birds—wading birds in fresh- and saltwater, raptors, songbirds, migratory birds—in the diverse marsh-beach habitat. Huguenot allows visitors to drive on the beach.

75 Camp Chowenwaw

Location: On 1.5 miles of shoreline on Black Creek and Peters Creek south of Jacksonville and north of Green Cove Springs adjacent to the St. Johns River (30° 2' 30" N, 81° 42' 54" W)

Season: Year-round

Sites: Site names date from the camp's years as a Girl Scout retreat

Hickory Flats—"Talahi": 8 sites for primitive tent camping with a centrally located bathhouse and dining hall with stove and refrigerator.

Magnolia Hill—"Adahi": 7 sites for primitive tent camping with a centrally located bathhouse and dining hall with stove and refrigerator.

Squirrel Run—"Inyanwastee": 7 cement block cabins with bunk beds sleeping 4 to 8 people. No electricity. Centrally located bathhouse and dining hall with stove and refrigerator.

Big Pine Shores—"Yamassee": 2 cabin/bunkhouses with no air-conditioning. Each cabin sleeps a maximum of 16 people. These cabins have electricity, and there is a centrally located bathhouse.

Treehouse Point: 9 tree houses, without electricity, sleep a maximum of 4 people per structure. There is a centrally located bathhouse, dining hall with stove and refrigerator.

Maximum length: Call for current information

Facilities: Picnic tables and grills available throughout the park and at each campsite; limited vehicle access; campsites and cabins accessible by walking trails

Fee per night: Primitive tent camp, $; cabins/tree houses, $$; group camping, reserving an entire site, $$$

Management: Clay County Board of County Commissioners

Contact: (904) 529-8058, www.claycountygov.com/Departments/Parks_Rec/Camp_Chow.htm

Finding the campground: From I-295 south of Jacksonville, take exit 10 south on US 17. Once you cross Black Creek, look for Ball Road on the right (west) side of the highway. Turn right on Ball Road and proceed to the campground.

About the campground: Camp Chowenwaw Park is a 150-acre site with 100 acres of wetlands and 50 acres of uplands. Formerly owned by the Girl Scouts of America, it was purchased by Clay County in 2006 as a place to provide environmental education as well as recreation. Besides camping, recreation includes picnicking, kayaking/canoeing, swimming, fishing, bird-watching, wildlife viewing, photography, and hiking.

At the mouth of Black Creek and near the St. Johns River, some of this site is prone to flooding and a tropical storm or hurricane can shut down access. Despite being close to a major city, its upland and wetland natural communities are in a relatively pristine state and many wading birds and raptors can be sighted here.

76 Bayard Wildlife Management Area

Location: Southeastern Clay County, south of Green Cove Springs (29° 59' 34" N, 81° 41' 02" W)

Season: Check with the WMD in advance to find out which areas are open for camping

Sites: Individual and group camping sites—first-come, first-served—available at most locations where camping is allowed in Bayard. Stay limited to 7 days. Camping in Bayard is primitive and many of Bayard's sites are reachable only by hiking, mountain biking, boating, or horseback riding. Camping is pack-in, pack-out.

Maximum length: Call for current information

Facilities: Expect camping to be primitive—no restrooms or potable water

Fee per night: No charge, but groups of seven or more should obtain a permit at least a week in advance

Management: Fish & Wildlife Conservation Commission and St. Johns River Water Management District (WMD)

Contact: (386) 329-4404 for permits, http://myfwc.com and www.sjrwmd.com/

Finding the campground: Drive south from Green Cove Springs on US 17. Bayard WMA is immediately on the left (east) between US 17 and the St. Johns River.

About the campground: Few rivers in America are as beautiful as the broad, north-flowing St. Johns. For most of its length, its banks alternate between jungle and zones of development.

Bayard is one of numerous managed areas designed as water recharge zones and to protect original ecological communities. It is comprised of more than 10,320 acres extending nearly 7 miles along the west bank of the river.

Low-lying and occasionally flooded forests line the St. Johns along the Bayard district, but as one moves west away from the river, elevation rises and hence the plant and animal communities change to pine flatwoods with vast stretches of palmetto scrub.

In Bayard, one can hunt, fish, hike, ride horses and mountain bikes, picnic, and watch for birds and wildlife. Deer, bald eagles, osprey, wild turkey, and the unusual dry land "gopher tortoise" are found here. While the area is easily accessible by water, there are no boat launches.

77 Etoniah Creek State Forest and Wildlife Management Area

Location: This state forest/wildlife management area is northeast of Florahome (29° 43' 57" N, 81° 53' 01" W) in northern Putnam County. Camping is allowed only by permit from the Division of Forestry. Permits may be obtained by calling (386) 329-2552.
Season: Year-round with a permit
Sites: 2 in the eastern part of the forest allow primitive camping
Maximum length: Call for current information
Facilities: Call for current information
Fee per night: $-$$
Management: Division of Forestry and Fish & Wildlife Conservation Commission
Contact: (386) 329-2552, www.fl-dof.com and http://myfwc.com
Finding the forest: Etoniah Creek State Forest and WMA is located in northern Putnam County in northeast Florida, 11.5 miles west of Palatka and the St. Johns River. The state forest headquarters is northeast of Florahome, 2 miles east to Holloway Road and then north on Holloway Road 2.6 miles to the second forest road on the right (Fieldhouse Road). The office is 0.5 mile down Fieldhouse Road.
About the forest: Recreational opportunities in the forest include hiking, horseback riding, biking, and bird-watching. This forest is 8,679 acres, and it is cut by several streams. There are a few trails for hiking and for horses. Several of the streams are very scenic and worth a visit.

This is one of the few areas in Florida where a camper may realistically see a black bear. Unfortunately most sightings take place at night as the bear is rummaging through your food supplies. Strict food discipline will prevent hassles for you (a torn tent, destroyed coolers) and perhaps save the bear's life as well, for problem or nuisance bears—if they have been relocated more than a few times—must sometimes be destroyed. Don't leave food out—or worse, keep it in your tent; keep dishes and cookware clean, and hang food in odor-free, bear-proof containers.

78 Marjorie Harris Carr Cross Florida Greenway

Location: Putnam, Marion, Citrus, and Levy Counties
Season: Year-round
Sites:

Rodman Campground: Rodman is on the east end of the Greenway, near Palatka (29° 38' 52" N, 81° 39' 05" W). There are 69 campsites with fire rings; 43 have electric and water hookups; 26 are primitive. There is a dump station and a boat launch, (386) 326-2846. Look for the visitor center at Buckman Lock.
Directions: From I-75, take SR 40/Silver Springs Boulevard (exit 352) east through Ocala and Silver Springs to CR 315. Turn left (north) on 315 and travel about 25 miles to CR 310. Turn right (east) on CR 310 for about 5 miles until it ends at SR 19. Turn right (south) and go over the Florida Barge Canal Bridge. Turn right (west) onto Rodman Road at the foot of the bridge. The campground is 3 miles on the right.

Santos Campground: In central Florida near Ocala (29° 11' 16" N, 82° 07' 50" W), the Santos area includes an equestrian-friendly campground and an equestrian day-use area, a mountain biking trail system, and barrier-free playground. Santos includes 24 campsites with water and electricity (30 and 50 amp), a picnic pavilion, bathhouse, potable water, and dump station. Santos is located on the Greenway south of Ocala, at the east end of the Santos Trailhead. Reservations can be made through the campground hosts, (352) 369-2693 on-site. Otherwise, campsites are first-come, first-served.

Directions: Take exit 341 from I-75 and head east on CR 484. Go approximately 2 miles and turn left (north) on CR 475. Take CR 475 north about 6 miles and turn right on SE 80th Street (east). Go about 3 miles and the Santos Trailhead and campground will be on your right.

Ross Prairie Campground: Near Dunnellon (29° 03' 00" N, 82° 27' 20" W). First-come, first-served campsites: 15 pull-through sites with electric (5 sites with 50-amp and 10 with 30-amp) and water hookups for recreational vehicles and campers. The day-use area has a large paved parking lot with restrooms and bathhouse, picnic pavilion, fire rings, picnic tables, and dump station. Horse grooming stations, a corral, tie-outs, and access to miles of riding trails make this campground popular with horse campers. A camp host is on duty 24/7 at (352) 427-4436.

Maximum length: Call for current information

Fee per night: Water and electricity, $$$; primitive camping, $$

Management: Dept. of Environmental Protection, Office of Greenways & Trails

Contact: (877) 822-5208 or (352) 236-7143, www.FloridaGreenwaysAndTrails.com, www.dep .state.fl.us/gwt/cfg/Campgrounds.htm

Finding the campgrounds: From I-75, take exit 341 (Belleview/Dunnellon) to CR 484. Take CR 484 west approximately 10 miles. Turn left at the stoplight on CR 200 and go south about 2 miles. The campground is on your left.

About the campgrounds: The Cross Florida Greenway stretches from the St. Johns River to the Gulf of Mexico. It is a 110-mile long corridor that encompasses a variety of natural habitats and offers more trails and recreation areas than you can explore on one vacation. Hiking, biking, equestrian trails, visitor centers, boat ramps, campgrounds, picnic shelters, plus Florida's natural beauty make this trail unforgettable. And to think that our politicians wanted to dredge and dam an enormous swath across Florida, just so that sea-going barges filled with phosphate could cut a day or two off their passage around the peninsula.

79 Caravelle Ranch Wildlife Management Area

Location: Between the Rodman Reservoir Dam and Rodeheaver Boy's Ranch on the St. Johns River in Putnam and Marion Counties a few miles south of Palatka (29° 38' 52" N, 81° 39' 05" W) near SR 19

Season: Year-round

Sites: Except during hunting season, primitive campsites along the Florida Trail and sites managed by the WMD are accessible. During hunting seasons, camping is permitted at designated campsites only.

Maximum length: Call for current information

Facilities: Call for current information

Fee per night: Call for current information

Management: Fish & Wildlife Conservation Commission and the St. Johns River Water Management District (WMD)

Contact: (386) 329-4404, http://myfwc.com, www.sjrwmd.com, www.floridatrail.org

Finding the campground: Take SR 19 south from Palatka. The camp is about 1 mile south of the old Cross Florida Barge Canal and east of the road.

About the campground: Caravelle Ranch, located between the Ocklawaha and St. Johns Rivers, is a big area: 26,467 acres. The lands of this WMA vary between hardwood river swamps, pine and palmetto flatwoods, and pastures punctuated with small depressions or runoff ponds and hardwood hammocks. The tract connects the Cross Florida Greenway with the Ocala National Forest.

You find a great diversity of wildlife in Florida's WMAs, from nesting bald eagles to alligators, black bears, snowy egrets, and manatees in the neighboring waters. Except for the bears and the snakes, which are generally shy, one stands a very good chance of seeing a real bounty of wild animals and birds at Caravelle Ranch.

During hunting season, access to the general public is restricted.

More than 20 miles of unpaved multi-use trail are available for hiking, biking, and horseback riding.

80 Murphy Creek Conservation Area

Location: On the east bank of the St. Johns River in Putnam County about 5 miles south of Palatka (29° 34' 30" N, 81° 40' 6" W)

Season: Year-round

Sites: Primitive camping is available with a permit

Maximum length: Call for current information

Facilities: None

Fee per night: Call for current information

Management: St. Johns River Water Management District

Contact: (386) 329-4404, http://sjr.state.fl.us

Finding the campground: From US 17 on the east side of the St. Johns River about 5 miles south of Palatka, turn west on Buffalo Bluff Road/CR 309B. A parking area is 0.5 mile on the north side of the road. Access to Murphy Island is by boat only.

About the campground: Murphy Creek is mostly swamp, and the island can only be reached by boat. The island has one of the rare highland areas on the St. Johns and the view of the riverine area from the high bluffs is fine.

Murphy Creek is only 1,842 acres and the best time to go to one of these primitive or group campsites is in cool weather as the mosquitoes and biting flies will be fewer then. Other flying animals—bald eagles, herons, and perhaps a bittern, for instance—and some walking on four legs—gopher tortoise, opossum, white-tailed deer, bobcats, and even foxes—are plentiful here. Hiking, off-road biking, and fishing are great here.

81 Dunn's Creek Wildlife Management Area

NOTE: Please contact the park(s) for more information regarding omitted camp specs and management as it is often changing.

Location: In eastern Putnam County, along the east side of Dunn's Creek (29° 34' 24" N, 81° 33' 18" W)

Season: Year-round

Sites: Only primitive tent camping at designated areas (during hunting periods, use restricted to those with valid quota hunt permits)

Management: Fish & Wildlife Conservation Commission and St. Johns River Water Management District

Contact: (386) 329-4404, www.sjrwmd.com, http://myfwc.com

Finding the campground: From the city of Palatka on the west bank of the St. Johns River, drive east on US 17 and turn left (east) on SR 100/20. Look for signs to the Tram Road on the right in about 2.5 miles. The campsite is 0.5 mile into the woods; watch for signs.

About the campground: This primitive campground is not on the creek after which it is named, and there is no boat ramp. At just 3,184 acres of swamp and wet hammock, this is a small WMA, and while there are many activities—hunting, fishing, wildlife viewing, hiking, horseback riding, bicycling, and of course camping—there are no amenities. You might see deer or raccoon or a fox, however, and hawks, which have made a great comeback throughout the U.S.

82 Welaka State Forest

Location: This forest is located in northeastern Florida, approximately 1 mile south of the town of Welaka (29° 28' 54" N, 81° 40' 18" W)

Season: Year-round

Sites: Primitive camping is available with horses and on the St. Johns River at Orange Point and John's Landing.

Maximum length: Call for current information

Facilities: Call for current information

Fee per night: $–$$

Management: Department of Agriculture & Consumer Services, Division of Forestry

Contact: (386) 467-2388, www.fl-dof.com/state_forests/welaka.html

Finding the forest: Approximately 17 miles south of Palatka, off US 17. The forest is on SR 309, 1 mile south of the town of Welaka.

About the forest: Welaka State Forest is located on the east bank of the St. Johns River. The forest is managed for sustained timber harvest. Its landscape of wetlands, flatwoods, hammocks, sandhills, and bayheads charms the many hikers that use the forest. Mud Spring Trail is a 2-mile self-guided loop to the Mud Spring Picnic Area. In the spring and summer, it is muddy, often thick. The Johns Landing Trail winds along old road beds to the river. The Sandhill Horse Trail is designed for horses as well as hiking. The forest manages an excellently cared-for 72-horse stable, with training and show horse arenas, all of which are available for rental. Pets are not allowed in the horse areas.

83 Ocala National Forest

Location: Between Ocala and Lake George
- Lake George Ranger District, 17147 East Highway 40, Silver Springs, FL 34488, (352) 625-2520
- Pittman Visitor Center, 45621 SR 19, Altoona, FL 32702, (352) 669-7495
- Ocklawaha Visitor Center, 3199 NE Highway 315, Silver Springs, FL 34488, (352) 236-0288
- Salt Springs Visitor Center, 14100 N. State Highway 19, Salt Springs, FL 32134, (352) 685-3070
- Seminole Ranger District, 40929 SR 19, Umatilla, FL 32784, (352) 669-3153

Season: Year-round, except when specifically noted otherwise

Sites: 14 developed campgrounds, primitive campsites, dispersed tent camping (permitted throughout the forest), 2 large cabins (at Lake Dorr and Sweetwater Spring); first-come, first-served, but reservations available at some sites (group campgrounds and forest cabins by reserva-

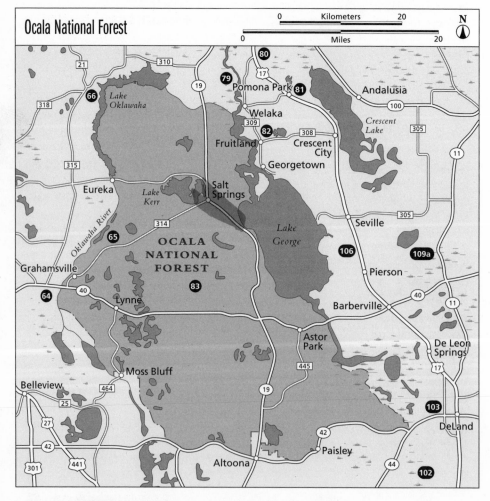

Ocala National Forest

tion only, cabins often by lottery because of high demand); 14-day stays for most sites are 7 days. Pets must be on a leash no longer than 6 feet and are not permitted in de swimming and picnicking areas. Detailed lists follow.

Maximum length: Call for current information

Facilities: Developed sites: hot showers, restrooms, picnic tables, charcoal grills, fire rings, lantern holders (no hanging lanterns on trees), drinking water, sanitation facilities, and trash receptacles; Salt Springs offers full hookup service; several campgrounds have dump stations, potable water, shower facilities.

Primitive campsites: No drinking water, few if any amenities. Dispersed tent camping: no facilities. Lake Dorr cabin, on a spring that flows into Juniper run, accommodates 10; Sweetwater Spring cabin sleeps 12.

Fee per night: At developed areas $ to $$$; primitive and dispersed camping is free

Management: Call for current information

Contact: www.fs.fed.us. Salt Springs, Juniper Springs, Alexander Springs, Clearwater Lake, Fore Lake, and Big Scrub are first-come first-served, but also can be reserved at (800) 326-3521 and www.reserveamerica.com. Cabins are managed by a concessionaire contracted by the Forest Service; call (352) 625-0546 for additional information and reservations.

Finding the forest: From I-75, take exit 352 onto SR 40 and drive east to the forest. From I-95, take exit 268 onto SR 40 and drive west to the forest.

About the forest: The Ocala National Forest is one of the largest and most diverse public recreation areas in the southeast U.S. The best time to visit is during the dry season, November to February, when weather is perfect for camping.

The other eight months of the year, temperatures can soar to near 100 degrees on any day and humidity can as well. Afternoon thunderstorms are frequent and hurricane season begins June 1.

Ocala National Forest vegetation varies from dank, black mud swamp to sunny, breezy pine uplands. There are cold, crystal springs and hot dry trails through the native scrub. Bugs are plentiful; alligators, snakes, bears, stray dogs, and the occasional unaccounted-for human make their home in the forest. Any negative, however, is easily balanced by the almost uncluttered starry night sky and a lonely wind slipping through high pines.

Forest vegetation consists of everything from native palms, wide-spreading live oaks, flowering magnolias, and scrubby sand pines. There's a campground in each of these settings, and most sites link to trails and boardwalks that lead you through the different bio-zones.

Developed Campsites

NOTE: Please contact the park(s) for more information regarding omitted camp specs and management as it is often changing.

Alexander Springs

Location: Forest Site 20, Lake County (29° 4' 42" N, 81° 34' 42" W)

Sites: 76 in 4 loops

Maximum length: 52 feet

Facilities: Hot showers, flush toilets, public phone in loop B, amphitheater, limited groceries at the beach, dump station

ree per night: $$$
Finding the campground: From Ocala, drive east on SR 40 to the hamlet of Astor Park. Turn right, almost 180 degrees back toward the west on Fairview Avenue/CR 445/445A. After 0.5 mile, CR 445 swings left (south) from SR 445A. The springs will be on your right side after about 5 miles.
About the campground: The campground is located in a subtropical forest of pines, oaks, bay, magnolia, and sable palm. The spring flows at a rate of 80 million gallons of water a day, and the water is cold and clear. Here, one can swim, picnic, hike, rent canoes, and when you are bored with the good, but often fairly basic food prepared over a camp stove, visit the concession store for a soda and snack.

Big Bass

Location: Forest Site 24, Marion County (28° 59' 12" N, 81° 47' 6" W)
Season: Oct 15 to Apr 15
Sites: 34
Maximum length: 59 feet
Facilities: Primitive camping: no hookups, but portable toilets, water from spigots, dump station
Fee per night: $
Finding the campground: From Ocala, drive south on US 441 through Belleview. About 7 miles past Belleview turn left (east) on SR 42. The Big Bass campground is not well marked but it is about 12 miles on the north side of the road. Look for the unpaved FR 588 and turn north onto it.
About the campground: Sites lie between small ponds in the woods—though not deep enough in the woods to muffle noise from SR 42. This is the most southerly campground in the forest.

Clearwater Lake

Location: Forest Site 26, Lake County (28° 58' 42" N, 81° 33' 6" W)
Season: Year-round
Sites: 42, a few overlooking Clearwater Lake
Maximum length: Largest RV apron is 55.5 feet
Facilities: Flush toilets, hot showers, drinking water, dump station, canoe rental
Fee per night: $$
Contact: Local reservations, (352) 625-3147; reservations, (800) 326-3521
Finding the campground: From Ocala, drive south on US 441 through Belleview and turn left (east) on SR 42. Clearwater is about 27 miles on the north side of the road via FR 536 near the hamlet of Paisley.
About the campground: This area offers swimming, hiking, and fishing.

Farles Prairie

Location: Forest Site 18, Marion County (29° 6' 54" N, 81° 40' 5" W)
Season: Camping from Nov 1 through Apr 5; the rest of the year is day use only
Sites: 75 camper maximum at this boat launch
Maximum length: Call for current information
Facilities: Call for current information
Fee per night: $
Finding the campground: From Ocala, drive east on SR 40 to SR 19 and turn right (south). About 4 miles on the right (west), turn onto FR 535. Farles is about 3 miles west.
About the campground: There's fishing, canoeing, and hiking—and a bombing range just to the west.

Fore Lake

Location: Forest Site 7, Marion County (29° 16' 12" N, 81° 55' 0" W)
Season: Year-round
Sites: 31
Maximum length: 64 feet
Facilities: Flush toilets, hot showers, dump station, picnicking (tables and grills), fishing pier
Fee per night: $
Finding the campground: From Ocala, drive east on SR 40 to CR 314 and turn left (north). Signs for Fore Lake will be on the left (north) side in about 5 miles.
About the campground: A fairly rustic campground less than 100 acres in size, it's adjacent to Fore Lake, so offers swimming and offers sites situated in a subtropical, pleasantly aromatic forest of pine and oak.

Hopkins Prairie

Location: Forest Site 9, Marion County (29° 16' 36" N, 81° 42' 24" W)
Season: Oct 1 to June 1
Sites: 21
Maximum length: 40 feet
Facilities: Restrooms, drinking water, boat ramp
Fee per night: $
Finding the campground: From Ocala, drive east on SR 40 to CR 314 and turn left (north). After about 7 miles, turn right on FR 86/Hopkins Prairie Road and follow it for about 12 miles to Hopkins Lake, which will be on the left (north) side.
About the campground: The site is located adjacent to Hopkins Prairie, sometimes a "prairie" sometimes a wetland, sometimes a lake. In other words, unless the lake is full of water, tall grass is the visible vegetation with intermittent potholes of water. The dominant vegetation is live oak and laurel oak. Some sites offer a scenic view of the prairie.

Juniper Springs

Location: Forest Site 15, Marion County (29° 11' 0" N, 81° 42' 48" W)
Season: Year-round
Sites: 19 tent and 60 RV sites
Maximum length: Call for current information
Facilities: Flush toilets, hot showers, dump station, swimming pool, concession stand with some groceries, canoe rental
Fee per night: $$
Contact: Local reservations (352) 625-3147; Reserve America reservations, (800) 326-3521
Finding the campground: From Ocala, drive east on SR 40 and Juniper will be on your left on the north side of the road about 4 miles before SR 19.
About the campground: The subtropical vegetation here on the edge of the Juniper Wilderness Area is not found in any other national forest. The Forest Service says the water flow from Juniper and Fern Hammock Springs is about 13 million gallons a day. Water temperature is a constant 72 degrees, which means it will feel exceptionally cold and refreshing on a hot day. You can hike the interpretive trail year-round.

Lake Delancy East

Location: Forest Site 2, Marion County (29° 25' 42" N, 81° 47' 18" W)
Season: Oct 1 to June 1
Sites: 29
Maximum length: RV parking with wide aprons, maximum length 35 feet
Facilities: Potable water from a hand pump
Fee per night: $
Finding the campground: From Ocala, drive east on SR 40 and turn left (north) on CR 314. Merge north on SR 19 at Salt Springs and continue north to FR 75. Turn left (west) and go 3.5 miles to the campground.
About the campground: The campground is adjacent to the National Forest's Delancy West campground and to Lake Delancy, which is, like most Florida lakes, a shallow lake encircled by prairie. In a wet year the lake is high and, it is said, might reach the edged campground, but wet years have become rare, and most of the time, tall prairie grass hides the water. Live oaks hung with moss give the site wonderful character. No off-road vehicles or horses are permitted in this campground, but one can launch a paddleboat. This campground is popular with RV families. This is bear country, too, so take special care with your food items.

Lake Delancy West

Location: Forest Site 1 in Marion County (29° 25' 18" N, 81° 46' 54" E)
Season: Year-round
Sites: 30
Maximum length: Call for current information
Facilities: Potable water, restrooms; hiking, off-road vehicles, and horses permitted
Fee per night: $
Finding the campground: From Ocala, drive east on SR 40 and turn left (north) on CR 314. Merge north on SR 19 at Salt Springs and continue north to FR 75. Turn left (west) to the campground.

Lake Dorr

Location: Forest Site 23, Lake County (29° 0' 48" N, 81° 38' 6" W)
Season: Year-round
Sites: 34
Maximum length: 55 feet
Facilities: Tables and grills; flush toilets, full restrooms with hot showers; cold showers for rinsing at the beach, private dump available
Fee per night: $$
Finding the campground: From Ocala, drive east on SR 40 to SR 19 and turn right (south). The campground will be on the left (east) in about 12 miles.
About the campground: On the northwest shore of the 1,760-acre Lake Dorr, this site offers excellent fishing, water skiing, and even some swimming, although the beach is small and unimproved. A cabin is also available but must be reserved well in advance.

Lake Eaton

Location: Forest Site 8, Marion County (29° 15' 18" N, 81° 51' 54" W)
Season: Oct 1 to June 1
Sites: 13 all-purpose sites
Facilities: Table, grill, fire ring, lantern post, parking spur available for tent or RV camping; vault toilets, no drinking water, boat ramp, 250-foot ADA accessible pier; campground host on premises
Fee per night: $
Finding the campground: From Ocala, drive east on SR 40 and turn left (north) on CR 314. After 7 miles, turn right (south) on CR 314A and after about 3 miles turn left (east) on FR 79. Within a few blocks, turn left (north) on FR 96A. Watch for signs and continue straight about 1 mile to the campsite.
About the campground: This is a very rich sub-tropical area and in the summer can be hot and muggy. Fishing is popular on the 292-acre lake.

Salt Springs

352-685-3070

Location: Forest Site 3, Marion County (29° 21' 18" N, 81° 44' 6" W)
Sites: 106 relatively open sites for RVs, 54 oak-shaded sites for tents. Maximum stay is 6 months (most public campgrounds in Florida have a 2-week limit).
Maximum length: 66 feet
Facilities: Full-service campground with hot showers, covered pavilions, drinking water, primitive or full-service hookups, boat ramp, canoe rental, dump station, grocery/post office/visitor center/ laundromat nearby
Fee per night: $$ (discount with Senior/Access Pass)
Contact: Local reservations, (352) 685-2048; Reserve America reservations, (800) 326-3521
Finding the campground: From Ocala, take SR 40 east to CR 314, turn left (north), and when CR 314 veers to a stop at SR 19, drive left (north) to Salt Spring, which will be almost immediately on your right (east).
About the campground: Salt Springs is one of the premier campgrounds in the forest. It's very popular with "snowbirds," who leave northern climates when the weather turns cold; many return year after year. All forest activities are available here or near here from swimming to snorkeling, fishing and hiking.

Shanty Pond

Location: Forest Site 5, Marion County (29° 19' 54" N, 81° 44' 0" W)
Season: Oct 15 to Apr 15
Sites: 106 designated camp spots and an open field for camping available
Maximum length: Call for current information
Facilities: Water from a hand-pump, some picnic tables that can be moved to accommodate your site preference, vault toilets, and rental toilets during camping season
Fee per night: $

www. Reserve.gov 6 mos. Advance
recreation

Finding the campground: From Ocala, take SR 40 east to CR 314, turn left (north), and when CR 314 veers to a stop at SR19, turn right and almost immediately watch for an unimproved road on the right and a sign.

About the campground: This site, only 1 mile south of the more popular and more highly developed Salt Springs, allows people to set up solar panels, according to the Forest Service. And of course, solar is strong in the Sunshine State, and a popular option for many of the "snowbirds" that flock to the area. Hunters also camp here during seasons in fall and winter. The pine and palmetto uplands area with numerous small ponds is popular for fishing, kayaking, and hiking. The Forest Service anticipates linking this site with the OHV (Off Highway Vehicle) trail system.

Undeveloped Group Campgrounds

NOTE: Please contact the park(s) for more information regarding omitted camp specs and management as it is often changing.

Lake Shore Group Camp

Location: Forest Site 6, Marion County (29° 16' 30" N, 81° 54' 12" W)
Sites: Group camping
Maximum length: Call for current information
Facilities: The campground has a bathhouse and shelter.
Fee per night: $$$, 2-night minimum
Contact: Reservations only, (352) 624-2520 or (800) 326-3521
Finding the campground: From Ocala, drive east on SR 40 to CR 314 and turn left (north). Fore Lake will be on the left (north) side in about 5 miles; watch for signs to the group camp.
About the campground: This is a wonderful lakeside spot opposite the developed Fore Lake Campground for family reunions or groups from church, civic organizations, or the scouts (boy or girl). Both swimming and fishing are popular, but fishing is only allowed from shore, from paddleboats, or from boats with electric motors.

Mill Dam Group Camp

Location: Forest Site 12, Marion County (29° 10' 54" N, 81° 49' 54" W)
Season: Oct 1 to Mar 15
Sites: Group camping for up to 150
Maximum length: Call for current information
Facilities: Drinking water, restrooms, picnic tables, pavilion, nearby boat ramp
Fee per night: $$$
Contact: Reservations only, (800) 326-3521
Finding the campground: From Ocala, drive east on SR 40 to FR 79, which will be on the left (north) side. Turn left and again take an almost immediate left; watch for the sign.
About the campground: The lake is favored for fishing, swimming, and water skiing.

Buck Lake Group Camp

Location: Forest Site 19, Marion County (29° 6' 0" N, 81° 39' 6" W)
Sites: Group site for up to 50
Maximum length: Call for current information
Facilities: Picnic tables, drinking water, boat ramp
Fee per night: $$$, 2-night minimum
Contact: (352) 625-3147; reservations only, (800) 326-3521
Finding the campground: From Ocala, drive east on SR 40 to SR 19 and turn right (south).
It will be about 4.5 miles to a right (west) turn on FR 535. Proceed to the camp on the left in
about 2 miles.
About the campground: Both fishing and hiking are popular here.

Doe Lake Group Camp

Location: Forest Site 21, Marion County (29° 2' 24" N, 81° 49' 12" W)
Season: Year-round
Sites: Group camp for up to 250
Maximum length: Call for current information
Facilities: Showers, potable water, restrooms, boat landing
Fee per night: $$$
Contact: Reservations only, (800) 326-3521
Finding the campground: From Ocala, drive east on SR 40 and turn right (south) on FR 579. In
about 9 miles, turn right (west) on FR 573 and proceed to the camp on the left in about 0.5 mile.
About the campground: Family and school reunion groups, plus church, scouting, and civic
groups all use this forest site. Fishing, swimming, and horseback riding are available.

Big Scrub

Location: Forest Site 22, Marion County (29° 3' 6" N, 81° 45' 24" W)
Season: Year-round
Sites: Designated off-road-vehicle site accommodating up to 250 campers
Maximum length: Call for current information
Facilities: Showers, restrooms, picnic tables
Fee per night: $$
Contact: Reservations only, (800) 326-3521
Finding the campground: From Ocala, drive east on SR 40 to FR 588 and turn right (south). It is
about 9 miles to the camp near the intersection with FR 573.
About the campground: There is no shade on the site, and the area is not one for lounging in a
hammock or admiring the area's natural beauty.

River Forest Group Camp

Location: Forest Site 27, Lake County (29° 0' 36" N, 81° 23' 30" W)
Season: Year-round
Sites: Group site accommodating a maximum of 150 campers

Maximum length: Call for current information

Facilities: Restrooms, hot showers, drinking water

Fee per night: $$$

Contact: Reservations only, (800) 326-3521

Finding the campground: From Ocala, drive south on US 441 through Belleview and turn right (east) on SR 42. River Forest Group Camp is located just before SR 42 intersects with SR 44. From that intersection left (east), it is only 0.25 mile to the St. Johns River.

About the campground: Here you can fish or hike the interpretive trail. River Forest is the National Forest's most southeasterly campsite and the city of DeLand is only a couple of miles to the east on SR 44.

The Space Coast Region

C ounties: St. Johns, Flagler, Volusia, Lake, Seminole, Orange, Brevard, Osceola, Polk, Indian River

	Hookup Sites	Total Sites[1]	Max RV Length	Hookups	Toilets	Showers	Dump Station	Recreation	Fee	Can Reserve
84 Lake Griffin State Park	40	40	40	WE	F	Yes	Yes	HFBL	$$	Yes
85 Lake Louisa State Park	63	63, T, C	115	WE	F	Yes	Yes	HSFBR	$$$	Yes
86 Polk County Parks	-	T	-	WE	F	Yes	Yes	HFBLRC	$-$$	Yes
87 Lake Wales Ridge State Forest	-	-	-	-	-	-	-	HFBLR, hunting	$-$$	No
88 Arbuckle WMA	-	-	-	-	-	-	-	HFBRC, hunting	$	Yes
89 Kicco WMA	-	-	-	-	-	-	-	HFBLRC, hunting	-	No
90 Lake Kissimmee State Park	60	64, T	58	WE	F	Yes	Yes	HFBR	$$	Yes
91 Three Lakes WMA	-	-	-	-	-	-	-	HFBLRC, hunting	-	No
92 Lake Marion Creek WMA	-	-	-	-	-	-	-	HFBRC, hunting	-	No
93 Osceola County Parks	-	-	-	-	-	-	-	HADVL	-	No
94 Moss Park	-	-	-	WE	F	Yes	Yes	HSBLC	$$	Yes
95 Orange County Parks	See individual listings for more detailed information. Sites vary from exceedingly primitive to well-equipped.							HSBLRC	$$-$$$	No
96 Little Big Econlockhatchee State Forest/WMA	-	-	-	-	-	-	-	HFBRC, hunting	$-$$	No
97 Seminole County Parks	-	-	-	-	F	Yes	No	HFBL	$$	Yes
98 Wekiwa Springs State Park	60	64, T	50	WE	F	Yes	Yes	HSFBRC, snorkel	$$$	Yes
99 Lower Wekiva River Preserve State Park	This park features horse camping. Call for additional information, reservations.									
	-	-	-	-	F	Yes	No	HRC	Varies[2]	Yes
100 Rock Springs Run State Reserve Park	Horse camping and canoe/kayak primitive camping. Call for more information.									
				-	F	Yes	No	HRBC[3]	Varies[2]	Yes
101 Seminole State Forest/WMA	-	-	-	-	-	-	-	HBRC,		
102 Hontoon Island State Park	-	12, T, C	-	-	F	Yes	No	HFBC	$$	Yes
103 Blue Spring State Park	51	51, T, C	30	WE	F	Yes	Yes	HSB	$$	Yes
104 Tiger Bay State Forest/WMA	Horse camping and group/primitive camping. Call for more information.									
				-	-	-	-	HFBRC, hunting	$-$$	No
105 Relay WMA	-	-	-	-	-	-	-	F, hunting		No
106 Lake George State Forest/ WMA/Conservation Area	-	-	-	-	-	-	-	HFBRC, hunting	$-$$	No
107 Faver-Dykes State Park	30	30, T	35	WE	F	Yes	Yes	HSFBLC	$$	Yes
108 Anastasia State Park	139	139	40	WE	F	Yes	Yes	HSFBC	$$	Yes
109 Flagler County Parks	-	-	-	-	-	-	-	HSFBLRC	$$	No
110 Gamble Rogers Memorial State Recreation Area	33	33	47	WE	F	Yes	Yes	HSFBLC	$$	Yes
111 Tomoka State Park	100	100, T	34	WE	F	Yes	Yes	HFBL	$$$	Yes

	Hookup Sites	Total Sites[1]	Max RV Length	Hookups	Toilets	Showers	Dump Station	Recreation	Fee	Can Reserve
112 Volusia County Parks	-	-	-	-	-	-	-	HFBRLC	$-$$	No
113 Canaveral National Seashore	-	16	-	-	No	No	No	HSFBLC	$	Yes
114 Buck Lake WMA	-	-	-	-	-	-	-	HFBLC, hunting	-	No
115 Seminole Ranch WMA/ Conservation Area	Primitive camping for through-hikers on Florida Trail.									
	-	-	-	-	-	-	Yes	hunting	$-$$	No
116 Tosohatchee WMA	-	-	-	-	-	-	-	HFBRC, hunting	-	Yes
117 Brevard County Parks	420	462	-	WE S	F	Yes	Yes	HSFBLC	$$-$$$	Yes
118 Bull Creek WMA	-	-	-	-	-	-	-	HFBRC, hunting	-	No
119 Triple N Ranch WMA	-	-	-	-	-	-	-	HRC, hunting	-	No
120 Upper St. John's River Marsh WMA	See individual listings for more detailed information. Sites are typically primitive with few amenities—even potable water.							HFBC, hunting	-	Yes
121 Fort Drum WMA/Conservation Area	-	-	-	-	-	-	-	HFBLR, hunting	-	No
122 St. Sebastian River Preserve State Park	Horse camping and group primitive camping. Call for more information.									
				-	NF	-	-	HFBRC	$	Yes
123 Sebastian Inlet State Park	51	51	50[4]	WE	F	Yes	Yes	HSFBLC, scuba, surfing,	$$$	Yes
124 Indian River County Parks	-	-	-	-	-	-	-	HFBLRC	-	No

Key:
Hookups: W = Water, E = Electricity, S = Sewer, C = Cable, P = Phone, I = Internet
Total Sites: T = Tents, C = Cabins, Y = Yurts
Maximum RV Length: Given in feet
Toilets: F = Flush, NF = No flush
Recreation: H = Hiking, S = Swimming, F = Fishing, B = Boating, L = Boat launch, O = Off-road driving, R = Horseback riding, C = Cycling

[1] T: Almost all Florida state parks, trails, greenways, etc., have prepared sites with water and electricity and a primitive camping (youth or group—tent-only) area with cold water available. Camping in the primitive area is regulated by number of occupants, not specific sites. C: cabins are available.

[2] Primitive equestrian camping fees can be obtained by calling (407) 884 2008.

[3] Each fall, areas of the reserve are closed to equestrians during weekends of special hunts. Canoes and kayaks cannot be launched within the reserve, but there are several places to launch outside that provide access to Rock Springs Run.

[4] The park Internet site says a maximum of 30 feet, while Reserve America claims 50 feet. A call to the park did not provide clarification. Recommend an advance call.

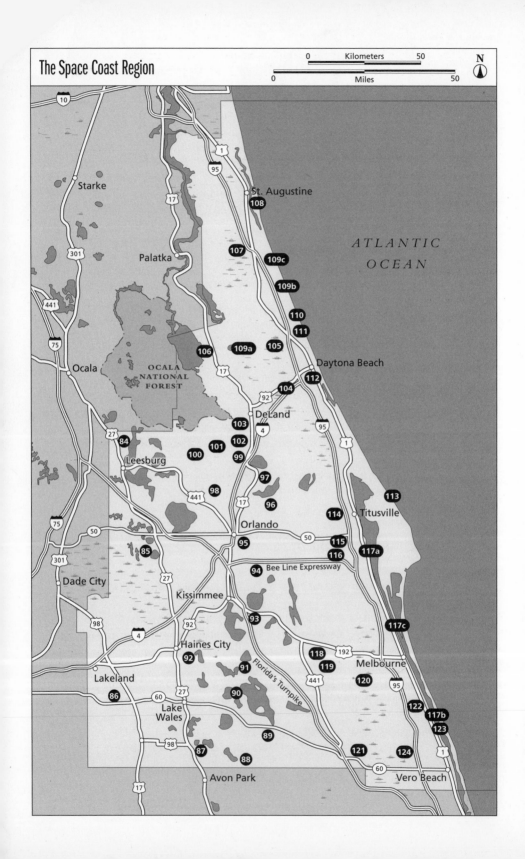

The Space Coast Region

0   Kilometers   50

0   Miles   50

N

ATLANTIC OCEAN

Starke

Palatka

Ocala

OCALA NATIONAL FOREST

St. Augustine
108

107
109c

109b

110
111

106   109a   105

Daytona Beach
104   112

92   DeLand

103
102
100   101   99

84
Leesburg
98
97
96

85

50

Dade City

Kissimmee
93

Haines City
92

Lakeland
86

Lake Wales
89

87   88

Avon Park

Orlando
95   50   115

94   Bee Line Expressway

113
114   Titusville

116   117a

117c

118   192
119

120
122
117b
123

121   124

Vero Beach
60

Florida's Turnpike

90
91
441
Melbourne

NOTE: The following state parks in this region do not offer camping at pres[...]
David Broussard Catfish Creek, Bulow Creek State Park, Bulow Plantatio[...]
Historic, Colt Creek, De Leon Springs, Dunn's Creek, Fort Mose, North P[...]
Ravine Gardens and Washington Oaks.

84 Lake Griffin State Park

Location: 3 miles north of Leesburg and 30 miles south of Ocala in Lake County (28° 51' 27.2"
N, 81° 54' 11.0" W)
Season: Year-round
Sites: 40 with 7 accommodating any RV length
Maximum length: 40 feet
Facilities: Full-facility camping; picnic tables, water, electricity, campfire grills; hot showers and
coin-operated laundry facilities
Fee per night: $$
Management: Florida Division of Recreation and Parks
Contact: (352) 360-6760, www.floridastateparks.org/lakegriffin/default.cfm; (800) 326-3521,
www.reserveamerica.com
Finding the campground: Take exit 289 on Florida's Turnpike and drive north on US 27 for about
15 miles. Past Leesburg, the park entrance is on the right (east).
About the campground: Although the park does not abut the lake for which it is named, it does
connect to it with a boat ramp and lake access via a canal to the Dead River. Established around
the river, this park has plenty of boating, fishing, and canoeing. Picnicking, walking the 0.5-mile
nature trail, and simple relaxing are quite popular here. The full-facility campground is washed with
shade and canoe rentals are available. Because of a healthy alligator population, no swimming is
allowed. Driving to theme parks is easy from this beautiful state park.

85 Lake Louisa State Park

Location: 7 miles south of SR 50 in Clermont on US 27 in Lake County (28° 27' 22.6" N, 81°
43' 19.0" W)
Season: Year-round
Sites: 60 full-facility sites, 2 primitive campsites, an equestrian campsite, and 20 fully furnished
cabins
Maximum length: 115 feet
Facilities: Full-facility camping plus primitive and primitive youth/group camping; cabins have two
bedrooms, two baths, full kitchen, dining and living room area and overlook Lake Dixie
Fee per night: $$$
Management: Florida Division of Recreation and Parks
Contact: 352-394-3969, www.floridastateparks.org/lakelouisa/default.cfm; (800) 326-3521,
www.reserveamerica.com

Finding the campground: Turn north at exit 55 on I-4 onto US 27 and drive about 20 miles to the entrance road on the left.

About the campground: Because this park is so close to Orlando and the immense population growth taking place in the cross-Florida axis (Tampa Bay–Orlando–Cape Canaveral), its 4,500 acres seem particularly delightful.

Numerous lakes ranging in size from the large Lake Louisa to tiny Dudes and Hook Lakes give this park its character. One can fish and swim without the roar of gasoline-powered outboard motors, which are not permitted. If you don't have a boat, fishing piers are available on Dixie and Hammond lakes.

Actually, the park is—for Florida—quite hilly, and thus its 20 miles of hiking trails are popular, as are its 15 miles of horse trails.

86 Polk County Parks

NOTE: Contact Polk County Leisure Services, 515 Boulevard St., Bartow, FL 33830, (863) 534-4340, for more information regarding camp specs and management as parks are often changing.

Saddle Creek Park: 3716 Morgan Combee Rd., Lakeland, FL 33801 (28° 3' 46" N, 81° 53' 0" W), www.saddlecreekpark.com/index.htm and www.floridabirdingtrail.com

Finding the campground: The park is just south of I-4, midway between Orlando and Tampa in Lakeland. Take exit 41 to CR 570, the Polk Parkway, and drive south to exit 18, Old Dixie Highway/Saddle Creek Road. Turn left (south) on Fish Hatchery Road and, in less than 1 mile, take another left (east) on Morgan Combee Road to the entrance.

About the campground: This 800-acre area was an open phosphate mine until the 1960s when it was given to the county. It has taken most of the time since then for nature to recover.

The campground for tents and RVs is in a lakeside area with shade from large oaks. There are electrical and water hookups, and a dump station ($: campers, $$: non-campers). Camping fees are $ for county residents, and several dollars higher for non-residents. You can fish here, and Saddle Creek is an important sector in the Great Florida Birding Trail. The park also has a gun range.

87 Lake Wales Ridge State Forest

Location: The Walk in the Water Tract is 2 miles east of Frostproof (27° 44' 44" N, 81° 31' 52" W) on CR 630. The Arbuckle Tract is 5 miles south of Frostproof on Lake Arbuckle Road. Both are in Polk County.

Season: Year-round

Sites: Primitive camping at 2 designated sites on the Florida Trail, which passes through the forest: the Reedy Creek Primitive Campground on the Arbuckle Tract and the Walk-in-Water Primitive Campground located on the Walk-in-Water Tract. Groups require a state forest use permit, which can be obtained from the forest office. NOTE: No drinking water is available. (Polk County operates a public, full-facility campground on Lake Arbuckle at the end of Lake Arbuckle Road.)

Maximum length: Call for current information

Facilities: Call for current information
Fee per night: $-$$
Management: Division of Forestry
Contact: (863) 635-8589, www.fl-dof.com
Finding the forest: Take exit 55 south off I-4 between Tampa and Orlando onto US 27. To reach the Walk in the Water Tract, turn left (east) on CR 630. It is 2 miles east of Frostproof. To reach the Arbuckle Tract, take the CR 630 exit, but continue straight onto Fort Meade Road rather than following CR 630. After about 2 miles, turn right (south) on Scenic Highway and then, after a couple blocks, left (east) on T. S. Wilson Road, which becomes South Lake Reedy Boulevard. After about 2 miles, Lake Arbuckle Road turns to the right; watch for the state forest signs.
About the forest: A sandy ridge runs from north to south through most of the Florida peninsula. At one time, sea levels rose to the point that only this ridge was out of the water, and consequently, a number of plants and animals evolved in relative isolation. The forest is named for this ridge.

The four separate tracts of Lake Wales Ridge State Forest are unique and beautiful, covering 28,563 acres of central Florida. Here, quite a few rare plants and animals flourish.

Fishing and canoeing are available year-round on the lakes as well as the numerous streams and creeks in the forest. Horseback riding is allowed on all roads and fire breaks.

88 Arbuckle Wildlife Management Area

Location: East of Avon Park and 5 miles south of Frostproof in Polk County (27° 42' 30" N, 81° 26' 48" W)
Season: Year-round
Sites: Designated campground near Rucks Dairy Road and designated sites along the Florida Trail; camping at other sites by special use permit issued by the Division of Forestry
Maximum length: Call for current information
Facilities: Call for current information
Fee per night: $; groups should reserve sites·
Management: Fish & Wildlife Conservation Commission and Division of Forestry
Contact: (863) 635-7801, http://myfwc.com, www.fl-dof.com, http://floridabirdingtrail.com, www .floridatrail.org
Finding the campground: Situated in the center of the Florida peninsula, Arbuckle WMA can be reached from I-95 via exit 147 and then driving west on SR 60 to turn left (south) on Polk CR 630. It is then about 11 miles to a left turn (southwest) onto Blue Jordan Road; 2 miles to a left turn (south) on North Lake Reed Boulevard; 2 miles to a left turn (southeast) on Lake Arbuckle Road; and 1 mile to a right turn (south) on Rucks Dairy Road (which becomes Schoolbus Road). The campground is on the west side of the road.
About the campground: This is a primitive site even though you must get a permit from the Division of Forestry and pay a fee. The management area is set aside to protect the land from development and the wildlife from disappearing once development takes place.

Arbuckle is a 3,531-acre area and part of Lake Wales Ridge State Forest. Fishing is also allowed, and a loop of the Florida Trail circles the property on the southwest side of Lake Arbuckle. There are ancient sand dunes here and the forested site is thick with scrub, home to Florida scrub jays and gopher tortoises.

There is also a short nature trail, and horseback riding is permitted. The WMA is part of the Great Florida Birding Trail. Look for short-tail hawks, abundant wading birds, eagles, osprey, and marsh limpkins feeding on snails.

89 Kicco Wildlife Management Area

Location: Along the channelized Kissimmee River south of SR 60 in Polk County (27° 48' 12" N, 81° 13' 6" W)
Season: During hunting seasons with special use permit
Sites: 5 sites for primitive tent camping. The first campsite is within 1 mile of the trailhead; the second, about 3 miles farther; and the third, another 3 miles beyond that. None is on the river-bank, but all are close. Primitive waterfront camping is also available on the opposite, east side of the Kissimmee River at Blanket Bay Slough. This sheltered campsite, accessible only by boat, is marked and can readily be seen from the river. There are no hiking trails on Blanket Bay, as it is mainly marsh.
Maximum length: Call for current information
Facilities: Call for current information
Fee per night: Call for current information
Management: Fish & Wildlife Conservation Commission and South Florida Water Management District
Contact: (800) 250-4200 or (863) 462-5260 for free permit, http://myfwc.com, www.floridatrail .org, https://my.sfwmd.gov, www.floridabirdingtrail.com
Finding the campground: From Florida's Turnpike, exit at Yeehaw Junction (193); take SR 60 west to the WMA. It is immediately on the south side of the highway after crossing the Kissimmee River and into Polk County.
About the campground: This is a water and wildlife area. Humans are a secondary element in the 7,000 acres. Thirteen miles of the Florida Trail cross the area although with any rain or high water event, miles of the trail may be under water. Wetland restoration construction indicates that the area will have more water, not less.

The WMA calls walking the 9-mile, shell-surfaced Kicco Grade Road "excellent," although those who enjoy true backcountry hiking will get off the road as soon as possible. There are no amenities in the WMA although several nearby dude ranches will accommodate campers.

90 Lake Kissimmee State Park

Location: Off SR 60, 15 miles east of Lake Wales in Polk County (27° 58' 8.7" N, 81° 22' 48.6" W)
Season: Year-round
Sites: 60 shaded family sites, 2 primitive sites, 2 primitive youth sites
Maximum length: 58 feet
Facilities: Full-facility camping in the family sites; none at the primitive sites, which are located within 13 miles of park hiking trails (everything must be backpacked in including water). Two primitive youth group sites with cold showers and restrooms are also available.

Fee per night: $$

Management: Florida Division of Recreation and Parks

Contact: 863-696-1112, www.floridastateparks.org/lakekissimmee/default.cfm; (800) 326-3521, www.reserveamerica.com

Finding the campground: From exit 55 on I-4, take US 27 about 40 miles due south to SR 60 in Lake Wales. Turn left (east), drive 9 miles to Boy Scout Camp Road and turn left (north). Boy Scout Camp Road becomes Barney Keen Road after it makes a sweeping counterclockwise curve, and after about 4 miles, Barney Keen dead-ends on Camp Mack Road. Turn right (east) and follow Camp Mack Road for about 6 miles to the park entrance.

About the campground: At Lake Kissimmee, you can camp or picnic under shady oaks and pines, picnic in the breeze beside a lake, stare into the embers of the fire in your fire ring, and look into the stars at night. You can hike miles of backcountry trails, keep lists or take pictures of magnificent bird life and wildflowers. This chain of central Florida lakes is, after all, known as the "Headwaters of the Everglades."

You might see deer and otters and wild hogs. For those with boats or paddle-craft, thousands of miles of streams and lakes are here for exploring and for fishing. If you have a horse, most parks welcome riders and are working to build facilities. Most of those things are available in abundance here, in a park dominated by three lakes, Lakes Kissimmee, Tiger and Rosalie.

One activity enjoyed by almost everyone is the reenactment of Florida's cowboy heritage. On weekends and holidays from October 1 through May 1, volunteers and their steeds regularly demonstrate the skills and way of life of "cow hunters" in an 1876-era cow camp.

91 Three Lakes Wildlife Management Area

Location: An hour's drive south of Disney World in Osceola County (27° 54' 30" N, 81° 8' 30" W)

Season: Year-round

Sites: At the Prairie Lakes Unit, primitive camping is allowed at designated campsites on non-hunting days. At the rest of Three Lakes, camping is permitted at hunter-designated areas during hunting seasons, and at designated sites on the Florida Trail throughout the year. (One primitive campsite is just west of the intersection of CR 523 and Road 5; the others generally lie between the smaller lakes, Jackson and Marian, and these are best accessed via Road 16.)

Maximum length: Call for current information

Facilities: Call for current information

Fee per night: A no-cost camping permit is required from the FWC

Management: Fish & Wildlife Conservation Commission (FWC)

Contact: (407) 435-1818 for permit, http://myfwc.com, www.floridabirdingtrail.com

Finding the campground: From the Orlando area, take US 441/92/17 south to Kissimmee. Here the roads split, but veer left (east) and follow US 441/192 to St. Cloud. In St. Cloud, turn right (south) on Vermont Avenue, which in 4 blocks becomes Canoe Creek Road/CR 523. Follow Canoe Creek Road for about 25 miles to the WMA, which is on the right (west) side of the road. Watch for road signs that direct you to the camping areas.

About the campground: Named for its three border lakes—Kissimmee, Jackson, and Marian—Three Lakes offers hunting, fishing, birding, hiking, horseback riding, and off-road biking. In the

WMA, the only boat ramp is on the smallest lake, Jackson, but ramps for Kissimmee and Marian are located just outside the WMA boundaries.

There are nearly 30 miles of trail and 25 miles of the Florida National Scenic Trail pass through. Flat stretches of dry prairie attract off-road cyclists and Three Lakes contains one the largest dry prairies remaining in the U.S. Still, thunderstorms can turn the area into a bog. Try the 10-mile interpretive trail; maps are available at the entrance kiosk.

Camping options are complex on this WMA as hunting seasons in the fall, winter, and spring require that recreational campers call ahead for a permit and for information about regulated activities and your own safety.

92 Lake Marion Creek Wildlife Management Area

Location: North and east of Lake Marion and 5 miles east of Haines City on SR 580 in Polk and Osceola Counties (28° 8' 0" N, 81° 32' 24" W)
Season: Year-round, except during hunting seasons
Sites: Primitive camping
Maximum length: Call for current information
Facilities: Call for current information
Fee per night: Call for current information
Management: Fish & Wildlife Conservation Commission, South Florida Water Management District and Polk County
Contact: (800) 250-4250 or (407) 858-6100 (in Orlando) for a special use permit, http://myfwc.com and https://my.sfwmd.gov
Finding the forest: This WMA is in the center of the state. From US 27 southwest of Orlando, turn left (east) in Haines City on US 92/17. In less than 2 miles, turn right on CR 580 and in about 5 miles you will be in the middle of the WMA; watch for signs as there are numerous unpaved parking areas.
About the forest: Even though a sliver of this wetlands and wildlife area is in Osceola County, the 8,083-acre area was purchased by the water management district and Polk County.

Because most of the area is a swamp, any recreational activity, including hunting for deer and hogs, hiking, and even camping while remaining dry, is going to be a challenge. Horseback riding is prohibited, and bicycling is only permitted with a permit. Still, there are marked and mapped hiking trails from designated entrances.

93 Osceola County Parks

NOTE: Contact Osceola County Parks & Recreation, 366 N. Beaumont Ave., Kissimmee, FL 34741, (407) 343-7173, www.osceola.org/index.cfm?IsFuses=department/Parks for more information regarding camp specs and management as parks are often changing.

This 132-acre undeveloped conservation area (28° 14' 56.0" N, 81° 24' 23.3" W) is inside northern Lake Tohopekaliga and can only be reached by boat. You will find primitive camping, restrooms, a boat and canoe ramp, hiking, fishing, pavilions, and mosquitoes.

Joe Overstreet Boat Ramp: 4900 Joe Overstreet Rd., Kenansville, FL 34739.

Directions: From US 441 south of Orlando, turn right (south) on Canoe Creek Road/CR 523. Turn right (southwest) on Joe Overstreet Road. Some RV camping is available on the east bank of Lake Kissimmee: two acres, two boat ramps, restrooms, and pavilions.

Southport Park: 2001 Southport Rd., Kissimmee, FL 34758 (28° 8' 16.8" N, 81° 21' 43.6" W).

Directions: Take US 17/92 south from Orlando, and turn left (south) on Pleasant Hill Road. Turn left (east) on Southport Road. RV camping is allowed on the south shore of Lake Toho-pekaliga: thirty-two acres, boat ramp, restrooms, concessions, and pavilions. (Operated by Boggy Creek Airboat Rides: contact East Lake Fish Camp, 407-933-5822.)

94 Moss Park

Location: Off the Central Florida Greenway (SR 417) southwest of Orlando in Orange County at 32832 Moss Park Rd., Orlando, FL 32838 (28° 22' 18" N, 81° 11' 30" W)

Season: Year-round

Sites: 48 tent/individual sites to full-service RV. Sites 1 to 4 are designated "multi-person" or small group sites and can be reserved for up to 18 people in 6 tents or 3 RVs/pop-up campers. Group sites A–E are designed for between 20 and 450 people. Campsites are situated among moss-hung oaks, cypress, and pines between lakes Mary Jane to the east and Hart to the west; all are in the back of the park. The campsites are large and are all back-ins, angled to make backing a trailer easy. Reservations are recommended.

Maximum length: Pull-through sites available

Facilities: Each relatively new site has electricity and water. Also here are bathrooms, shower, picnic facilities, boat ramp, pier on Lake Mary Jane for fishing, available dump station.

Fee per night: $$; multi-person sites, $$$

Management: Fish & Wildlife Conservation Commission (FWC)

Contact: (850) 488-4676, (407) 273-2327, http://myfwc.com/, www.orangecountyfl.net/dept/cesrvcs/parks/ParkDetails.asp?ParkID=29

Finding the campground: From Orlando, drive east on SR 408, the East-West Expressway, to exit 18B, SR 417, the Central Florida Greenway, and turn right (south). At exit 22, turn right (north) on Narcoosee Road and then right on Moss Park Road. Follow it east then south to the park entrance. The boat ramp is to the left of the park office.

About the campground: Ownership and responsibilities become complicated and often difficult when bureaucrats from various agencies become involved. In this case, the FWC owns the double-lane boat ramp and an associated unimproved parking lot capable of accommodating 30 vehicles. The balance of the 1,551-acre park is generally supervised and maintained by Orange County.

The park has many hiking trails through an attached forest so visitors can take to the trails as well as to boats. Swimming in Lake Mary Jane is popular too, but there is no lifeguard.

95 Orange County Parks

NOTE: Please contact the park(s) for more information regarding omitted camp specs and management as it is often changing.

Clarcona Horse Park

Location: 3535 Damon Rd., Apopka, FL 32703 (28° 37' 36" N, 81° 30' 6" W), www.orange countyfl.net/dept/cesrvcs/parks/ParkDetails.asp?ParkID=10

Finding the campground: From Florida's Turnpike, take exit 267 and drive north on SR 429/Western Expressway. Turn east at exit 26, and after 1 block, turn left (east) on Clarcona-Ocoee Road. Follow it through several turns to the intersection with North Apopka-Vineland Road and turn left (north). Turn left (west) on East McCormick Road and right (north) on Damon Road and watch for signs.

About the campground: RV camping is available at this horse park built on 40 acres in northwest Orlando. The site has show rings with bleacher seating, judging towers, horse stalls, and dressage show rings. Clarcona links to the 22-mile West Orange multiuse trail (hiking, cycling, jogging, and skating) with an equestrian path. The park also houses the Mid-Florida Midget Race Track and Association. A midget car is a special vehicle designed for children ages 6 to 16. For more information about this pastime, call (407) 886-6255.

Hal Scott Preserve

Location: 5150 Dallas Blvd., Orlando, FL 32833 (28° 28' 18" N, 81° 5' 42" W), www.orange countyfl.net/dept/cesrvcs/parks/ParkDetails.asp?ParkID=17

Finding the campground: Drive east on the Bee Line (or Beach Line) Expressway/SR 528 in south Orlando. Take exit 24 north onto Dallas Boulevard and follow the signs to the preserve.

About the campground: Hal Scott has three primitive campsites (Canal 3, Yates, and Hancock) for tents only. Each has fire rings and picnic tables, but you won't find portable toilets or potable water here. Access is by foot, bicycle, or horseback only. The nearest campsite to the parking lot (Canal 3) is about 2 miles. All sites are first-come, first-served; no reservations or fee required. Miles of hiking trails wind through this 9,000-acre sanctuary on the shoreline of the Econlockhatchee River. The St. Johns River Water Management District actually manages the park. Recreational opportunities consist of bird-watching, hiking, cycling, horseback riding, and fishing. Contact (407) 836-6200.

Kelly Park/Rock Springs

Location: 400 East Kelly Park Rd. Apopka, FL 32712 (28° 45' 30" N, 81° 30' 12"), www.orange countyfl.net/dept/cesrvcs/parks/ParkDetails.asp?ParkID=22

Finding the campground: From I-4, take exit 101 and proceed west on SR 46. Turn left (south) on Plymouth Sorrento Road; left again (east) on Kelly Park Road.

About the campground: This is a very nice 245-acre urban park that charges lower fees for Orange County residents ($$) than it does for non-residents ($$$). There will be a lot of daytime activity here—team sports such as volleyball, for instance—especially on holidays and weekends in the summer All campsites—RV, trailer, tent—have water and electrical hookups. Amenities include a free-flowing natural spring for tubing, full-service concession, picnic pavilions, playground, and hiking and swimming opportunities. Contact (407) 889-4179. (The gates close when it hits capacity so if you visit this park go early.)

Magnolia Park

Location: 2929 South Binion Rd. Apopka, FL 32703 (28° 38' 6" N, 81° 33' 0" W), www.orange countyfl.net/dept/cesrvcs/parks/ParkDetails.asp?ParkID=26

Finding the campground: From Florida's Turnpike, take exit 272 east on SR 50 to the intersection with SR 429, the Daniel Webster Western Beltway, and turn left (north). Take exit 30 onto Ocoee-Apopka Road/CR 437, and the park is on the left, adjacent to Lake Apopka.

About the campground: Sunsets can be very pleasant from this urban campground, which offers primitive tent and RV camping in the shade of large live oaks, southern magnolias, and hickories. RVs 40 feet in length have access to 18 campsites with cement pads, water, picnic tables, and fire rings. All campers can expect restrooms with hot showers, a dump station, and playground. Orange County residents pay $$; non-residents pay $$$. (Fees also vary by age, older campers receiving a small break. Because this park is very nice, reservations are recommended.) There is a boat launch for fishing and boating on Lake Apopka. Team sports such as volleyball and basketball are popular. Each year in April, the park hosts a Bluegrass (music) Festival in October, a Pumpkin Fest & Hayride; and in December a meet-Santa get-together. Contact (407) 886-4231.

Trimble Park

Location: 5802 Trimble Park Rd. Mt. Dora, FL 32757 (28° 41' 8" N, 81° 39' 22.3" W), www .orangecountyfl.net/dept/cesrvcs/parks/ParkDetails.asp?ParkID=40

Finding the campground: From Florida's Turnpike exit northbound on the Daniel Webster Western Beltway/SR 429. Exit to the northwest on US 441, the Orange Blossom Trail, and just past the crossroads called "Tangerine," turn left (west) on Lake Ola Drive, which swings left (west) onto Earlwood Avenue and then right (north) on Trimble Park Road.

About the campground: Trimble is a 71-acre park with 10 RV sites with electrical/water hookups, 5 RV sites with electrical only, and 1 group site that accommodates 50 campers. The group site can be split into 5 sites with 10 campers each.

Trimble is set in a hammock of magnolias, oaks, and pines, on a peninsula between Lakes Beauclair and Carlton. It has a boat ramp, docks, a lakeside picnic area, and even a short nature trail. Swimming, fishing, bird-watching, and picnic pavilions are available. Reservations are recommended; Fees are $$–$$$, depending on one's age, place of residence, and type of camping. Contact (352) 383-1993.

96 Little Big Econlockhatchee State Forest/ Wildlife Management Area

Location: 3.3 miles east of the town of Oviedo on CR 426 in Seminole County (28° 39' 35" N, 81° 11' 45" W)

Season: Year-round

Dawn fog lifts over the wetlands revealing white-tailed deer and migrating pintails.

Sites: Primitive camping for paddlers of canoes and kayaks with a special use permit from the forest office. Paddling the Econ is a great way to spend a day and improved launch areas have been built along the river.

Maximum length: Call for current information

Facilities: Trailhead parking areas

Fee per night: $-$$

Management: Division of Forestry and Fish & Wildlife Conservation Commission

Contact: (407) 971-3500, www.fl-dof.com/state_forests/little_big_econ.html, http://myfwc.com, www.floridabirdingtrail.com, www.floridatrail.org

Finding the forest: From Orlando, take the East-West Expressway/SR 408 east to the Central Florida Greenway/SR 417 and swing left (north). Take exit 41 to the right (east) toward Oviedo on Mitchell Hammock Road and turn left (north) on Lockwood Road until it intersects with Oviedo Road/CR 426 and turn right. Follow the signs to the forest, which will be on the right.

About the forest: Florida's Little Big is named after the Little Econlockhatchee River and the larger Econlockhatchee River, both of which flow through the state forest.

Although not in the separate Kilbee Unit to the east, paddlers are going to love the Econlockhatchee, the forest's most notable feature, because it provides sweet scenic beauty in a winding stream with plenty of what makes Florida wonderful: herons and alligators, possibly a river otter, wild turkeys, and bald eagles. In places old, moss-hung hardwoods arch over the golden-brown stream providing complete shade, and it is possible that you will see snakes dangling from tree limbs over the water. The area is part of the Great Florida Birding Trail and the Florida National Scenic Trail and is used by hikers to cross the Econlockhatchee River. Besides the birding and hiking, and the canoeing and kayaking along the river, visitors enjoy horseback riding, mountain biking, fishing, picnicking, and nature study.

97 Seminole County Parks

NOTE: Please contact the park(s) for more information regarding omitted camp specs and management as it is often changing.
General location: Seminole County, 1101 East First St., Sanford, FL 32771, (407) 665-0311

Lake Mills

Location: 1301 Tropical Ave., Chuluota, FL 32766 (28° 37' 54" N, 81° 7' 24" W), www.seminole countyfl.gov/leisure/parks/parkInfo.asp?id=10
Finding the campground: From Orlando, take SR 408/East-West Expressway east and turn right (east) on SR 50/Colonial Drive/John Cheney Highway. Turn left (north) on CR 419/Chuluota Road, right (east) on Lake Mills Road, and left (north) on Tropical Avenue.
About the campground: This smallish 50-acre park in Seminole County is east of Oviedo. It offers an up-close look at a hardwood swamp and highlands of oak and pine. Picnic pavilions are shaded by 150-year-old oaks. Go to Lake Mills for camping, cookouts, and fishing from boardwalks. For small children, there is a playground with a tot lot. Contact the Seminole County Softball Complex, (407) 788-0609.

Mullet Lake

Location: 2368 Mullet Lake Park Rd., Geneva, FL 32732 (28° 47' 24" N, 81° 8' 12" W), www .seminolecountyfl.gov/leisure/parks/parkInfo.asp?id=13
Finding the campground: From Orlando, take I-4 east and use exit 101 to drive east on SR 46A/H.E. Thomas Parkway/25th Street. Turn left (north) on Mullet Park Lake Road.
About the campground: This 151-acre park is associated with Mullet Lake, which is part of a chain of lakes and wetlands northeast of Orlando. There are primitive campsites with restrooms, a pavilion for picnicking, fishing, and boat launch with access to the St. Johns River basin. Contact the Seminole County Softball Complex, (407) 788-0609.

98 Wekiwa Springs State Park

Location: 20 minutes north of Orlando, just west of I-4 in Orange County (28° 46' 12" N, 81° 30' 04" W)
Season: Year-round
Sites: 60, plus 2 primitive campsites for youth group camping and 2 canoe-accessible sites on Rock Springs Run (Otter Camp and Big Buck Camp) that can only be accessed by canoe or kayak. Travel to either site can begin from any livery along the Wekiva River or inside Wekiwa Springs State Park.
Maximum length: 50 feet
Facilities: Full-facility campsites with water, electricity, in-ground fire circle with grill, picnic table; ADA-accessible campsites available
Fee per night: $$$

Management: Florida Division of Recreation and Parks

Contact: (407) 884-2008/4311, www.floridastateparks.org/wekiwasprings/default.cfm; (800) 326-3521, www.reserveamerica.com

Finding the campground: Wekiwa Springs is 20 minutes north of Orlando and 45 minutes north of the tourist attractions. It is easily located off I-4 at exit 94. Take SR 434 west to Wekiwa Springs Road. Turn right on Wekiwa Springs Road and travel approximately 4 miles to the entrance, which is on the right.

About the campground: This park surrounds the springs and headwaters of the Wekiva River, and it is quite a beautiful place and feels more remote than it actually is. Florida looked much like this just prior to the arrival of European and African settlers.

This is one of a number of urban and suburban parks in the Orlando area. Swimming is popular in the large, clear springs, which maintain a constant temperature of 72 degrees year-round. Canoeists/kayakers can paddle the Wekiva River and Rock Springs Run. There are 13 miles of multiuse trails for hiking, bicycling, and horseback riding. Options for camping include a full-facility campground and primitive camping areas. Canoe and kayak rentals are available.

99 Lower Wekiva River Preserve State Park

Location: 9 miles west of Sanford on SR 46 and stretching north toward SR 44 along the Wekiva River in Lake and Seminole Counties (28° 48' 56.3" N, 81° 24' 18.7" W)

Season: Year-round

Sites: Primitive horse camping on a first-come, first-served basis

Maximum length: None allowed overnight

Facilities: Shower and wheelchair-accessible restroom in the horse camping area; corrals and stalls for horses

Fee per night: $$ (Fees are dependent upon the ratio of campers to horses: horse campers must make reservations, but their RVs and horse trailers are welcome)

Management: Florida Division of Recreation and Parks

Contact: (407) 884-2008, www.floridastateparks.org/lowerwekivariver/default.cfm

Finding the campground: The northern entrance is located off of SR 44 in Pine Lakes. From SR 44, turn east onto Oak Avenue and then right on County Road. Jog east on Jack Lake Drive for a block, and then turn right (south) onto Swift Rd. Follow Swift Road to the end of the paved road and turn south into the preserve (38015 Fechtel Rd., Eustis, FL 32726). The southern entrance is 9 miles west of Sanford on SR 46. The park entrance is on the right (8300 West State Road 46, Sanford, FL 32711).

About the campground: Lower Wekiva is an unusual place with no continual on-site attendant, two entrances and little in the way of amenities. Camping is restricted to the northern entrance for equestrians and their steeds. Trails wind through the preserve. From the north, an 18-mile multiuse trail is designed for horses, cyclists, and hikers. At the southern end, where no horses are allowed, there is a 2.5-mile trail. Although paddlers are welcome on the Wekiva, there is no official launch in this 18,000-acre park.

Warning: Google maps does not correctly show park boundaries. The Web site shows the incorrect park (Wekiwa Springs State Park) when you "Download the Park Brochure." Although the two parks are situated along the same wetlands system and are less than an hour apart by automobile, this creates confusion.

100 Rock Springs Run State Reserve

Location: In Sorrento, approximately 30 miles north of Orlando off SR 46 in Lake County (28° 48' 36.0" N, 81° 27' 26.3" W)

Season: Year-round

Sites: Horse camping—sites vary depending upon numbers of people and horses in a group. Canoe/kayak primitive camping—2 sites can be reached only from Rock Springs Run, and there is no launching available in the park.

Maximum length: Horse trailers and accompanying RVs

Facilities: Horse camping—pack in all food, water, and firewood and pack out all trash; bathhouse/restroom facility available. Ground grills are provided and fires are only permitted in these grills. Tents are permitted but can only be pitched in designated camping areas. The collection of firewood is prohibited. RV and trailer parking, horse stalls and corrals are first-come, first-served. There are posts for tethers, but temporary fencing is not permitted. Nonpotable water is available for horses, and there are troughs in several locations.

Fee per night: Horse camping fees vary by number of people/horses. Canoe/kayak primitive camping is $ per person per night.

Management: Florida Division of Recreation and Parks

Contact: (407) 884 2008, www.floridastateparks.org/rockspringsrun/default.cfm

Finding the campground: Rock Springs Run State Reserve is located in Sorrento, approximately 30 miles north of Orlando. From I-4, take exit 101C and travel west on SR 46 for approximately 10 miles to the park entrance located at the beginning of CR 433. This road is not marked. It begins at the entrance to the park. The park entrance is on the left (south side) if traveling from I-4 and is framed by a very tall chain-link fence. The entrance is about 3 miles west of the Wekiva River bridge on SR 46.

About the campground: There is plenty to do in this lovely state preserve, especially along the 17 miles of trails: off-road biking, horseback riding, and hiking plus bird-watching. It is one of the few state parks where guided trail rides and horse rentals are available. The trails can be closed in hunting seasons or when the staff is conducting prescribed burns of the undergrowth. Primitive campsites on Rock Springs Run and the Wekiva River are accessible only by canoe. Reserve the canoe or horse campsites by calling Wekiwa Springs State Park, (407) 884-2008.

101 Seminole State Forest/Wildlife Management Area

Location: Off SR 46 approximately 14 miles west of the town of Sanford in Lake County (28° 47' 36" N, 81° 16' 36" W)

Season: Year-round

Sites: 3 primitive campsites (but each has a fire ring and picnic table) and 5 primitive campsites along hiking trails. Moccasin Springs Camp, on the bank of Blackwater Creek, accommodates 5 people; Oaks Camp and Jumper Camp, adjacent to open fields, can accommodate up to 20 people. State forest use authorization required.

Maximum length: Call for current information

Facilities: Call for current information

Fee per night: $-$$

Management: Division of Forestry and Fish & Wildlife Conservation Commission

Contact: (352) 360-6675/6677, www.fl-dof.com/state_forests/seminole.html, http://myfwc.com, and www.floridabirdingtrail.com

Finding the forest: The first entrance is reached from I-4 via exit 101C to SR 46. It is approximately 14 miles west of the town of Sanford. Parking areas, entrance gates, and trailheads are located at the second entrance, which is located west of the Wekiva River on SR 44 in Cassia, approximately 12 miles east of the town of Eustis.

About the forest: Camping in a state park is an excellent vacation or "staycation." Florida's state parks are well managed and well apportioned, but camping in one of them can also feel a little too managed, too apportioned. That's when it's time to try your equipment and your ingenuity at a primitive campground, such as one of those along the Florida Trail or in a WMA. Primitive camping—where there are no rowdy neighbors except the wildlife, no concessionaires selling soft drinks, and the complexity of rules for how high or how far or how much slackens—is a real way to shake off the scales of civilization for a few hours. Off-road bicycling is permitted where designated.

102 Hontoon Island State Park

Location: 6 miles southwest of DeLand off SR 44 (28° 58' 36.7" N, 81° 21' 23.4" W)

Season: Year-round

Sites: 12 tent sites, 6 cabins, primitive/youth camping for groups up to 35

Maximum length: Call for current information

Facilities: Picnic table, ground grill, access to water spigot, central restroom facilities and hot showers. Cabins (1-room) have bunk beds with vinyl-covered mattresses (ugh), ceiling fan, overhead lighting, one electrical outlet plus picnic table, ground grill, screened porch with table and chairs. No restroom facilities, cooking facilities, heating or air-conditioning inside the cabins. Cooking is only permissible outside the cabins at the ground grill or on a personal camp stove.

Fee per night: $$

Management: Florida Division of Recreation and Parks

Contact: (386) 736-5309, www.floridastateparks.org/hontoonisland/default.cfm; (800) 326-3521, www.reserveamerica.com

Finding the campground: From I-4, take exit 118 west on SR 44. In west Deland, veer left (southwest) onto CR 4110, which after 2 miles turns left (south) and becomes Hontoon Road. Make a left on River Ridge Road and proceed to the entrance and ferry.

About the campground: The campground is in a hammock area so it is shaded (and buggy). This beautiful, shaded campground surrounded by oaks, tall pines, magnolias, and palm trees is on an island in the St. Johns River and only accessible by private boat or the park ferry, which operates from 8:00 a.m. to an hour before sunset. On land, watch for deer, and in the water, look for manatees. Protective insect repellent will help you enjoy this beautiful site even more. Hontoon Island offers overnight boat slips (fee $$ includes 30-amp electrical service), first-come, first-served.

103 Blue Spring State Park

Location: West of Orange City in Volusia County (28° 57' 8.2" N, 81° 20' 1.2" W)
Season: Year-round
Sites: 51, plus 6 cabins and primitive camping (requiring a 4-mile hike to and from the site, carrying your food and water)
Maximum length: 30 feet
Facilities: Full-facility camping, table, water, electricity, grill
Fee per night: $$
Management: Florida Division of Recreation and Parks
Contact: 386-775-3663, www.floridastateparks.org/bluespring/default.cfm; (800) 326-3521, www.reserveamerica.com
Finding the campground: From I-4, take exit 114 and follow the signs or go west on CR 472 to US 17/92. Turn south on US 17/92 to Orange City, about 2 miles, and then right (west) onto French Avenue to the park's entrance.
About the campground: Blue Spring is the largest upwelling of pure, cold water on the St. Johns River. The bubble of water is clear as glass and a constant 72 to 73 degrees. After the first shock of cold, your body quickly becomes accustomed to the temperature and swimmers, tubers, snorkelers, and certified scuba divers may enjoy the waters almost year-round.

It is also a designated manatee refuge because from November through March, West Indian Manatees flock to this area.

The river is popular for fishing, canoeing, and boating. Rentals are available and you can book boat tours from St. Johns River Cruises, (386) 917-0724. The park has plenty of picnic areas, boat ramps, and a hiking trail.

104 Tiger Bay State Forest/Wildlife Management Area

Location: Tiger Bay State Forest/WMA extends north and south of US 92 and west of Daytona Beach in Volusia County (29° 12' 26" N, 81° 02' 16" W)
Season: Year-round
Sites: Both primitive and primitive youth camping are available by permit in the Rima Ridge Unit. An equestrian campground has been added to the Rima Ridge Tract with 5 primitive campsites, a 16'- by-16' horse corral, nonpotable water supply, and water trough for horses.
Maximum length: Call for current information
Facilities: Call for current information
Fee per night: $-$$
Management: Division of Forestry and Fish & Wildlife Conservation Commission
Contact: (386) 226-0520 for permits, www.fl-dof.com/state_forests/tiger_bay.html, http://myfwc.com/RECREATION/WMASites_TigerBay_index.htm
Finding the forest: Tiger Bay is located in the central section of Volusia County, 7 miles west of Daytona Beach. Take exit 261 from I-95; the forest extends north and south of US 92.
About the forest: In 1998, 15,000 acres of this 27,330-acre forest burned in what foresters call a "wildfire firestorm." Damage was extensive and, although much reforestation has been undertaken,

ars from this fire are still visible. Otherwise, much of Tiger Bay is swamp with about 40 percent of the forest in embedded pine islands and a large pine ridge. Camping is prohibited in some sections entirely, and you really must call ahead both for a permit and to discuss which sections are open.

The forest includes two lakes and several ponds. Coon Pond is natural, but Rattlesnake Pond, Woody Pond, and Ranch Pond are man-made and available for fishing.

105 Relay Wildlife Management Area

Location: South of the crossroads of Cody's Corner in Flagler County (29° 18' 30" N, 81° 16' 18" W)
Season: Year-round
Sites: Primitive camping at one site is available during hunting season with a permit
Maximum length: Call for current information
Facilities: Call for current information
Fee per night: Call for current information
Management: Fish & Wildlife Conservation Commission and Plum Creek Timber Company
Contact: (386) 226-0520 for permits, http://myfwc.com
Finding the campground: From I-95, take exit 268 onto SR 40 west. At SR 11, turn right (north), and 1.6 miles before the Cody's Corner crossroad with Dupont Road, signs will appear to the WMA on the right (east side) and the camping area in about 6 miles into the WMA.
About the campground: Relay WMA would not be your first choice of campground unless you were a hunter with a license and a permit. It is a 19,672-acre privately owned timber plantation with white-tailed deer, feral hogs, and wild turkeys. Primitive camping and fishing are allowed during hunting seasons. This WMA consists of pine flatwoods, bottomland hardwoods, and scattered hammocks and cypress heads. Migratory birds are common.

106 Lake George State Forest/ Wildlife Management Area/Conservation Area

Location: Near the towns of Barberville and Astor in Putnam and Volusia Counties (29° 09' 50" N, 81° 32' 04" W)
Season: Year-round
Sites: Primitive camping only
Maximum length: Call for current information
Facilities: Call for current information
Fee per night: $–$$
Management: Cooperatively managed by the Division of Forestry, Fish & Wildlife Conservation Commission, and the St. Johns River Water Management District
Contact: (386) 985-7822 at the forest headquarters for a use permit for primitive camping or for vehicle access to portions of the Mary Farms and Dexter Units (except during Special Opportunity

Hunts), www.fl-dof.com/state_forests/lake_george.html, http://myfwc.com, www.sjrwmd.com

Finding the forest: Lake George State Forest and the WMA/Conservation Area is located in northwestern Volusia County near Barberville and Astor. To reach Astor, take exit 268 from I-95 and drive east on SR 40. To access the forest north of SR 40 (Astor Tract), take Riley Pridgeon Road, located 0.5 mile east of the town of Astor. To access the 14,377 acres of forest and the campground south of SR 40 (Mary Farms/Dexter Tracts) take St. Johns River Road, located 0.5 mile east of Astor. This goes to the Bluffton Recreation Area.

About the forest: It is difficult at times to know what is happening on Florida's wild lands. Some are closed to camping during hunting seasons; others are open to hunters; others are open regardless. It is best to call and ask; that is certainly the case here in the 19,468-acre Lake George State Forest because multiple government agencies claim prerogatives and responsibilities. An additional impediment to informed camping is cutbacks in governmental operations, so the telephone will not always be answered, or sometimes it will be answered by a willing, but poorly informed volunteer. Be persistent. The answers are out there.

On the eastern shore of Lake George, the land alternates between low cypress and bay wetlands, oak and hickory hammocks, and pine and palmetto uplands. Several disjointed tracts have been administratively combined into this forest, and the St. Johns River borders it for 3.5 miles, providing plenty of opportunities for fun.

107 Faver-Dykes State Park

Location: 15 miles south of St. Augustine near the intersection of I-95 and US 1 in St. Johns County (29° 40' 4.1" N, 81° 16' 5.6" W)
Season: Year-round
Sites: 30, including a primitive youth and group camping area accommodating up to 100 people
Maximum length: 35 feet
Facilities: Full-facility camping with water, electricity, in-ground fire circle with grill and picnic table, hot showers, restrooms. Group camping area with pitcher pump for water, fire circle, and pit toilet.
Fee per night: $$
Management: Florida Division of Recreation and Parks
Contact: (904) 794-0997, www.floridastateparks.org/faver-dykes/default.cfm; (800) 326-3521, www.reserveamerica.com
Finding the campground: Take exit 298 off I-95 and drive north on US 1 for 300 yards. Turn right (east) on Faver-Dykes Road and travel 1.5 miles to the park entrance.
About the campground: At Faver-Dykes campers can hike the nature trails, picnic, join evening campfire circles and ranger programs for the full flavor of camping under the stars of virtually unspoiled Florida. Although it is only 6,045 acres, the long south side of the park borders Pellicer Creek, which meanders slowly toward the Intracoastal Waterway and, ultimately, the Atlantic Ocean. Pellicer is slow and boggy in places, but more than a hundred species of birds live here, from warblers to falcons, egrets and storks to eagles and pelicans.

You can launch a small boat or kayak to explore the area or to fish as both freshwater and saltwater species can be landed in Pellicer Creek. (Canoe rentals are available at the park, and if you don't have a boat, you can fish from the dock.)

108 Anastasia State Park

Location: Just south of St. Augustine on Anastasia Island in St. Johns County (29° 52' 47.87" N, 81° 17' 6.46" W)
Season: Year-round
Sites: 139
Maximum length: 40 feet
Facilities: Full-facility camping with electricity and water, picnic table, in-ground grill, fire ring
Fee per night: $$
Management: Florida Division of Recreation and Parks
Contact: (904) 461-2033, www.floridastateparks.org/anastasia/default.cfm; (800) 326-3521, www.reserveamerica.com
Finding the campground: From I-95, take exit 318 east on CR 16 to US 1 and turn right (south). Turn left (east) on CR 214/King Street and, merging with US 1A at the Bridge of Lions in downtown St. Augustine, cross the bridge. The road becomes US1A/Anastasia Boulevard, and the entrance to the park is a little more than 1 mile on the left.
About the campground: This is a popular park because the beach is magnificent and it is a short drive to the old city, the old Castillo de San Marcos National Monument, and to a lighthouse that you can climb for a wonderful view.

Anastasia offers great camping, and there is plenty to do. Surf fishing only requires a license and a little bit of gear. You will find windsurfers and surfers, beachcombers, swimmers, and sunbathers. There are nature trails and paddling in the ocean and on the Intracoastal Waterway.

Hundreds of thousands of people visit Anastasia because its 4 miles of beach are backed by sand dunes and a shady oak hammock. The campground is in a wooded area within easy walking distance of the beach, and anything you might not have on hand is available for purchase or rental within a few minutes of the campground. Island Joe's (904-461-9322) camp store, rental shop, and grill sells beach sundries and camping and fishing supplies and rents bicycles, beach chairs, ocean toys, and umbrellas. Anastasia Watersports (904-460-9111) rents canoes, sailboards, paddleboats, and kayaks, and lessons are available. Fort Mose Historic State Park, the first free black community in North America, is just a short drive north on US 1.

109 Flagler County Parks

NOTE: Flagler County Parks offer campers a choice of four campgrounds, three featured here. Please contact the parks for more information regarding camp specs and management as information is often changing.
Contact information for the following three Flagler County Parks sites: Flagler County Parks and Recreation, 160 Sawgrass Rd., Bunnell, FL 32110 (next to the Agricultural Center, adjacent to the Flagler County Fairgrounds), (386) 437-7490, www.flaglerparks.com/recreation/camping.htm

Haw Creek Preserve

Location: Southwest Flagler County at Haw Creek (29° 23' 42" N, 81° 23' 0" W)
Sites: Primitive camping
Facilities: Walking trails, restrooms, elevated boardwalk, canoe or kayak launch, picnic pavilion, grills
Management: Flagler County Parks and Recreation
Contact: (386) 437-7490 for permit
Finding the campground: From I-95, take exit 284 west on SR 100 through the town of Bunnell. Turn left (south) on CR 305. Turn right (west) on CR 2006W. Turn left (south) on CR 2007.
About the campground: This remote 1,005-acre park borders Haw Creek, which flows into Dead and Crescent Lakes and past the marshy Mud Lake for approximately 2 miles along its southern boundary. It retains a wild flavor, perhaps because it is not overpublicized.

Haw Creek is thickly lined with Mayhaw trees, which produce the small applelike fruit from which the creek gets its name. The fruit is popular for making jelly.

A winding boardwalk overlooking the creek preserves the cypress, oak, and hardwood swamp along the water.

Princess Place Preserve Pellicer Creek

Location: 2500 Princess Place Rd. off Old Kings Road (29° 39' 30" N, 81° 14' 18" W)
Fee per night: $$
Management: Flagler County Parks and Recreation
Contact: (386) 437-7490
Finding the campground: From I-95 take exit 298 and drive south on US 1. Turn left (east) on North Old Kings Road and left (north) again on Princess Place Road.
About the campground: This little park is located on a hill overlooking the confluence of Pellicer Creek and the Intracoastal Waterway. There are plenty of hiking trails through the scenic wood and places to launch paddle boats and fish. Kayaks can be rented and guides arranged by calling (386) 445-0506.

The 1,505-acre park has an interesting history, having been built in 1886 as a hunting lodge. Consequently, it is the oldest-standing structure in Flagler County. When the owner died, his wife married a Russian prince and thus became a princess, hence the name of the park.

River-to-Sea Preserve

Location: Near Marineland at 9805 N. Oceanshore Blvd./SR A1A in extreme northeast Flagler County (29° 39' 54" N, 81° 12' 42" W)
Sites: Primitive group camping
Facilities: Restroom, pavilions, beach parking and access, beachside boardwalk
Management: Flagler County Parks and Recreation
Contact: (386) 437-7490
Finding the campground: From I-95, take exit 289 and drive east on CR 1424. At SR A1A, turn left (north) and drive to the park.
About the campground: This tiny county preserve—just 90 acres—straddles the island and SR A1A, so campers can swim in the ocean and kayak on the Intracoastal Waterway without picking up and moving. Jointly owned by Flagler County and the town of Marineland, the preserve is one of five public beach access parks in Flagler County. All offer off-beach parking and all have facilities.

There are hiking trails, and a multiuse path that runs alongside A1A for 19 miles is excellent for nonmotorized uses (no horses). This wide-open path connects to additional paths in the county and one can make a long day of it simply exploring.

110 Gamble Rogers Memorial State Recreation Area

Location: Immediately south of Flagler Beach along SR A1A in Flagler County (29° 26' 19.7" N, 81° 6' 31.7" W)
Season: Year-round
Sites: 33
Maximum length: 47 feet
Facilities: Full-facility camping with water, electricity (20, 30, or 50 amps at each site), picnic table, fire ring
Fee per night: $$
Management: Florida Division of Recreation and Parks
Contact: (386) 517-2086, www.floridastateparks.org/gamblerogers/default.cfm; (800) 326-3521, www.reserveamerica.com
Finding the campground: From I-95, take exit 284 east on SR 100 until it dead-ends on SR A1A in Flagler Beach. Turn right (south). Gamble Rogers is about 3 miles on both sides of the road.
About the campground: The beach at Gamble Rogers is popular for swimming, sunbathing, beachcombing, and surf fishing; the best surfing in the area is north on A1A at Matanzas Inlet between Marineland and St. Augustine. The nature trail winds through a coastal forest of scrub oak and saw palmetto, and one must understand that the low, twisted oaks are magnificent in their ability to adapt to poor soils and a salty environment. There is a boat ramp on the Intracoastal Waterway, but the park's full-facility campground overlooks the Atlantic Ocean and is just a short walk along a boardwalk from the beach.

111 Tomoka State Park

Location: 3 miles north of Ormond Beach on North Beach Street in Volusia County (29° 20' 30.4" N, 81° 5' 4.2" W)
Season: Year-round
Sites: 100
Maximum length: 34 feet (11 feet in height)
Facilities: Full-facility sites with picnic table, grill, electricity, water (sites are generally well-shaded); 3 bathhouses with hot showers, 1 ADA compliant
Fee per night: $$
Management: Florida Division of Recreation and Parks
Contact: (386) 676-4050/673-0022, http://www.floridastateparks.org/tomoka/default.cfm; (800) 326-3521, www.reserveamerica.com
Finding the campground: From I-95, take exit 278 and head southeast about 3.5 miles on CR 4011. Follow the signs to the entrance as this road runs through the middle of the park.

About the campground: Indians dwelling here lived off the area's fish-filled lagoons, which are accessible by a boat ramp. The waters still are popular for paddling, boating, and fishing. You will have good opportunities at Tomoka to observe the native dugong, the West Indian manatee. The park is also popular with bird-watchers, especially during migrations in spring and fall.

This scenic and popular park has a half-mile nature trail, museum, and park store with canoe rentals.

112 Volusia County Parks

NOTE: Please contact the park(s) for more information regarding omitted camp specs and management as it is often changing.

Contact information for the following five sites: Volusia County Leisure Services, (386) 736-5953 (West Volusia), (386) 257-6000 ext. 5953 (Daytona Beach); or (386) 423-3300 ext. 5953 (Southeast Volusia), http://volusia.org/parks/links.htm

Fee per night for the following five sites: Fees fluctuate seasonally, but remain within the $$ range. There is a $ per night charge for electricity, if available. There is a $ RV dumping fee for non-camping related sewage. Firewood is $ per site per night, or campers can bring their own. At parks charging admission, the entry fee is included in the camping charge.

Gemini Springs Park

Location: 37 Dirksen Drive, DeBary, FL 32713 (28° 52' 0" N, 81° 18' 42" W), (386) 668-3810, http://volusia.org/parks/gemini.htm

Finding the campground: Take exit 108 just north of Sanford and drive west on Dirksen Drive/CR 4162.

About the campground: Tent camping only. Situated on DeBary Creek, this 210-acre park offers a lot of recreation in a small area: camping, canoeing, fishing, a nature trail, a bike trail, a fishing dock, picnic pavilions, and a children's playground. The two springs pump 6.5 million gallons of freshwater every day. The picnic pavilions may be reserved: (386) 668-3810.

Lake Ashby Park

Location: 4150 Boy Scout Camp Rd., New Smyrna Beach, FL 32168 (28° 56' 12" N, 81° 5' 6" W), http://volusia.org/parks/ashbypark.htm

Finding the campground: From exit 249 on I-95, take SR 44 west and turn left (south) onto SR 415/Tomoka Farms Road. Turn left (east) onto Lake Ashby Road and left again onto Boy Scout Camp Road.

About the campground: Primitive tent camping only. Lake Ashby Park is a 64-acre park in a "rural setting" with primitive tent camping, playground, volleyball court, 3,500-square-foot playground, nature and horse trails, boardwalks, fishing pier, pavilions with picnic tables, and grills. A free public boat ramp is nearby.

Lake Monroe Park

Location: 975 U.S. Hwy 17/92, DeBary, FL 32713 (28° 50' 30" N, 81° 19' 24" W), (386) 668-3825, http://volusia.org/parks/LkMonroe.htm
Sites: RV camping; rates $$$ include taxes and electric; tent camping $$
Finding the campground: Take exit 108 from I-4 northeast of Orlando onto CR 4162/DeBary Avenue.
About the campground: Because it is centrally located and well maintained, Lake Monroe is one of the county's oldest and most popular parks. A $1.2-million improvement included new restrooms, floating docks, picnic pavilions, improved parking, and a trailhead for the Lake Monroe-Gemini Springs–DeBary Hall multiuse trail. Here you will find boardwalks, boat ramps, fishing docks, pavilions, picnic areas, nature trails, a playground, and a volleyball court.

River Breeze Park

Location: 250 H.H. Burch Rd., Oak Hill, FL 32759, (28° 53' 42" N, 81° 51'6" W), (386) 345-5525, http://volusia.org/parks/riverbreeze.htm
Finding the campground: From I-95 south of Daytona, take exit 244 east on CR 442/Indian River Boulevard. Turn right (south) on US 1 and drive about 7 miles to H.H. Burch Road. Turn left (east) to the park.
About the campground: Tent and RV camping. A small, but fine 37-acre park with camping for every rig from backpackers to million-dollar RVs and 5 acres of park are right on the Indian River (Intracoastal Waterway). While not "unspoiled" as park brochures suggest, it is quite close to that utopian vision, with soft sunrises over the lagoon. Bird-watching, picnicking, fishing on the pier, and photography are popular here.

Spruce Creek Park

Location: 6250 Ridgewood Ave., Port Orange, FL 32127, (29° 5' 36" N, 80° 58' 18" W), (386) 322-5133, http://volusia.org/parks/spruce.htm
Finding the campground: From exit 256 on I-95 just south of Daytona Beach, turn east on CR 421/Taylor Road. Within a block, follow Taylor Road to the right (southeast) and then left on Spruce Creek Road to SR 5A/Nova Road. Turn right (south) on US 1/Ridgewood Avenue.
About the campground: Tents only. Spruce Creek's 1,637 acres include a boardwalk, nature trails, and a 15-foot observation tower overlooking the marsh. With its playground and canoe launch, the creek is great for bird-watching, paddling, and picnicking.

113 Canaveral National Seashore

Location: On the east coast of Merritt Island east of Titusville in Brevard County (coordinates of the Titusville headquarters: 28° 35' 28.4" N, 80° 49' 11.7" W)
Season: Year-round (beach camping is closed from May 1 to Oct 31 to protect nesting sea turtles)
Sites: 16 total sites: 2 sites on the beach at Apollo Beach and 14 Natural Island campsites and Spoil Island campsites. Access by boat, canoe, or kayak.
Maximum length: None permitted

Facilities: Primitive camping with no freshwater or sanitation facilities. Campers are advised to bring insect repellent: Mosquito infestation can be severe. All necessities need to be packed in and all trash packed out.

Fee per night: $

Management: U.S. National Park Service

Contact: (386) 428-3384. Camping permits can be obtained at the information center, 0.25 mile south of Turtle Mound on SR A1A, between 9:00 a.m. and 4:30 p.m. Beach camping permits will only be issued on the day camping begins, but for lagoon island camping, you can apply up to seven days in advance. You can call the information center, (904) 428-3384, for site availability. A park brochure is available at www.nps.gov/cana/planyourvisit/upload/camping-02.pdf.

Finding the campground: Canaveral National Seashore and Merritt Island National Wildlife Refuge are located midway on Florida's east coast between Daytona Beach and Melbourne. They are accessible via US 1, I-95, and SR 528 (BeeLine or Beach Line Expressway). The northern access, Apollo Beach, is on SR A1A at the southernmost end in New Smyrna Beach. Seminole Rest is located east of US 1 in Oak Hill on River Road. In Oak Hill, turn east onto Halifax Avenue, located by the flashing caution light on US 1. Take Halifax Avenue east to River Road. Turn north on River Road. Seminole Rest is 0.2 mile on the east side of River Road. The southern access, Playalinda Beach in Titusville, is on SR 406/402. Playalinda Beach is reached via SR 402/Beach Road. From I-95, the exit number for the north district (Apollo Beach) is 249. For the south district (Playalinda), the exit number from I-95 is 220. At both exits, go toward the east and follow the signs.

About the campground: The U.S. has set aside ten national seashores and these treasures—on the Atlantic, Pacific, and Gulf coasts—preserve a little of the original flavor of shoreline unencumbered by souvenir shops and condominiums. Canaveral has saved 24 miles of beach and dune; it is the longest stretch of undeveloped coastline remaining in Florida.

Canaveral's backcountry campsites are mostly located among the low, marshy islands in the northern part of Mosquito Lagoon, and they can only be reached by boat. The Atlantic Ocean beach is closed to backcountry camping from May 1 through October 31, to protect the endangered sea turtle during its nesting period, and a no-fee backcountry permit is required to stay overnight.

Due to NASA security requirements, no camping is allowed south of the Volusia County line on the beach and beach camping is prohibited the night before a shuttle launch, which makes planning difficult since shuttle launches are often delayed or postponed at the last minute.

114 Buck Lake Wildlife Management Area

Location: Adjacent to I-95 and east of the St. Johns River in Volusia and northwestern Brevard Counties (28 40' 0" N, 80 53' 18" W)

Season: Year-round, except in hunting season

Sites: No-charge primitive camping first-come, first-served at Buck Lake, Freshwater, and Old Timer's camps in Brevard County. Pack-in, pack-out. Permit required.

Maximum length: Call for current information

Facilities: None

Fee per night: Call for current information

Management: Fish & Wildlife Conservation Commission and St. Johns River Water Management District

Contact: (386) 329-4500, http://myfwc.com and www.sjrwmd.com

Finding the campground: This WMA borders I-95 just north of Titusville. Take exit 223 onto SR 46 and the entrance is about 1 mile on the right (north) side of the road.

About the campground: This WMA is part of an extensive, though not integral, system of lands designed to preserve Florida's natural wild heritage. At 9,638 acres, Buck Lake consists of marsh and interspersed cabbage palm hammocks with pine flatwoods and oak scrub. Although it borders I-95, sections are wild and remote. The area is part of the Great Florida Birding Trail. Other opportunities for fun include hunting, fishing, wildlife viewing, hiking, biking (on roads), and horseback riding. Camping is prohibited during periods open to hunting.

115 Seminole Ranch Wildlife Management Area/ Conservation Area

Location: On the west bank of the St. Johns River in Orange County (28° 32' 18" N, 80° 58' 54" W)

Season: Year-round

Sites: Camping is permitted only at the designated through-trail campsite on the Florida Trail just north of SR 50 "provided that access is by the Florida Trail."

Maximum length: Call for current information

Facilities: Call for current information

Fee per night: Call for current information

Management: Fish & Game Conservation Commission

Contact: http://myfwc.comping, www.floridatrail.org, www.floridabirdingtrail.com

Finding the campground: The campground is reserved for individuals through-hiking the Florida Trail. It is due east of Orlando on the north side of SR 50 approximately 20 miles, or due west of exit 215 on SR 50 from I-95 approximately 6 miles. It is 10 miles west of Titusville.

About the campground: This 6,000-acre WMA is part of the 29,145-acre Seminole Ranch Conservation Area. It is a mosaic of pasture, marsh, and hardwood and cabbage palm hammocks and part of the Great Florida Birding Trail with roseate spoonbills, white pelicans, bald eagles, painted buntings, wild turkeys, and sandhill cranes.

For fun, one can hunt, fish, watch for birds, ride horses (except during hunting season), hike, camp (completely primitive), paddle kayaks, cycle, and picnic. More than 4 miles of the Florida National Scenic Trail run through, generally north-to-south. Trails are seasonally flooded.

116 Tosohatchee Wildlife Management Area

Location: Eastern Orange County

Season: Year-round

Sites: Primitive camping at an equestrian camp, group camp, and a campsite for through-trail hikers on the Florida National Scenic Trail. Car and RV camping are not available. During established hunting seasons, camping is permitted only to through-hikers.

Maximum length: Call for current information

Facilities: Call for ...
Fee per night: Cal ...
Management: Fish ...
Contact: (407) 56 ... [obscured] ...org
Finding the camp ... e Bee Line
Expressway/SR 52 ... in 5 to 6 miles,
however, at SR 520 ... (north) and drive
about 3 miles to B ...
About the campgr ... questrians.
Popular fishing spo ... erous creeks and
ditches throughout ... to March.

This WMA cove ... t features mean-
dering creeks, dam ... freshwater marsh.
Of course, there is a ... ds and orchids,
enjoy the Spanish n ... xtensive logging in
the early twentieth cen ...

[handwritten note: Thurs, 2/26, 27, 28 → O, Elec., Tree, Sewer? on H₂O]

117 Brevard County Parks

Brevard County offers visitors a choice of three campgrounds:

Manatee Hammock

Location: 7275 S. U.S. Hwy 1, Titusville, FL 32780 (28° 30' 12" N, 80° 46' 54" W). The Manatee Hammock is across the Indian River from Cape Canaveral and the Kennedy Space Center.
Season: Year-round
Sites: 182 (147 RV sites with water, electric, sewer; 35 tent campsites with water and electric); plus group tent camping (Apr 1 through Dec 15)
Maximum length: None
Facilities: Hot showers, laundry facilities, swimming pool for campers, pavilion, Internet hookup, fishing (shoreline and 197-foot pier), and short, rustic 0.2-mile walking trail
Fee per night: $$$ (a higher rate applies to non-county residents)
Management: Brevard County Parks & Recreation
Contact: (321) 264-5083, manateehammock@brevardparks.com, www.campingspacecoast.com
Finding the campground: From I-95, take exit 215 and go east for 3 miles on SR 50. Turn right (south) on US 1 and go 3.5 miles to the entrance on the east side of the highway.
About the campground: Manatee Hammock is on the west bank of Indian River Lagoon in a quiet, well-shaded hammock of pines and palms. Just 26.5 acres, the campground offers a spectacular view of launches at Kennedy Space Center.

Campers have access to the park's recreation hall, which has a small swimming pool and reception grill area, a fire ring, a mid-sized pavilion, 2 shuffleboard courts, and a horseshoe pit. Reservations are recommended, especially any time near a space shuttle launch. Launches are often delayed or postponed, however. In such a case, a visit to Canaveral National Seashore will never disappoint.

Location: On the east bank of the Indian River in Brevard County located off of SR A1A, 1.5 miles north of Sebastian Inlet, and 20 miles south of Melbourne. Mailing address is 700 Long Point Rd., Melbourne Beach, FL 32951 (27° 52' 30" N, 80° 28' 6" W)

Season: Year-round

Sites: 170 (On the waterfront: 113 semi-improved campsites with water and electric, 15 improved campsites with water, electric, and sewer. Off the water: 26 semi-improved campsites with water and electric and 16 overflow campsites. Group tent camping available on Scout Island.)

Maximum length: None

Facilities: Showers and restrooms, laundry facilities, one-lane boat ramp, fish cleaning station, pavilions (2 small, 3 midsize), playground, horseshoe pits, swimming pond (guarded during swim season), volleyball

Fee per night: $$$ (higher rates apply to non-county residents)

Management: Brevard County Parks & Recreation

Contact: (321) 952-4532, www.campingspacecoast.com or email at longpoint@brevard parks.com *Waterfront no trees*

Finding the campground: From US 192/Melbourne Causeway, drive 16 miles south on SR A1A and turn right (west) into the park. From Sebastian Inlet, go 1 mile north on SR A1A.

About the campground: Don't expect shade here in the Indian River Lagoon. It's hot and you are only a foot above sea level, so bring plenty of bug repellent. If you are looking for a great getaway spot though, this is about as isolated as it gets on Florida's Atlantic coast. Plus the 84.5-acre park has stocked up on things to do, especially for boaters. Whether you have a power boat to cruise the Intracoastal Waterway and make waves, or prefer the slower speed of a paddleboat (canoe or kayak) to ease around the shoreline looking for birds and gators, or perhaps paddle to the primitive camping areas on the adjacent Scout Island, this is an ideal park for you and your family. Or you can fish—with or without a boat. The fishing's fine from the shoreline, bridge, or dock too. When you're tired of the water, there is a short nature trail, too.

Wickham Park

Location: 2500 Parkway Drive, Melbourne, FL 32935 (28° 9' 30" N, 80° 39' 48" W) between I-95 and the coast in North Melbourne

Season: Year-round

Sites: 110 sites (88 with water and electricity, 22 overflow campsites, and a youth campground with no amenities)

Maximum length: None

Facilities: Picnic tables and 8 pavilions, amphitheater, 18-hole disc golf course, archery range, horseshoe pits, softball fields, volleyball courts, dog park, playground, multi-purpose and soccer fields

Fee per night: $$$ (higher rates apply to non-county residents)

Management: Brevard County Parks & Recreation

Contact: (321) 255-4307, www.campingspacecoast.com or email at wickham@brevardparks.com

Finding the campground: From I-95, take exit 191, Wickham Road east. Follow it 8.4 miles as it curves south to Parkway Drive. Turn left (east) on Parkway Drive. The entrance is on the left and unmistakably marked.

In the vastness of southwest Florida this kayaker paddles through the tides to find the right creek with his GPS.

About the campground: This is a true metro park and sports are emphasized, with multiple sports facilities, two seasonally guarded swimming lakes and 3 small fishing lakes. Encouraging hikers is a 0.25-mile trail with exercise stations and a 0.5-mile nature trail. There are also horse trails, a horse stable, and a show ring.

The 391-acre park features open pine woods and small lakes with a central campground. Community events and special interest activities are often scheduled in open areas at the south end and at a large pavilion (includes a banquet kitchen and seating for up to 1,500 people) at the north end. An amphitheater is centrally located near the campgrounds. An all-in-one park office/visitor reception facility and a small community center are located near the park entrance.

118 Bull Creek Wildlife Management Area

Location: Near Holopaw in Osceola County (28° 08' 09" N, 81° 04' 34" W)
Season: Year-round
Sites: Designated campgrounds during hunting seasons, designated sites year-round for through-hikers along the Florida National Scenic Trail
Maximum length: Call for current information
Facilities: Call for current information
Fee per night: Call for current information
Management: Fish & Wildlife Conservation Commission and St. Johns River Water Management District

Contact: (352) 732-1225, http://myfwc.com; (386) 329-4404, www.sjrwmd.com

Finding the campground: From I-95, take exit 180 and drive west on US 192/SR 500. The WMA is on the south side of the road.

About the campground: Primitive camping in the pines and palmetto will not provide much cool shade, but it is excellent exposure to a real Florida habitat. This WMA is 23,646 acres, and a section of the Florida Trail passes through it; one trail section forms a great loop around the WMA, including the primitive camping area.

Note that numerous streams come together in the forest, and during the rainy season, extensive areas of Bull Creek are wet. This breeds mosquitoes and tends to concentrate snakes on high ground, so use your bug dope unsparingly and look inside your tent before crawling into your summer sleeping bag. Hunting, fishing, wildlife viewing, hiking, bicycling, horseback riding, and paddling are among the activities available. Levee 73 is open for hiking and bicycling.

119 Triple N Ranch Wildlife Management Area

Location: South of US 192 and east of the hamlet of Holopaw in Osceola County (28° 08' 09" N, 81° 04' 34" W)

Season: Year-round

Sites: Primitive camping is permitted at designated campsites during specific hunting seasons. The camping area is near the WMA entrance south of US 192.

Maximum length: Call for current information

Facilities: Call for current information

Fee per night: Call for current information

Management: Fish & Wildlife Conservation Commission

Contact: (850) 488-4676, http://myfwc.com

Finding the campground: From the Kissimmee–St. Cloud area south of Orlando, take US 441/192 east. At the hamlet of Holopaw, US 441 splits south, but continue east on US 192/SR 500 to the WMA on the right or south side of the road. The WMA is about 17 miles from St. Cloud, and the camping area is near US 192 on Area Road 1.

About the campground: Ecologists find small variations in plant and animal complexes in the Sunshine State and develop names for them. They soon become known as "fast-disappearing native ranges." The 16,295-acre Triple N Ranch WMA has one, although you will need to get down on your hands and knees with a magnifying glass to discover it. Still, a network of internal roads lets visitors take a look—as well as hike, watch for wildlife and birds, bike, and ride horses. Hunting is allowed in season.

120 Upper St. John's River Marsh Wildlife Management Area

Location: In Orange, Brevard, and Indian River Counties

Season: Year-round

Sites: During hunting season, tent camping is permitted at the designated campsites below. During periods closed to hunting, camping is regulated by the St. Johns River Water Management District.

Buzzard's Roost Camp: South of Lake Poinsett on the west side of the St. Johns River—4 tent platforms, 1 fire ring, 1 picnic table, and 2 benches

Pontoon Camp: North of Lake Winder on the west side of the St. Johns River—3 tent platforms, 1 fire ring, 1 picnic table, and 2 benches

Palms Camp: On the northwest shore of Lake Winder—2 tent platforms, 1 fire ring, 1 picnic table, 1 bench

Highwater Camp: On the west shore of Lake Winder—4 tent platforms and 1 fire ring

Lake Poinsett Camp: On the west shore of Lake Winder—3 tent platforms, 1 fire ring, 2 picnic tables, and 2 benches

Spike Camp: On the west shore of the St. Johns River and south of Lake Winder

Winder Mound Camp: South of Lake Winder on the west side of the St. Johns River

Persimmon Mound Camp: South of Lake Winder on the east side of the St. John's River—2 tent platforms, 1 fire ring, 1 picnic table

Wolf's Head Camp: South of Lake Winder on the west side of the St. Johns River

Oak Trees Camp: South of Lake Winder on the east side of the St. Johns River

East Union Cypress Camp: South of US 192 on the south end of Lake Sawgrass—2 tent platforms, 1 fire ring, 1 picnic table, 1 bench

North Indian Field Camp: South of Lake Sawgrass, east of the river channel

Spade Island Camp: North of the Bulldozer Canal and the Three Forks Water Management Area

Bulldozer Canal Camp: South of Lake Hell 'n' Blazes and west of Three Forks Run—3 tent platforms, 1 fire ring, 1 picnic table

Great Egret Camp: Southwest corner of Three Forks Water Management Area, just east of C-40—3 tent platforms, 1 fire ring, 1 picnic table

North Camp: East of US 512 and part of the Blue Cypress Water Management Area

Winter Camp (north): East of US 512 and part of the Blue Cypress Water Management Area

Winter Camp (south): East of US 512 and part of the Blue Cypress Water Management Area

Maximum length: Call for current information

Facilities: Call for current information

Fee per night: Call for current information

Management: Fish & Wildlife Conservation Commission and St. Johns River Water Management District (WMD)

Contact: (386) 329-4500, (352) 732-1225, www.sjrwmd.com, http://myfwc.commping

Finding the campground: The Upper St. Johns River Marsh is located west of I-95 between the interstate and the St. Johns River in Orange, Brevard, and Indian River Counties. Take exits 156 to 202 and watch for signs.

About the campground: This is a very expansive and disarticulated area, which is not altogether bad as the camping is dispersed, and you have to learn "the system" to be able to camp along here effectively. Once you learn the WMD's way of conducting business, however, and if you stay informed and enjoy primitive riverine camping, an elegant world of opportunities awaits along the St. Johns River. This WMA consists of 124,623 acres and another 150,000 acres of marshlands are being restored. According to the WMD, this should re-create fish and wildlife habitat, and improve water quality. The WMA's 62 miles of levees offer a range of recreation: fishing, wildlife viewing, hiking, bicycling, hunting, and paddling.

121 Fort Drum Wildlife Management Area/ Conservation Area

Location: 15 miles west of Vero Beach on SR 60 in southwestern Indian River County (27° 37' 11" N, 80° 24' 42" W)

Season: Year-round

Sites: Primitive, first-come, first-served camping on Hog Island at the end of a boardwalk. Campsite coordinates on the Hog Island "White Loop" are 27° 36' 34" N, 80° 45' 46" W; "Yellow Loop," 27° 36' 29" N, 80° 45' 28" W.

Maximum length: Call for current information

Facilities: Call for current information

Fee per night: Call for current information

Management: Fish & Wildlife Conservation Commission and St. Johns River Water Management District

Contact: (386) 329-4404, www.sjrwmd.com, http://myfwc.com

Finding the campground: From I-95, take exit 147 at SR 60 and go west to "20-Mile Bend." Access is located 10.9 miles west of CR 512 and 10 miles east of Yeehaw Junction.

About the campground: Two things the camper can expect in any WMA are miles of wilderness, much of it wet, and few amenities. Fort Drum is a patchwork of wet and dry areas, 20,858 acres of pine and palmetto interspersed with muddy bogs and marsh.

The camper who gets out on the hiking trail is liable to see everything and the bird life begins with honking formations of sandhill cranes. Keep your eyes open here and you may see wild turkeys and wild hogs. Do watch your step, however, for the diamondback rattlesnake is not rare.

A boardwalk through a swamp leads to Hog Island where the Florida Trail Association has developed trails and primitive campsites. A picnic pavilion and tables are adjacent to Horseshoe Lake. Vehicle access to Horseshoe Lake during non-hunting periods requires a permit. Hunting, fishing, wildlife viewing, horseback riding, hiking, biking, paddling, and camping are permitted. Indeed, they are encouraged.

122 St. Sebastian River Preserve State Park

Location: Just east of I-95 in Brevard and Indian River Counties (27° 49' 39" N, 80° 33' 37" W)

Season: Year-round

Sites: Primitive tent camping at 6 hike-in campsites, 2 on the north side of the preserve in Brevard County and 4 on the south in Indian River County; 5 primitive tent campsites for groups to 20 persons; 3 primitive campsites for horse camping that accommodate groups to 20. Eagle Camp is a ride-in-only site requiring a 5-mile ride each way from the parking area. All camping is pack-in, pack-out; collection of firewood prohibited.

Maximum length: Primitive camping only

Facilities: Storytelling Camp in Brevard County: paddocks, nonpotable water for horses, a pitcher pump, picnic pavilion, one portable toilet, campfire ring, and benches. Ranch Camp in Indian River County: paddocks, nonpotable water for horses, campfire ring, and benches. Eagle Camp in Indian

River County: one large paddock, pitcher pump, three raised tent platforms, a lean-ring, and benches. An ADA-accessible Clivus Multrum (large Port-o-let) is located of the park.

Fee per night: $

Management: Florida Division of Recreation and Parks

Contact: (321) 953-5004/5005, www.floridastateparks.org/stsebastian/default.cfm

Finding the campground: The south entrance is off CR 512/Fellsmere Road 1.8 miles east of I-95. The north entrance for the visitor center and Manatee Vista is off CR 507/Babcock Street just north of the C-54 Canal. Exit I-95 at CR 514 to reach CR 507. (Note that Google Maps has not been updated to reflect the north entrance.)

About the campground: Horse people will love this preserve, which is mostly open grassy forests of longleaf pine; these were once commonplace in Florida, but were logged almost to destruction for this variety of pine's hard, straight-grained wood. The uplands, scrub, and swamps are home to at least fifty protected species. Photographers and bird-watchers can explore miles of trails on foot, bicycle, or horseback. Canoeing, boating, and fishing on the St. Sebastian River are popular. Launching facilities are available outside the preserve at Dale Wimbrow Park, and there are private ramps along the river nearby.

123 Sebastian Inlet State Park

Location: On a barrier island off the Atlantic coast 15 miles south of Melbourne Beach in Brevard County (27° 52' 27.5" N, 80° 27' 20.4" W)

Season: Year-round

Sites: 51

Maximum length: 50 feet

Facilities: Full-facility camping with water, electrical hookups, fire ring with grill, picnic table, restroom facilities, dump station, coin laundry, pay phones

Fee per night: $$$

Management: Florida Division of Recreation and Parks

Contact: (321) 984-4852, www.floridastateparks.org/sebastianinlet/default.cfm

Finding the campground: From the south on I-95, take the Fellsmere/Sebastian exit 156 and travel east on CR 512. After 2 miles, turn right on CR 510. This road intersects US 1. Continue east, over the Indian River, to SR A1A. Turn left (north) and go 7 miles on SR A1A to the park. From the north on I-95, take US 192 exit 180 and drive east to SR A1A in Indialantic. Turn right (south) on SR A1A and drive 18 miles to Sebastian Inlet.

About the campground: A boat ramp at this campground allows saltwater fishing from the jetties. The "jetties" here are long piles of boulders designed to stabilize the seabed and channel—dangerous to walk on and not at all scenic, but apparently necessary. Surfing, swimming, scuba diving, snorkeling, and sunbathing on the 3 miles of white sand beach are very popular. Several museums emphasize the area's nautical history: The McLarty Treasure Museum features the 1715 Spanish treasure fleet, and the Sebastian Fishing Museum tells of the area's fishing industry. You can canoe and kayak in the Indian River Lagoon or walk the mile-long Hammock Trail. Waterfront pavilions and picnic areas are available.

124 Indian River County Parks

NOTE: Please contact the park(s) for more information regarding omitted camp specs and management as it is often changing.

Location: Indian River County Parks Department, 5350 77th St., Wabasso, FL 32970, (772) 589-9223, www.ircgov.com/Departments/Public_Works/Parks_Maintanence_Division/Index.htm

Sites:

Donald MacDonald Park: 12315 Roseland Rd., Roseland, FL 32957, (772) 589-0087. MacDonald Park is on the southeast bank of the Sebastian River in northern Indian River County (27° 49' 11.68" N, 80° 30' 28.30" W). It has 29 primitive campsites, one with electricity; observation boardwalk, boat launch, restrooms with showers, fire pits, and concrete picnic tables. The park is open every day. No reservations; camping is first-come, first-served. The ranger's office has a multipurpose room available for rent.

Blue Cypress Park: 7400 Blue Cypress Lake Rd., Vero Beach, FL 32966, (772) 589-9223. The park is 23 miles west of I-95 and due west of Vero Beach, north of SR 60. Turn right (north) on Blue Cypress Lake Road (27° 42' 18" N, 80° 46' 54" W). Primitive camping is allowed and there are quite a few amenities for a rural area, including two boat launches, a floating dock, paved parking with grass, overflow parking, restroom facilities with hot showers and two covered pavilions. Activities include bird-watching, wildlife viewing, fishing, hunting, bicycling, kayaking, and hiking along miles of levees. An airboat launch is also available.

Prange Islands Conservation Area: (772) 589-9223. Primitive camping is allowed on these two islands—just 27 acres—in the Indian River Lagoon. They lie just south of the 17th Street Bridge in Vero Beach (27° 37' 24" N, 80° 21' 24" W) on the eastern side of the Intracoastal/lagoon. The islands contain native maritime hammock, and the larger was the historic homestead of the Prange Family from the early 1900s. A small boat dock was built on the east side of the island in 2002. There is great fishing, bird-watching, and plenty of relaxing on these exotic little islands.

Carson Platt Estate: Located on CR 512, just west of the CR 510/512 intersection, (321) 953-5004. From I-95, take exit 156 east on 95th Street/Sebastian Boulevard. The park is on the left (north) side of the road (27° 46' 6" N, 80° 31' 0" W). This park's 5,334 acres are managed in the state's St. Sebastian Buffer Preserve. Recreational opportunities include horseback riding, hiking, primitive camping at designated sites, off-road bicycling, canoeing, boating, studying nature, bird-watching, and fishing. This land provides habitat for rare birds including wood storks, roseate spoonbills, Florida scrub jay, bald eagle, and red-cockaded woodpecker.

The Magic Coast Region

C ounties: Hernando, Sumter, Pasco, Pinellas, Hillsborough, Manatee, Sarasota, Hardee, DeSoto, Highlands, Glades, Charlotte, Lee, Monroe, Collier

	Hookup Sites	Total Sites[1]	Max RV Length	Hookups	Toilets	Showers	Dump Station	Recreation	Fee	Can Reserve[2]
125 Lake Panasoffkee WMA	-	-	-	-	F	-	-	HFBLRC, hunting	-	No
126 Withlacoochee State Forest	-	250	-	WE	F	Yes	Yes	HFSBLRC, hunting	$-$$	Yes
127 Pasco County Parks	-	T, C	-	-	-	-	-	HFBLRC	$-$$$	Yes
128 Anclote Key Preserve State Park	-	T	-	-	NF	-	-	HSFB	-	No
129 Cypress Creek	-	-	-	-	-	-	-	HFBRC	-	No
130 Green Swamp WMA East/West	-	-	-	-	-	-	-	HFBRC, hunting	-	No
131 Hillsborough River State Park	112	112, T	90	WE	F	Yes	Yes	HFSBC	$$$	Yes
132 Upper Hillsborough WMA	-	-	-	-	-	-	-	HF, hunting	-	Yes
133 Edward Medard County Park	-	40	50	WE	F	Yes	Yes	HFBLRC	$$	Yes
134 Lithia Springs County Park	40	40	-	E	F	Yes	Yes	HFBLC	$$	No
135 Alafia River Corridor	-	-	-	-	-	-	-	HRBR	-	No
136 Alafia River State Park	30	30, T	55	WE	F	Yes	Yes	HFBRC	$$	Yes
137 Little Manatee River State Park	34	34, T	60	WE	F	Yes	Yes	HFBLR	$$$	Yes
138 E.G. Simmons County Park	50	88	-	E	F	Yes	Yes	FSBLC	$$	No
139 Fort DeSoto County Park	236	236	90	WE	F	Yes	Yes	HFSBLRC, scuba, snorkeling	$$$	Yes
140 Lake Manatee State Park	60	60	65	WE	F	Yes	Yes	HFBL	$$	Yes
141 Manatee County Parks	-	T	-	-	F	Yes	No	HFBLRC	$$	Yes
142 Myakka River State Park	76	81, T, C	35	WE	F	Yes	Yes	HFBLRC	$$$	Yes
143 Turtle Beach County Park	40	4	-	WEC	F	Yes	Yes	HFSBLC	$$$	Yes
144 Oscar Scherer State Park	104	104, T	36	WE	F	Yes	Yes	HFBLC, snorkeling	$$$	Yes
145 DeSoto County Parks	12	26	-	WE	F	Yes	Yes	HFBRC	$-$$$	Yes
146 Myakka State Forest	-	-	-	-	F	-	-	HFBRC, hunting	$-$$	No
147 Fred C. Babcock Cecil M. Webb WMA	-	-	-	-	-	-	-	HFBLRC, hunting	-	No
148 Cayo Costa State Park	-	30, C	-	No	F	Yes	No	HFSBC, scuba, snorkeling	$$	Yes
149 Koreshan State Historic Site	48	60	40	WE	F	Yes	Yes	HFBLC	$$$	Yes
150 Lee County Parks	-	-	-	-	-	-	-	HBRC	$$	Yes
151 Lake Okeechobee and Okeechobee Waterway	89	89	-	WE	F	Yes	Yes	FBLC	$$-$$$	Yes
152 Highlands Hammock State Park	140	159, T	50	WE	F	Yes	Yes	HRC, in-line skating	$$	Yes
153 Kissimmee River PUA	-	-	-	-	-	-	-	HFBLRC, hunting	-	No
154 Hickory Hammock WMA	-	-	-	-	-	-	-	HFBRC, hunting	-	No
155 R.K. Butler Campground	8	8	-	WE	F	Yes	Yes	HFBLRC	$$	Yes
156 Fisheating Creek WMA	45	245, C	-	WES	F	Yes	Yes	HFBL, hunting	$$-$$$	Yes
157 Okaloacoochee Slough State Forest/WMA	-	-	-	-	-	-	-	HFBRC, hunting	$-$$	No
158 Dinner Island Ranch WMA	-	-	-	-	-	-	-	HFRC, hunting	-	No
159 CREW WEA	-	-	-	-	-	-	-	HFB, hunting	-	No

	Hookup Sites	Total Sites[1]	Max RV Length	Hookups	Toilets	Showers	Dump Station	Recreation	Fee	Can Reserve[2]
160 Picayune Strand State Forest/WMA	-	-	-	-	-	-	-	HFBR, hunting	$-$$	No
161 Collier-Seminole State Park	137	137, T	60	WE	F	Yes	Yes	HFSBC	$$	Yes
162 Big Cypress National Preserve/WMA	26	195	-	E	F	Yes	Yes	HFBCO, hunting	0-$$	No
163 Everglades National Park	342	388	-	-	F/NF	Yes	Yes	HFBLC	$-$$	Yes
164 John Pennekamp Coral Reef State Park	47	47	62	WE	F	Yes	Yes	HSFBL, scuba, snorkeling	$$$	Yes
165 Long Key State Park	60	60	45	WE	F	Yes	Yes	HSFB, snorkeling	$$$	Yes
166 Curry Hammock State Park	28	28	70	WE	F	Yes	Yes	HSFBC, in-line skating, snorkeling	$$$	Yes
167 Bahia Honda State Park	64	86, C	71	WE	F	Yes	Yes	HSFBLC, scuba, in-line skating, snorkeling	$$$	Yes
168 Dry Tortugas National Park	-	8	-	-	NF	No	No	HSFB, snorkeling	$	No

Key:
Hookups: W = Water, E = Electricity, S = Sewer, C = Cable, P = Phone, I = Internet
Total Sites: T = Tents, C = Cabins, Y = Yurts
Maximum RV Length: Given in feet
Toilets: F = Flush, NF = No flush
Recreation: H = Hiking, S = Swimming, F = Fishing, B = Boating, L = Boat launch, O = Off-road driving, R = Horseback riding, C = Cycling

[1] T: Almost all Florida state parks have prepared sites with water and electricity and a primitive camping (youth or group—tent-only) area with cold water available. Camping in the primitive area is regulated by number of occupants, not specific sites. C: cabins are available.

[2] Many public entities that control lands in Florida, the Water Management Districts, for example, require that campers, even in authorized, but primitive sites with no improvements, acquire permits. Permits are not the same as reservations, however, and are usually at no charge to the camper.

NOTE: The following state/national parks in this region do not offer camping at present: Charlotte Harbor, Dade Battlefield Historic, Delnor-Wiggins Pass, DeSoto National Memorial, Don Pedro Island, Egmont Key, Estero Bay Preserve, Fakahachee Strand Preserve, Fort Foster State Historic Site, Gamble Plantation Historic, Gasparilla Island, Honeymoon Island, Lake June in Winter Scrub, Lovers Key, Madira Bickel Mound State Archeological Site, Mound Key Archeological State Park, Paynes Creek Historic (camping only for organized youth groups), Skyway Fishing Pier, Stump Pass Beach, Werner-Boyce Salt Springs and Ybor City Museum.

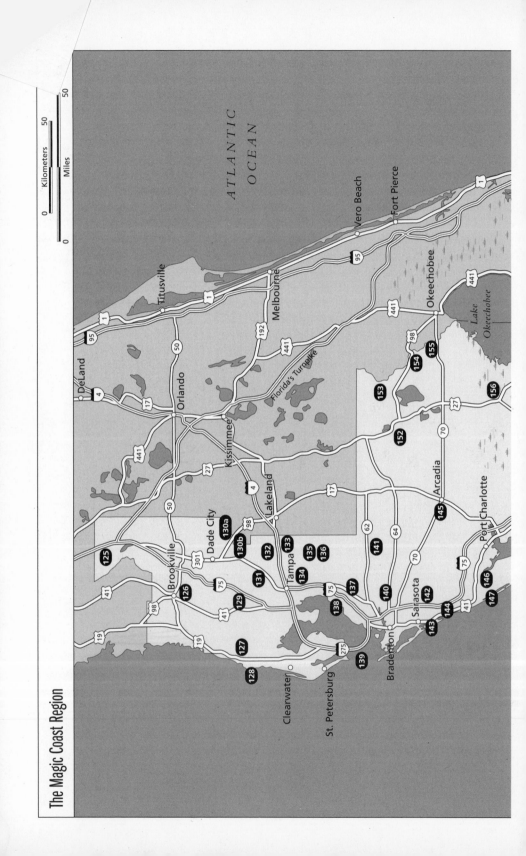

The Magic Coast Region

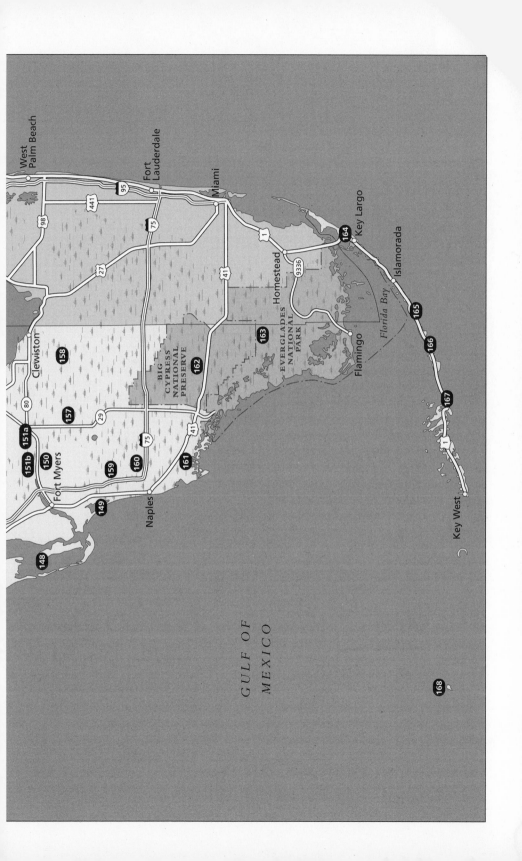

Lake Panasoffkee Wildlife Management Area

Location: Along the eastern shore of Lake Panasoffkee in north central Sumter County (28° 51' 54" N, 82° 8' 0" W)

Season: Year-round

Sites: Primitive equestrian and group campsites on the northern end of the WMA. A pavilion and campsites may be reserved for group use through the Water Management District.

Maximum length: Call for current information

Facilities: Call for current information

Fee per night: Call for current information

Management: Fish & Game Conservation Commission and Southwest Florida Water Management District

Contact: (850) 488-4676, (352) 796-7211 ext. 4470, http://myfwc.com, www.sfwmd.state.fl .us, http://floridabirdingtrail.com

Finding the campground: Take exit 329 from I-75 in central Florida and drive west on SR 44 to the designated entrance on the left (south). The campground is about 1 mile further south.

About the campground: At 8,676 acres, this WMA is a great park for enjoying the lake and the trails if you also enjoy primitive camping, for there is nothing except a primitive pavilion here. Boaters discover that the public boat launch is on the southeast end of the lake and requires a 14-mile one-way drive. There are 8.5 miles of shared trails for bicycling and hiking, and another 18 for horseback riding and hiking. Hunting is seasonal. Much of the park is low and marshy while pine and oak scrub cover the higher elevations. The WMA is part of the Great Florida Birding Trail.

126 Withlacoochee State Forest

NOTE: Includes Citrus, Croom, Jumper Creek, and Richloam Wildlife Management Areas

Location: Within two hours driving time from Cape Canaveral, Orlando, and several other points of interest, Withlacoochee State Forest's various locations (it is not a single, contiguous area) provide convenient access. The forest complex is located in west central Florida and its headquarters is on US 41, 7 miles north of Brooksville and 50 miles north of Tampa (28° 33' 13" N, 82° 23' 19" W).

Season: Year-round

Sites within the Withlacoochee State Forest Recreation Areas: It is best to call the local forestry office, (352) 754-6896, to check for a permit prior to arriving on site, even if most areas offer no-charge, first-come, first-served camping.

Management: Division of Forestry and Fish & Wildlife Conservation Commission

Contact: (352) 754-6896, www.fl-dof.com/state_forests/withlacoochee.html, http://myfwc.com

Finding the forest: From I-75, take exit 301 and travel west on US 98 approximately 10 miles to Brooksville and the intersection with US 41.

About the forest: The 157,479-acre Withlacoochee is the third-largest state-managed forest in Florida. The interwoven WMAs make this a huge and primitive area since building and even developing amenities is not at present high on Florida's shrinking state budget.

Numerous rivers and streams flow through the forest and several are designated O[...]
Florida Waters because of their beauty. These rivers are overhung with cypress, oak, Spa[...]
Southern magnolia, gum, hickory, and tall pines.

Campers can hike and kayak for weeks and never repeat the same trail. In the spring you can
expect an abundance of wildflowers.

The forest has been declared one of the "10 Coolest Places You've Never Been in North
America" by the World Wildlife Fund. More than 600,000 people visit annually.

Silver Lake Campgrounds
1st come, 1st served (handwritten)

Silver Lake: On the northern end of Silver Lake on a gently sloping grassy area, campsites are
shaded by large oak trees. Most sites have a view of open water. 23 sites have electricity and
water. Canoe/kayak and small boat launch site, nature trail, boardwalk. *(handwritten: H&O E/e)*

Cypress Glen: High above Silver Lake and shaded by oaks and pines, 34 campsites have
electricity and water; restrooms and showers.

Crooked River: 26 non-electric campsites are surrounded by a screen of vegetation. A stair-
case provides access to the Withlacoochee River.

Hog Island Campground

Hog Island: Campsites are screened by understory vegetation. 20 non-electric campsites,
dump station, canoe/kayak launch. For campers arriving by canoe, there is a campsite available near the river. Youth group area requires reservations, (352) 754-6896.

River Junction Campground

River Junction: 20 non-electric campsites and a boat/canoe launch located at the junction of
the Little Withlacoochee and Withlacoochee Rivers at the southern end of Silver Lake Croom
Motorcycle Campground.

Buttgenbach Mine: 50 campsites with electricity are designated for off-road motorcycle and
ATV use. Campers may ride through the area's 2,600 acres into the surrounding off-road rid-
ing area. The gate, open seven days a week from 8:00 a.m. to 5:00 p.m., is behind the Best
Western Hotel at exit 301 off I-75.

Holder Mine Campground

Holder Mine: Open seven days a week, the campground has 27 shaded sites with electricity
and available dump station. The site is popular with hunters during archery and small game
seasons.

Mutual Mine Campground

Mutual Mine: 13 nonelectric campsites beside a rain-filled lake, formerly a mine pit. No
showers. Call for reservations for the nearby youth group area, (352) 754-6896.

Tillis Hill Campground

Tillis Hill: 37 campsites with water and electricity require reservations, (352) 344-4238.

There is a dining hall and pavilion. Popular with horse owners, the park has horse stalls, tie-outs, and a communal corral; 2 of the 20 stalls are designed for stallions.

Shell Island (Sumter County)

A 10,552-acre primitive site with boat ramp, technically part of the associated Jumper Creek WMA, offers camping that can only be reached by boat. Because water depth varies and in-water obstacles are many, canoes or kayak are recommended—even for turkey hunters.

Richloam (Hernando, Lake, Pasco, and Sumter Counties)

Sites: Named primitive camps include: Flag's Ford, Pless Place, Megs Hole, Cow Camp, East Tower, Raulerson House, Powder House, South Loop, McKinney Sink, and Bay Lake (camping is prohibited in the Baird Unit).

Road wash-outs are common, requiring a great deal of energy and determination on a bicycle or in a 4x4 truck. Please wear blaze orange clothing during hunting seasons. Portable toilets are occasionally found in the camping areas, but maintenance is an issue in a time of dramatically shrinking budgets.

127 Pasco County Parks

NOTE: Please contact the park(s) for more information regarding omitted camp specs and management as it is often changing.
General location: Pasco County Office of Tourism, 7530 Little Rd., New Port Richey, FL 34654, http://visitpasco.net/ or Parks & Recreation at http://portal.pascocountyfl.net/portal/server.pt/community/home/202

Crews Lake Wilderness Park

Location: 16739 Crews Lake Dr., Shady Hills, FL 34610, (727) 861-3038 (28° 22' 30" N, 82° 32' 0" W)
Finding the campground: From I-75 north of Tampa, take exit 285 and drive west on SR 52 to Shady Hills Road (just prior to the Suncoast Parkway/CR 589). Turn right (north) and then turn right (north) on Lenway Road. Turn right (east) on Crews Lake Drive into the park.
About the campground: Tent camping at an 111-acre park with bike trails, nature trails, boardwalk, canoe access, boat ramp, fishing pier, restrooms, volleyball, and an earth stage.

Jay B. Starkey Wilderness Park

Location: 10500 Wilderness Park Rd., New Port Richey, FL, 34655, (727) 834-3247 (28° 15' 6" N, 82° 39' 0" W)
Finding the campground: From I-75 north of Tampa, take exit 275 and drive west on SR 54/56 to Starkey Boulevard. Follow Starkey to the entrance on Wilderness Park Road.
About the campground: Tent camping and cabins at an 8,069-acre park offering bike trails, equestrian trail, nature and interpretive trails, picnic area and shelters, playground, and restrooms. Cabins

have bunk beds, a fan, light, and electricity, and cost $$ per night; tent sites are $ per night. Hikers and horseback riders with reservations can camp for free at primitive camping facilities.

Withlacoochee River Park

Location: 12449 Withlacoochee Blvd., Dade City, FL 33525, (352) 567-0264/521-4104 (28° 20' 37" N, 82° 7' 26" W)
Finding the campground: From I-75 north of Tampa, take exit 285 and drive east on SR 52 to Dade City. Turn right (south) at the intersection with US 98/Lakeland Road for about 3 blocks and take a left (east) across the railroad tracks on Tuskeegee Avenue. After a long block, angle right (southeast) on Sumner Lake Road and follow it as it becomes River Road. Turn right (south) on Auton Road and then left (east) on Withlacoochee Boulevard. The park is straight ahead.
About the campground: Tent camping at a 408-acre park with canoe access, restrooms, hiking, nature trails, 40-foot tower, picnic area, fishing pier, playground, and bike trail.

128 Anclote Key Preserve State Park

Location: 3 miles off the coast of Tarpon Springs in the Gulf of Mexico in Pinellas County and accessible only by private boat (28° 11' 16" N, 82° 50' 44" W)
Season: Year-round
Sites: Primitive camping only
Maximum length: Call for current information
Facilities: Restrooms available (not wheelchair-accessible)
Fee per night: Camping is free, but before you go you must call (727) 469-5942 and check in. Have your boat registration number, number of campers, arrival and departure dates, and a contact phone number in the event of an emergency.
Management: Florida Division of Recreation and Parks
Contact: (727) 469-5942, www.floridastateparks.org/anclotekey/default.cfm
Finding the campground: 3 miles off Tarpon Springs, accessible only by private boat. Take your GPS because the Gulf is a big place.
About the campground: Florida has made an effort to draw everyone who is an outdoor enthusiast into its state park system and Anclote Key Preserve, miles out in the Gulf, is a good example. You can get there only by private boat; there is no ferry or shuttle.

The preserve has a pristine 4-mile-long beach for swimming, sunbathing, fishing, or snorkeling. The water is normally mild, the surf is gentle, and the sand is snow white. There are restrooms, but no other facilities. There is no water and no electricity: bring your own. A satellite phone would be nice, too.

An old lighthouse on the south end and 50 species of bird life make this an island worth visiting.

129 Cypress Creek

Location: East of Land O' Lakes in Pasco County (Cypress Creek, Parkway Boulevard entrance—28° 14' 17" N, 82° 25' 50" W)

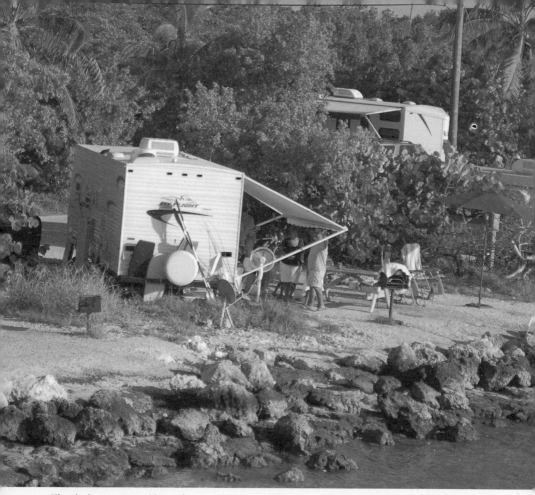

Florida has many public and private campgrounds along the Gulf of Mexico. Reservations are always required for these sites.

Season: Year-round
Sites: Primitive camping, including group campsite near Parkway Boulevard and also an equestrian camping area
Maximum length: Call for current information
Facilities: Nonflush toilets, picnic table and fire ring at group site, portable restroom and nonpotable water at equestrian site
Fee per night: Call for current information
Management: Southwest Florida Water Management District
Contact: (800) 423-1476 (Florida only) or (352) 796-7211 ext. 4470, www.swfwmd.state.fl.us/recreation/areas/cypresscreek.html
Finding the campground: Take exit 275 from I-75 and drive west on SR 54. Turn right (north) on US 41/SR 45 and right once again on Ehren Cutoff. Turn right (east) on Parkway Boulevard. The primary access is 0.7 mile north of Pine View Middle School off Parkway Boulevard.
About the campground: This park is not the easiest to find, but for equestrians, the 12 miles of trails, beginning at the Parkway Boulevard access, are terrific. The horse needs exercise, and the pine

and palmetto ridges are paths to fine riding in an urbanizing area. Camping is primitive, and if you do not own a horse, this is a fine park to explore your bicycling or in-line skating and hiking abilities. During periods of high water, you can fish Cypress Creek or in one of the man-made ponds.

130a Green Swamp Wildlife Management Area (East)

Location: Northeast of Zephyrhills in Lake, Polk, and Sumter Counties (28° 14' 14" N, 82° 10' 46" W)
Season: Year-round
Sites: Primitive camping is permitted year-round at designated campsites and along the Florida Trail (permit required during non-hunting periods)
Maximum length: Call for current information
Facilities: Call for current information
Fee per night: None
Management: Fish & Wildlife Conservation Commission and Southwest Florida Water Management District (WMD)
Contact: (800) 423-1476, (352) 796-7211 (WMD) for free permit, www.floridatrail.org, www.swfwmd.state.fl.us, http://myfwc.com
Finding the campground: From I-75, exit 279, take SR 54 east through Zephyrhills to US 98. Jog right (southeast) for 1 mile and turn left (north) on SR 471. It is about 6.3 miles to a primary entrance to the WMA.
About the campground: The Green Swamp lives by a reputation as fierce as that of the Okefenokee. Within this vast swamp, 49,768 acres is dedicated to recharging the water supplies of the aquifer and the boggy wetlands support four rivers: the Hillsborough, Withlacoochee, Ocklawaha, and Peace. This portion is thus incorporated into the WMA.

Freshwater fishing is good along the Withlacoochee, but paddling the river east of SR 471 is not recommended due to the poorly defined channel and numerous logjams. More than 20 miles of the Florida Trail, 13.1 miles of which are part of the Florida National Scenic Trail, cross the area; portions are wet in all but the driest years.

130b Green Swamp Wildlife Management Area (West)

Location: In Pasco County east of Zephyrhills (28° 14' 14" N, 82° 10' 46" W) and Dade City (28° 21' 42" N, 82° 11' 36" W)
Season: Year-round
Sites: Primitive camping, including an equestrian campground with well-water for horses. Closed to the public during hunts except for through-hikers on the Florida National Scenic Trail.
Maximum length: Call for current information
Facilities: Call for current information
Fee per night: Call for current information
Management: Fish & Wildlife Conservation Commission and Southwest Florida Water Management District

Contact: (800) 423-1476, www.floridatrail.org, www.floridabirdingtrail.com, http://www.swfwmd .state.fl.us, http://myfwc.com

Finding the campground: From I-75 exit 279, take SR 54 east through Zephyrhills to US 98. After a couple miles, turn left (north) on CR 35A. Cross US 98 to Messick Road and turn right; after 1 mile turn left on Singletary Road and proceed to the marked entrance.

About the campground: Green Swamp West has 42 miles of trails for hikers, off-road, nonmotorized cyclists, and horseback riders. In addition, more than 50 miles of the Florida National Scenic Trail can be hiked when water conditions permit. Hikers and those entering the Florida backcountry for bird-watching or hunting must remember to take more water than they think they will need and to carry an insect repellent with DEET. Even in the summer, lightweight long-sleeve shirts are preferred because Florida mosquitoes can carry several dangerous diseases.

Horse-drawn buggies are allowed on appropriately marked trails; there are good spots to launch canoes from River Road and in Withlacoochee River Park as the scenery is excellent and fishing is good. Paddlers should be aware of fluctuating water levels.

131 Hillsborough River State Park

Location: 12 miles north of Tampa and 6 miles south of Zephyrhills on US 301 in Hillsborough County (28° 8' 41.2", 82° 13' 29.1" W)

Season: Year-round

Sites: 112, plus a primitive camp, which is located across the river and available via foot trail. The youth camp can handle groups of 60.

Maximum length: 90 feet

Facilities: Full-facility camping with water, electrical hookups, fire ring, picnic table. Campground has full-facility bathhouse, coin-operated laundry, and dump station. Pets allowed with restrictions.

Fee per night: $$

Management: Florida Division of Recreation and Parks

Contact: (813) 987-6771, www.floridastateparks.org/hillsboroughriver/default.cfm; (800) 326-3521, www.reserveamerica.com

Finding the campground: Hillsborough River is 9 miles north of Tampa and 6 miles south of Zephyrhills on US 301. From I-75, take exit 279, SR 54/Wesley Chapel Boulevard east to US 301. Turn right (south) and travel 6 miles. The park will be on your right. From I-4, take exit 10 and drive north on CR 579/Mango Road to US 301. Follow the signs north 7 miles to the park on your left-hand side.

About the campground: Fort Foster at Hillsborough River is a replica of the 1837 fort built during the Second Seminole War. Park rangers and historical reenactors give tours and demonstrations to help audiences understand an era and way of life.

Canoeing and kayaking are popular. The river flows over a series of very small rapids, caused by hardened limestone shelves, and this makes being on the water exciting because most of Florida's rivers and streams are flat and tranquil. A launching point is available, and visitors can fish the river.

The park concession rents canoes and bicycles, serves breakfast and lunch, and stocks some food, beverages, picnic supplies, and souvenirs. The park also has an ADA-accessible swimming pool.

For landlubbers, there are 7 miles of nature trails used by hikers, and the Wetlands Restoration Trail also accommodates bicycles. Several playgrounds are available.

132 Upper Hillsborough Wildlife Management Area

Location: On either side of the Hillsborough River on CR 54 east of Zephyrhills in Polk and Pasco Counties (28° 14' 14" N, 82° 10' 46" W)
Season: Year-round
Sites: Camping at designated campsites during hunting seasons and at other times with written permission from the WMD
Maximum length: Call for current information
Facilities: The Alston campsite has nonpotable water, picnic shelters, and portable toilet.
Fee per night: No-charge camping
Management: Fish & Wildlife Conservation Commission, Southwest Florida Water Management District (WMD) and Hillsborough River Basin Board
Contact: (800) 423-1476, (352) 796-7211 ext. 4470, http://myfwc.com, www.swfwmd.state.fl.us
Finding the campground: From I-75, take exit 279 east on SR 54 to Zephyrhills, where the road jogs north and again east. It is about 2.5 miles to the designated entrance (Main Grade), and the campsite is about 0.5 mile south.
About the campground: This is a typical Florida WMA with 5,178 acres in pine and saw palmetto with swamps along the Hillsborough River. This area was purchased for water management purposes and recreation is a secondary concern, but hunting for deer, wild hogs, and turkey is popular. Bicyclists, hikers, and horseback riders are also found here in good numbers when the area is dry. There are no boat ramps in the WMA. Be sure to check directly with the WMD regarding this non-elected body's written permission to camp.

133 Edward Medard County Park (and Reservoir)

Location: 5737 Turkey Creek Rd., Plant City, FL 33567 in east Hillsborough County, south of SR 60 (27° 55' 16" N, 82° 9' 35" W)
Season: Year-round
Sites: 40 campsites—RV, tent, and 2 group sites
Maximum length: 50 feet
Facilities: Full-facility campsite with table, water, electricity, fire ring; 2 restrooms with showers, drinking fountains, dump station
Fee per night: $$ group camping; $ per person
Management: Hillsborough County Parks, Recreation and Conservation Department (and Southwest Florida Water Management District)
Contact: (813) 757-3802, www.hillsboroughcounty.org/parks/parkservices/regionalsites.cfm?fa cilitydetailid=364&selparks=-1&selcategory=25&zipcode=&First=1&Last=5, www.swfwmd.state.fl .us/recreation/areas/medard.html
Finding the campground: From I-4, take exit 21 south through Plant City on SR 39. Turn right (west) about 7 miles south onto SR 60; the park is about 15 miles on the left (south) side of the road.
About the campground: Edward Medard has a 730-foot boardwalk/fishing pier that leads to an observation tower on a small island within the reservoir. With its improved boat launch, the lake

An RV is a great way to experience Florida, even with high gas prices. Most public campgrounds have limits, however, on the length of visitor stays.

is popular with anglers. You can fish or use your binoculars to watch osprey catch fish from the boardwalk, too.

Formerly known as Pleasant Grove, this 1,281-acre county park has picnic areas with shelters, hiking, and equestrian trails, easy places to launch canoes and kayaks, a playground, and restrooms. No mountains in Florida? Go climb the "Sacred Hills," leftovers from the days of phosphate excavation.

134 Lithia Springs County Park

Location: 3932 Lithia Springs Rd., Lithia FL 33547 in Hillsborough County (27° 52' 01" N, 82° 13' 51" W)
Season: Year-round
Sites: 40
Maximum length: None
Facilities: 2 shower houses
Fee per night: $$
Management: Hillsborough County Parks, Recreation and Conservation
Contact: (813) 744-5572, www.hillsboroughcounty.org/parks/parkservices/regionalsites.cfm ?facilitydetailid=525&selparks=525&selcategory=-1&zipcode=&First=1&Last=5

Finding the campground: Take exit 257 from I-75 and drive east to Brandon on SR 60. Turn right (southeast) on CR 640/Lithia Road. The entrance to Lithia Springs County Park is on the right (south side) after crossing the Alafia River.

About the campground: Reviews of this 160-acre park routinely stress its beauty—cypress, oaks, magnolias—and the cold, clear springs that bubble up here not only give it its name, but its personality as well. It is a wonderful place to swim, snorkel, and paddle a canoe or kayak. There is a full bathhouse. The water from the springs remains at a constant 72 degrees, year-round. On a hot and sweaty day in summer, the spring water is an extreme joy.

135 Alafia River Corridor

Location: The primary access—other than by the Alafia River—is at the Pinecrest baseball field parking area next to Alderman's Ford Park east of Lithia in Hillsborough County (27° 52' 6.5" N, 82° 8' 43.4" W)

Season: Year-round

Sites: Primitive and group sites in the northern end of the corridor

Maximum length: No RVs

Facilities: Restroom facilities and water fountains at Alderman's Ford Park

Fee per night: $$

Management: Hillsborough County Parks, Recreation and Conservation and Southwest Florida Water Management District (WMD)

Contact: (813) 672-7876 Hillsborough County for permit, (352) 796-7211 WMD, www.hills boroughcounty.org/parks, www.swfwmd.state.fl.us/recreation/areas/alafiarivercorridor.html

Finding the campground: From I-75 east of Tampa, take exit 257 and drive east on SR 60. Turn right (south) on SR 39 and in about 6 miles you will cross the Alfia River. There is a walk-through on the north side of the parking area. Access to trails in the northern portion of the property is through Alderman's Ford Park. To access the horse trails, go a little further south on SR 39, then left (east) on Old Welcome Road to the parking area.

About the campground: Purchased by the WMD and Hillsborough County, the corridor is now managed by the county. There is a great deal to do in the Tampa Bay area, and a lot is available in this corridor park. Trails wind through natural areas—hardwood swamps and upland fields and hammocks—of this 3,992-acre corridor, as well as along the old and revegetated phosphate mine pits. Equestrians may use 8 miles of marked trails on the southern portion of the property adjacent to the Alafia River State Park. Campers can use the picnic shelters and can fish from shore or from a kayak.

136 Alafia River State Park

Location: 20 miles southeast of Tampa on CR 39 in Hillsborough County (27° 46' 48.4" N, 82° 8' 41.1" W)

Season: Year-round

Sites: 30

Maximum length: 55 feet

Even in an era of diminishing finances, Florida is taking steps at all levels—state, county, and municipal—to protect its hundreds of magnificent springs.

Facilities: Full-facility family and equestrian sites have water, 50-amp electrical service, dump station, restroom facilities, showers, and wheelchair-accessible picnic shelters.

Fee per night: $$

Management: Florida Division of Recreation and Parks

Contact: (813) 672-5320, www.floridastateparks.org/alafiariver/default.cfm; (800) 326-3521, www.reserveamerica.com

Finding the campground: From I-75, take exit 246 and turn right (east) onto Big Bend Road. Keep straight on Big Bend Road for approximately 1 mile. Turn right (south) onto US 301. Keep straight on US 301 for approximately 1.5 miles and turn left (east) onto CR 672/Balm Road. Follow CR 672 for approximately 12 miles and turn left (north) onto CR 39. Keep straight on CR 39 for approximately 1.5 miles to the main park entrance on the right (east) side. From the east, take I-4 west to exit 21A and turn south onto CR 39/North Wheeler Street. In Plant City, CR 39 turns left (east) as Reynolds Street and after 2 blocks turns right (south), becoming South Collins Street. Follow CR 39 to the main park entrance, which will be on the left.

About the campground: This park is known for its challenging off-road bicycling trails. Formerly, this 6,312-acre park was mined for phosphate and that means radical changes in elevation. There are 20 miles of trails available to hikers and horseback riders. Trails wind through hardwood forests, pine flatwoods, and rolling hills. The riverine environment is home to many species of birds that will delight bird-watchers. You can canoe, kayak, and fish in the region's lakes and on the south prong of the Alafia River. There are picnic pavilions, a playground, a horseshoe pit, and a volleyball court.

137 Little Manatee River State Park

Location: 4 miles south of Sun City Center, off US 301 on Lightfoot Road in Hillsborough County (27° 39' 54" N, 82° 23' 22" W)
Season: Year-round
Sites: 34 RV campsites, 8 for horse camping, youth group campground that accommodates up to 20, primitive camp on the hiking trail (reservation needed)
Maximum length: 60 feet
Facilities: Full-facility with electricity, water, fire ring, picnic table
Fee per night: $$$
Management: Florida Division of Recreation and Parks
Contact: (813) 671-5005, www.floridastateparks.org/littlemanateeriver/default.cfm; (800) 326-3521, www.reserveamerica.com
Finding the campground: From I-75 southeast of Tampa, take exit 240A onto SR 674/Sun City Center Boulevard for about 3 miles and turn south on US 301. Drive south 4 miles and turn right onto Lightfoot Road. The park is on the right on Sundance Trail.
About the campground: The Little Manatee River is part of the unfortunately named Cockroach Bay Aquatic Preserve. If you come to this 2,416-acre park, plan to paddle the river, and if fishing is your thing, toss in a line for bluegill and catfish. Canoe rentals are available.

Hikers and equestrians are well served by Little Manatee. There is a 6.5-mile trail through the park's northern wilderness area, with a primitive campsite along the trail. For equestrians, the park maintains 12 miles of trails and 8 equestrian campsites.

The campground is shaded, and thick brush generally gives campers some privacy as a great deal of the mature vegetation—sabal palm, saw palmetto, pine, and scrub oak—is intact, even after campsite renovation. A riverside picnic area has tables, grills, and pavilions. Pavilions can be reserved for a fee or are available first-come, first-served.

138 E. G. Simmons County Park

Location: 2401 19th Ave. NW, Ruskin FL 33570 in Hillsborough County (27° 44' 24" N, 82° 27' 56" W)
Season: Year-round
Sites: 88 individual sites (1 camper vehicle and 8 people per site), 1 group site
Maximum length: None
Facilities: 50 sites have electricity; campground has picnic area with grills, 5 restrooms, hot showers, pay telephone, dump station, water fountains, playground, screened pavilion, boat launch, fishing pier, and waterfront view *no water*
Fee per night: $$
Management: Hillsborough County Parks, Recreation and Conservation
Contact: (813) 671-7655, www.hillsboroughcounty.org, www.ruskinonline.com
Finding the campground: From I-75, take exit 240 and drive west to the town of Ruskin on CR 674. Turn right (north) on US 41 and left (west) in less than 2 miles on 19th Avenue NW, which goes straight to the park.

he campground: Near the town of Ruskin on the east shore of Tampa Bay, the 469-acre ~~park~~ ~~has~~ a public beach. Its boat launch provides access to saltwater fishing and boating or for personal watercraft. The park also has fishing piers and areas for bank fishing.

Bird-watching is very popular among the shallow waters of surrounding mangrove swamps. Manatees and flamingoes are occasional visitors.

139 Fort DeSoto County Park

Location: 3500 Pinellas Bayway South, Tierra Verde, FL 33715 in Pinellas County (27° 36' 56" N, 82° 44' 09" W)
Season: Year-round
Sites: 236 total (1–85 for tent, van, or pop-up campers only, 86–236 for any camping unit). About 25 sites are reserved for walk-in campers. A primitive group campground is available near the entrance.
Maximum length: Unlimited in some sites
Facilities: Water, electrical hookups, picnic table, charcoal grill; convenience store, dump stations, modern restrooms with showers and laundry. Pets only in sites 86–164. One camping area is on St. Jean Key; two are on St. Christopher Key. Many sites have ocean views, but shade is a premium. A shade cloth over your tent or camper trailer will be invaluable in managing the heat.
Fee per night: $$$
Management: Pinellas County Parks and Recreation
Contact: Park office: (727) 582-2267 ext. 10 or (727) 464-3347; campground office: (727) 582-2267; www.pinellascounty.org/park/05_Ft_DeSoto.htm
Finding the campground: From I-75 north of Tampa/St. Petersburg, curve right (also south) onto I-275 and follow it south through Tampa and then St. Petersburg. Prior to the Sunshine Parkway Bridge, swing off to the right at exit 17 and turn right (west) at CR 682/54th Avenue South. This four-lane highway becomes Pinellas Bayway South, and in about 2.5 miles, prepare to turn left at the traffic light (onto Pinellas Bayway South—the names make this a bit confusing) and follow the signs.
About the campground: The beach at DeSoto is one of the top public playgrounds in America, and that is not all this park offers. Consequently, it is worth every penny you spend here. There is a nineteenth-century fortress that is only reached by ferry and a popular multiuse path stretching the length of Mullet Key on which you can skate, bike, run, push strollers, or just walk. Within arm's reach, it seems, cruise liners wind around the tip of the park, ruffling its calm waters. You can fish, windsurf, or launch your personal watercraft in the shallow, aquamarine lagoons between the five interconnected islets.

Dedicated as a public park in perpetuity in 1963, it receives about three million visitors a year. Holidays are very crowded.

140 Lake Manatee State Park

Location: 9 miles east of I-75 on SR 64 in Bradenton in Manatee County (27° 28' 34.4" N, 82° 20' 49.1" W)

Season: Year-round

Sites: 60

W E

Maximum length: 65 feet

Facilities: Full-facility camping

Fee per night: $$

Management: Florida Division of Recreation and Parks

Contact: (941) 741-3028, www.floridastateparks.org/lakemanatee/default.cfm; (800) 326-3521, www.reserveamerica.com

Finding the campground: From I-75 southeast of Tampa, take exit 220. The park is 9 miles east on SR 64 in Bradenton.

About the campground: This wonderful 549-acre park extends along 3 miles of the south shore of the 2,400-acre Lake Manatee. The lake is a reservoir that supplies water for southwest Florida. Almost by accident, it provides great fishing, from the park's dock or from a boat as long as any mounted motor does not exceed 20 hp. Kayaking (and canoeing) are popular on 5 miles of designated trails, and of course, you can scoot out onto the lake whenever you wish. There is a 6.5-mile trail for hiking, horseback riding, and bicycling. Swimming is permitted in a designated area; showers are nearby.

141 Manatee County Parks

NOTE: Please contact the park(s) for more information regarding omitted camp specs and management as it is often changing.

General contact and location: Parks and Recreation Department, 5502 33rd Avenue Dr. West, Bradenton, FL 34209, (941) 742-5923

Duette Park

Location: 2649 Rawls Rd., Duette, FL 33834 in Manatee County (27° 32' 7.4" N, 82° 6' 38.8" W)

Contact: (941) 776-0900/2295, www.mymanatee.org

Facilities: Tent camping only

Fee per night: $$

Finding the campground: From I-75 south of Tampa, take exit 229 and drive east on Moccasin Wallow Road. Turn right (south) at US 301, and within 0.5 mile, take a left (east) on SR 62. Rawls Road is about 22 miles on the right.

About the campground: A county-owned upland park, the 22,000-acre Duette Park has trails for horses, bicycles, and hiking. Hunting is popular here, in season, and there ar~ ~i~~ grills under the pines. If your family suffers from nature deficit disorder, Duett~ them for a touch of history—old homestead sites and "Indian mounds"—stret~ the land's first human inhabitants.

tra.

County at 751 Rye Wilderness Trail, Parrish, FL 34219 (27° 30' 47.9" N, 82°

/76-0900/2295, www.mymanatee.org/internet/homemanatee_site.nsf?open

Facilities. tent campsites at $$ per night, first-come, first-served; restrooms and hot showers. The typical campsite has a picnic table, barbecue grill, and campfire circle.

Finding the campground: From I-75 south of Tampa, take exit 220 and drive east on SR 64 to Rye Road. Turn left (northeast) and proceed to Rye Wilderness Trail on the right (east) side of the road.

About the campground: This small county park packs a great many options into a small space, and there is a ranger station on site. Rye Wilderness is only 145 acres, but it occupies both north and south banks of the Manatee River. Because it is wrapped around a river, Rye naturally has a boat ramp for fishing, paddling, and exploring. It has a fitness trail and trails for hikes, off-road bicycles, horses, and campers who appreciate a stroll in nature.

Although its name implies that it is a wilderness, facilities include restrooms, horseshoe pits, picnic tables and grills, a public pay telephone, and a playground.

142 Myakka River State Park

Location: East of Sarasota on SR 72 in Sarasota County (27° 14' 22" N, 82° 19' 0" W)
Season: Year-round
Sites: 76 plus 5 cabins (6 primitive campgrounds, all set in shady oak hammocks, offer 3 camp-sites each; 3 group camping areas accommodate 20 people each)
Maximum length: 35 feet
Facilities: Full-facility and primitive camping. All full-facility campsites are within 40 yards of restrooms with hot showers. All have a dirt base; few have vegetation buffers. 5 modernized palm log cabins date from the 1930s.
Fee per night: $$$
Management: Florida Division of Recreation and Parks
Contact: (941) 361-6511, www.floridastateparks.org/myakkariver/default.cfm; (800) 326-3521, www.reserveamerica.com
Finding the campground: From I-75 south of Tampa, take exit 205 east on SR 72/Clark Road. It is about 9 miles to the park.
About the campground: Florida's Loxahatchee and Wekiva Rivers have national "Wild & Scenic" status, but the Myakka was so designated by the state legislature in 1985 (www.myakkariver .org). The river flows through a natural setting replete with Spanish moss and alligators. Paddlers and anglers are welcome on the 14 miles of river that flow through the park; canoes, kayaks, and bicycles can be rented at the park concession, Myakka Outpost (which also sells a variety of camping and outdoor supplies); a boat ramp provides access to Upper Myakka Lake. Airboat tours are offered on the two lakes in the park.

Large expanses of rare dry prairie are available for hikers and bird-watchers. Backcountry ꓤ tours are offered from mid-Dec through May. An amazing boardwalk over Upper Myakka Lake extends to higher levels in the tree canopy—truly a one-of-kind experience in Florida's state parks. There are playgrounds and 14 miles of looped horse trails.

143 Turtle Beach County Park

Location: On Siesta Key in Sarasota County (27° 16' 31" N, 82° 33' 09" W)
Season: Year-round
Sites: 40 sites for RVs (no pull-through sites) and tents
Maximum length: Call for current information
Facilities: Electrical, water, and cable-television hookups
Fee per night: $$$
Management: Sarasota County Parks and Recreation
Contact: 8862 Midnight Pass Rd., Sarasota, FL 34242, (941) 349-3839, or email at turtlebeach campground@scgov.net
Finding the campground: I-75's exit 205 leads to Clark Road. Drive west for 3.8 miles and bear left onto Stickney Point Road for 1.7 miles. Turn left (south) onto Midnight Point Road and drive 2.5 miles into the campground.
About the campground: Sarasota County purchased a private trailer park called "Gulf Beach Travel Trailer Park" in 2006. Today the tiny 14-acre park has 2,600 linear feet on the Gulf, and offers campers a boat ramp, canoe/kayak launch, horseshoe pits, fishing, parking, picnicking, grills, playground, restrooms, swimming, and a volleyball court. It is named for the beach's many sea turtle nests.

144 Oscar Scherer State Park

Location: On US 41, 6 miles south of Sarasota in Sarasota County (27° 10' 13.6" N, 82° 28' 33.1" W)
Season: Year-round
Sites: 104 tent sites with a separate organized youth and adult group camp
Maximum length: 36 feet
Facilities: Full-facility: pavilion, campfire circle, restroom, cold-water shower; no electricity; limited to 60 people; no pets allowed
Fee per night: $$$
Management: Florida Division of Recreation and Parks
Contact: (941) 483-5956, www.floridastateparks.org/oscarscherer/default.cfm; (800) 326-3521, www.reserveamerica.com
Finding the campground: Take exit 200 off I-75 south of Sarasota and drive southwest on CR 681. After 3 miles, turn right (north) onto US 41/Tamiami Trail Scenic Highway. The park entrance is about 2 miles north on the right (west) side of the road.
About the campground: This park protects scrubby pine woodlands that are home to the threatened Florida scrub jay. Fifteen miles of trails provide hiking, bicycling, and wildlife viewing, while small craft can paddle along South Creek, a black-water stream that flows to the Gulf of Mexico (kayak rentals are available); motorized boats are not permitted.

Freshwater and saltwater fishing are available along the creek or along the shores of Lake Osprey, the park's swimming hole. Picnic areas along South Creek are equipped with grills; pavilions can be reserved for a fee. The park's nature center has exhibits and movies about natural communities.

145 DeSoto County Parks and Recreation

NOTE: Please contact the park(s) for more information regarding omitted camp specs and management as it is often changing.

General contact and location: 201 East Oak St., Arcadia, FL 34266 (863) 993-4800, www.co .desoto.fl.us

Brownville Park

Location: 1885 NE Brownville St., Arcadia, FL 34266 (27° 17' 54" N, 81° 50' 42" W)

Sites: 12 RV sites and 10 tent sites beneath heavily shaded and moss-hung oaks, some with electricity, dump station available for RVs, nearby restrooms with showers. Also 4 primitive sites along the river and 3 nonprofit primitive group sites, each accommodating 20 people.

Fee per night: $$$: RV sites with electricity, water, grill, picnic table, fire ring, and use of the dump station; $$$: tent sites with electricity, water, picnic table, and fire ring; $$: tent sites with water, picnic table, and fire ring, without electricity; $$: primitive sites, call (863) 491-5333 for required reservations. For other sites, reservations not required, but recommended for holiday weekends and the busy winter season.

Finding the campground: From I-75, take exits 205/SR 72 or 217/SR 70 and drive east. Just before Arcadia, these roads intersect and become Oak Street in Arcadia. Turn left (north) on US 17, left again (west) on 102nd Street/Brownville Street, and the park will be on the left.

About the campground: This well-apportioned 75-acre park is on the east bank of the Peace River. The central feature of Brownville Park is the boat ramp, and the river is picturesque. Florida has many rivers and streams that are memorable, but the Peace is rich in history. The river's fossil beds are famous for significant discoveries, and the river itself has been a source of commercial phosphate; thus, mining scars run deep in the ecology and the sociology. Barred owls often gather in a hammock of nearby oaks in the evening and serenade the campground. Ideal for the kids, a short loop nature trail is located on the south side of the park. On the north side are more extensive trails. During high water events, these campsites do flood.

Deep Creek Park

Location: Southwestern DeSoto County, east of Port Charlotte on the Peace River (27° 3' 36" N, 82° 0' 12" W) and adjacent to the Southwest Florida Water Management District park of the same name. Land Resources Department, Southwest Florida Water Management District: (800) 423-1476 (Florida only) or (352) 796-7211 ext. 4470.

Sites: Primitive campsites available with permit for equestrian, group, and river camping via the nearby boat ramp. Equestrian and group sites are accessible with vehicles, and horses have access to 9 miles of multiuse trails.

Finding the campground: From I-75, take exit 170 and drive northeast toward Arcadia King's Highway/CR 769. In about 3 miles, turn right (east) on Peace River Street and loc signs to the campground.

About the campgrounds: Fishing and boating—power or paddle—are popular here. Half of Deep Creek is pine flatwoods; the other half is marsh and bog, and so when it rains heavily, you will be wet to your knees and trails will become inhospitably boggy. This wooded area is surprisingly close to Charlotte Harbor and the Gulf of Mexico, close enough that tidal swamp, bordered by small areas of salt marsh and mangrove forest, dominate the floodplain.

146 Myakka State Forest

Location: 7 miles west of Port Charlotte between the Myakka River and the Gulf of Mexico in Sarasota County (River Road access—26° 59' 24" N, 82° 18' 12" W)
Season: Year-round
Sites: Primitive campsite accessible by hiking or boat
Maximum length: Call for current information
Facilities: 2 restrooms
Fee per night: $–$$
Management: Division of Forestry
Contact: (941) 460-1333, www.fl-dof.com/state_forests/myakka.html
Finding the forest: Myakka State Forest is located in southern Sarasota County approximately 10 miles southeast of Venice and 7 miles west of Port Charlotte. Most of the forest falls within the city limits of North Port. Access is available from River Road, about 11 miles south of I-75.
About the forest: Pines, palmetto, and sand with a few swampy depressions are the ecological stories of this forest. The 2.5 miles of forest frontage on the Myakka River is beautiful and very southern: cypress, wispy Spanish moss, blue and green dragonflies searching lazily for a meal in the hot sun. Hiking and horseback riding on the trails in the forest are popular in the cooler months, while in the warmer months visitors take to the river for fishing, boating, and paddling. Other popular forest activities are off-road bicycling, wildlife viewing, and hunting.

147 Fred C. Babcock/Cecil M. Webb Wildlife Management Area

Location: Southwest of Punta Gorda in Charlotte County (26° 54' 57" N, 82° 02' 52" W)
Season: First-come, first-served camping is permitted in designated primitive campgrounds along Webb Lake and Webb Lake Road. During hunting season, camping is allowed seven days a week; during nonhunting periods, camping is permitted from 5 p.m. Friday to 9 p.m. Sunday and on Memorial Day, Independence Day, Martin Luther King Jr. Day, and Labor Day. Camping is prohibited entirely on the Yucca Pens Unit.
Sites: Camping is only permitted in designated primitive campgrounds
Fee per night: None

Management: Fish & Wildlife Conservation Commission

Contact: (850) 488-4676, http://myfwc.com

Finding the campground: Exit 158 from I-75 between Port Charlotte and Fort Myers on Florida's southwest Gulf coast will put a driver close to the primitive camping areas and the shooting range in this WMA.

About the campground: Even though at 79,013 acres Babcock-Webb is an enormous tract of land, it is surrounded by residential and commercial strip development. This WMA is a particularly good example of why Florida's WMAs are so treasured. In the midst of urban development, this one protects the last wet pine flatwoods in the southwest corner of the state.

Here, within a few miles of the coast, you can still hunt wild coveys of bobwhite quail—a rare treat for any bird hunter—and take part in bird dog field trials. You can also fish and mountain bike and ride horses, assuming you bring your own. Deer and feral hogs are also popular *objet de chasse* (object of chase).

In winter, a variety of warblers, the American woodcock, and common snipe are present. In spring, the rare and beautiful pawpaw and other wildflowers bloom in the pine flatwoods. During the summer rainy season, a majority of the area is likely to be flooded.

148 Cayo Costa State Park

Location: West of Cape Coral and North Ft. Meyers in Lee County (26° 41' 9.9" N, 82° 14' 44.2" W)

Season: Year-round

Sites: Primitive tent camping and 12 primitive cabins

Maximum length: None

Facilities: Campsites near beach and trails have picnic table and ground grill, plus access to modern bathrooms with potable water. Cabins have no electricity or any other amenities and cooking is by outdoor grill. Access is by boat so supplies must be carried on; no concessions on the island. All trash or discarded items must be removed upon departure.

Fee per night: $$

Management: Florida Division of Recreation and Parks

Contact: (941) 964-0375; (800) 326-3521, www.reserveamerica.com. For ferry information and reservations: Pineland Marina, 13921 Waterfront Drive, Pineland, FL 33945 at (239) 283-0015.

Finding the campground: Cayo Costa is south of Boca Grande and west of Pine Island and North Ft. Meyers. Several charter boat services provide access, if you don't own your own boat. A passenger ferry, Tropic Star of Pine Island, also carries passengers from Pineland, Florida (Pine Island). Reservations are required, and there is a fee for the service: (239) 283-0015.

About the campground: This subtropical barrier island lies in the Gulf of Mexico, just off the west coast of south Florida. Its 9 miles of beach are sparkling white and it is never thronged with crowds, even on holidays—almost certainly because you can only reach the island by boat.

Campers can fish, swim, or snorkel, with excellent chances of seeing manatees and pods of dolphins. These southwest Florida beaches are also known for the best shelling in the state, especially during the winter. Several nature trails allow hiking and even off-road cycling for those adventuresome enough to venture on the ferry with their bicycle.

An amphitheater allows park rangers to present educational programs about the island's ecology and history.

So -barrier

149 Koreshan State Historic Site

Location: Intersection of US 41 and Corkscrew Road at Estero in Lee County (26° 25' 52.4" N, 81° 48' 53.1" W)
Season: Year-round
Sites: 60; 12 next to the Estero River are tent only
Maximum length: 40 feet
Facilities: Full-facility camping with electricity, water, grill, fire ring, and table; centrally located bathhouse with laundry facilities
Fee per night: $$$
Management: Florida Division of Recreation and Parks
Contact: (239) 992-0311, www.floridastateparks.org/koreshan/default.cfm; (800) 326-3521, www.reserveamerica.com
Finding the campground: From I-75, take exit 123/Corkscrew Road and head west for 2 miles. Cross US 41 and continue approximately 1,000 yards to the entrance of the park.
About the campground: "The world as we know it is a crazy place, but relaxing beside the Gulf of Mexico it seems as though the world is a bowl with you at the center. Overhead, an arching sky and on either side the earth, spreading like the wings of a gull, rises gently up to meet the blue of day." Cyrus Reed Teed handed his followers a new faith that he called Koreshan Unity. He believed the above paragraph was literally true and he moved a colony of believers here in 1894 to build a "New Jerusalem." The social movement eventually dissolved in the heat and the storms.

Bordering the Estero River, this park offers many twenty-first-century recreational activities. You can fish, picnic, boat, and hike where Teed's visionaries once carried out experiments to prove the horizon curves upward. There is a boat ramp, canoe rentals, playground, short nature trail, and ranger-guided tours. There is no beach and consequently no swimming here.

150 Lee County Parks

Caloosahatchee Regional Park

Location: 19130 North River Rd., Alva, FL 33920 (26° 43' 30" N, 81° 39' 18" W)
Season: Year-round
Sites: 27 walk-in tent campsites (2 tents or 8 people per site), plus 6 group and 2 equestrian sites
Maximum length: Call for current information
Facilities: Water, outdoor showers, grills, picnic tables, modern restrooms, but no electricity for individual sites; group and equestrian sites at an additional charge
Fee per night: $$-$$$
Management: Call for current information
Contact: (239) 694-0398, www.leeparks.org/
Finding the campground: From I-75, take exit 143 and drive east on SR 78 to the park.

About the campground: Spanish moss hanging from old oak trees provides a quiet, beautiful backdrop for all the activities this lovely 768-acre park offers. On the 400-acre north side of SR 78, there are picnic tables and 10 miles of trails for horses, bikes, and hiking. Horses and bicycles are prohibited on the 12 miles of trail on the south side of the highway bordering the Caloosahatchee River. This is great canoeing and kayaking, and hence fishing, country. You can rent a kayak nearby or fish from the park's dock. Lee County makes a special effort to notify park visitors that Florida has fire ants, an invasive swarming and biting ant with distinctive above-ground mounds. Annual special events include the "River, Roots, and Ruts" trail run in January and the Palm Grass Bluegrass Music Festival in March.

151 Lake Okeechobee and Okeechobee Waterway

Ortona Lock A *East of Ft Myers*

Location: Glades County (campground office is at 26° 47' 15" N, 81° 18' 29" W)
Season: Year-round
Sites: 51 *no - via boat*
Maximum length: 45 feet
Facilities: Full-facility campsites with electricity, water, sewer; showers, dump station, laundry facility; no group sites
Fee per night: $$–$$$
Management: U.S. Army Corps of Engineers, www.usace.army.mil/
Contact: (800) 326-3521, www.reserveamerica.com
Finding the campground: To Ortona South from Fort Myers, drive 33 miles east on SR 80 and turn left at the sign on a paved road (Dalton Lane) to the lock and follow into campground.
About the campground: Ortona is not a recreational camping experience unless you have a boat and an RV. In that case the campground, located on the Caloosahatchee River section of the Okeechobee Waterway, is a good getaway: a spot to launch your boat or fish from the piers, picnic, and watch boats and even manatees going through the lock. Occasionally, an alligator will swim with a boat, and that brings people to their feet out of curiosity. Park attendants are on-site, and the nearby town of LaBelle offers normal amenities: groceries, hardware stores, restaurants. The Ortona campground received only 13,000 visitors last year.

W. P. Franklin Lock B

Location: Lee County (campground office is at 26° 43' 26" N, 81° 41' 33" W)
Season: Year-round
Sites: 38, 30 for tents/RVs and 8 boat sites
Facilities: All sites have electric and water hookups. Campground has trailer dump station, hot showers, public phones, fishing pier, and boat ramp. No toilets. Boat (cruiser) sites are only for boats that have onboard sleeping facilities. You may not dock a boat and pitch a tent.
Maximum length: 40 feet
Fee per night: $$–$$$

The vastness of south Florida is echoed in the Lake Okeechobee Scenic Trail atop the dike around the 730-square-mile lake, which averages a mere 9 feet deep.

Management: U.S. Army Corps of Engineers, www.usace.army.mil/
Contact: (800) 326-3521, www.reserveamerica.com. Reservations must be made 3 days in advance.
Finding the campground: To W. P. Franklin North from I-75, take exit 141/SR 80. Travel east to SR 31, turn north, and follow to SR 78. Turn east on SR 78 and drive 5 miles to North Franklin Lock Road. Turn south on North Franklin Lock Road and follow into the campground.
About the campground: Franklin North Campground, like the Ortona campground, is located on the Caloosahatchee River section of the Okeechobee Waterway, but on the north side. There is a tropical atmosphere here with swimming, fishing, picnicking, boating, and bird-watching.

Not far away, Fort Myers offers flea markets, grocery stores, malls, the historic Thomas Edison/ Henry Ford Home, and Gulf beaches. These amenities are all within 15 minutes drive.

152 Highlands Hammock State Park

Location: Off US 27 on SR 634/Hammock Road, 4 miles west of Sebring in Highlands County (27° 28' 16.1" N, 81° 31' 52.4" W)
Season: Year-round
Sites: 159 total, 140 having full hookups, primitive and youth/group areas, primitive horse camp
Maximum length: 50 feet
Facilities: Nearly all full-facility sites offer shade and easy access to nature trails, the picnic area, a Civilian Conservation Corp Museum and the Hammock Inn concession. The primitive horse camp

area is located at the start of an 11-mile trail; there is no electricity and restrooms are a short drive away. Self-contained units and generators are welcome in this area. There is room for trailer parking; tie-outs and a water trough are provided.

Fee per night: $$

Management: Florida Division of Recreation and Parks

Contact: (863) 386-6094, www.floridastateparks.org/highlandshammock/; (800) 326-3521, www.reserveamerica.com

Finding the campground: From I-75 south of Tampa, take exit 220 onto SR 64 east. Turn right (south) when SR 64 intersects US 17 in the town of Zolfo Springs. In about 0.5 mile, turn left (east) onto SR 66. After about 16 miles, turn left (north) onto CR 635 and proceed to the park entrance.

About the campground: Once considered for a national park but deemed too small, this park now measures more than 9,000 acres because Florida citizens have encouraged its growth. Consequently, it has something in the way of recreation for everyone and is beautiful as well.

Campers find nine multiuse trails and a 3-mile bicycle loop. Elevated boardwalks take families through cypress swamps, and ranger-led tours are scheduled each week. There is a restaurant (863-385-7025), a museum, and a tram for tours. Unlike most south Florida areas, this is not a park built about water activities, but has more to offer horseback riders—including a sterling 11-mile day-use trail—and campers wearing out their hiking boots.

153 Kissimmee River Public Use Area

Location: Adjacent to KICCO and Hickory Hammock WMAs along the Kissimmee River from SR 60 south to Lake Okeechobee in Glades, Highlands, Okeechobee, Osceola, and Polk Counties (US 98 bridge over the Kissimmee River—27° 21' 54" N, 81V 3' 6" W)

Season: Year-round

Sites: In designated locations with a WMA special use permit

Maximum length: Call for current information

Facilities: Call for current information

Fee per night: Call for current information

Management: Fish & Wildlife Conservation Commission and South Florida Water Management District

Contact: (800) 250-4200 for a water management district special use permit, www.sfwmd.gov, http://myfwc.com, www.floridatrail.org

Finding the campground: Taking US 98 west and north from the town of Okeechobee will put you in the middle of the PUA when you come to the Kissimmee River.

About the campground: Emphasizing the area's opportunities for boaters, access to and enjoyment of this 24,873-acre WMA/PUA stretching along the Kissimmee River is primarily by boat, and a number of boat ramps from its northern end to its southern extremity facilitate fishing and boating. Although bikers are allowed on the roads in the PUA, horseback riders need a WMA special use permit and are restricted to certain areas. Hunting is excellent and a portion of the Florida Trail is available. Otherwise, for campers, this is a warm, humid, and usually buggy experience.

154 Hickory Hammock Wildlife Management Area

Location: About halfway between Sebring and Okeechobee near the southwest border of Highlands County (27° 24' 18" N, 81° 10' 30" W)

Season: Year-round

Sites: 2 designated primitive campsites located along the Florida Trail for through-hikers. All other campers must possess a special use license.

Maximum length: Call for current information

Facilities: Call for current information

Fee per night: Call for current information

Management: Fish & Wildlife Conservation Commission and Southwest Florida Water Management District (WMD)

Contact: (863) 462-5260, (800) 250-4200 (WMD) for special use license, ww.sfwmd.gov, http://myfwc.com, www.floridabirdingtrail.com, www.floridatrail.org

Finding the campground: From the town of Okeechobee on the north end of Lake Okeechobee, take US 98 west. The entrance to Hickory Hammock is on US 98, about 8 miles west of the Kissimmee River Bridge and the hamlet of Fort Basinger and just north of the Istokpoga Canal.

About the campground: This small WMA was purchased for water reasons, but 7.5 miles of the Florida Trail run through its pine and palmetto, oak and grassland grounds. Begun in the 1960s, the Florida Trail is now part of the National Scenic Trail system with more than 1,400 miles marked and mapped from Pensacola to Miami. The hiking section in Hickory Hammock is a wonderful part of the trail. Bicycling and horseback riding require advance permits from the WMD.

155 R. K. Butler Campground

Location: 992 Boat Ramp Rd., Butlers Bluff Rd., Lorida, FL 33857 in Highlands County (27° 18' 0" N, 81° 1' 6" W)

Season: Year-round

Sites: 8 improved campsites

Maximum length: Call for current information

Facilities: Playground, restrooms, showers, picnic facilities with grills, electrical hookups, dump station, basketball court, boat ramp, and pull-through sites

Fee per night: $$

Management: Highland County Board of County Commissioners, Parks and Recreation

Contact: (863) 763-3113

Finding the campground: From I-75, take exit 217 and go east on SR 70 through Arcadia and past US 27 to CR 721. Turn left (north) and drive 4.5 miles to Boat Ramp Road. Turn right (east) and drive about 2 miles to the campground. Turn west off I-95 at exit 129 onto SR 70 and drive through Okeechobee. Go approximately 15 miles to CR 721 and turn right (north). Turn right (east) on Boat Ramp Road in 4.5 miles and drive to the end.

About the campground: Located on the Kissimmee River, a resident manager is on site for security and assistance. Canoeing, kayaking, fishing, and hiking opportunities are all available at this rural county park.

156 Fisheating Creek Wildlife Management Area

Location: Palmdale, west of Lake Okeechobee, Glades County (26° 56' 42" N, 81° 18' 59" W)

Season: Year-round   *863-675-5999*

Sites: 45 full hookup RV sites and 200 primitive campsites, air-conditioned cabins sleeping five. During established hunting seasons, individuals are encouraged to camp at the Palmdale campground or at designated sites along Fisheating Creek. Primitive camping is otherwise permitted year-round throughout the area.

Maximum length: Call for current information   *Sewer,*   *#$$*

Facilities: Call for current information   *yc*

Fee per night: RVs: full hookup $$$, no hookup $$; other campsites: regular and primitive $$, waterfront $$$

Management: Fish & Wildlife Conservation Commission

Contact: (863) 675-5999 (Palmdale concessionaire), http://fisheatingcreekresort.com, http://myfwc.com/

Finding the campground: From I-75 in Fort Myers on the Gulf coast, take exit 141, SR 80 east to LaBelle and the intersection with SR 29. Turn left (north) and, in about 13 miles at the intersection with US 27, turn left (north). The campground is on the left in about 1 mile—just past Fisheating Creek.

About the campground: Fisheating Creek is a recreation area, a protective zone for Florida's water resources, and a critical connective wildlife zone related to Big Cypress Swamp, Lake Okeechobee, and the Lake Wales Ridge. Big animals—black bears, Florida panthers, or whooping cranes, for instance—require big areas to forage, hunt, and wander in the search for mates. Thus, the 18,272 acres of this WMA, which stretch for 40 miles along the course of the only free-flowing tributary to Lake Okeechobee, are a privilege to visit. Wonderful for paddling, hunting, and exploring.

A1-A8, B1-B10, C1-C11, D1-D5,
+ F1-F9

157 Okaloacoochee Slough State Forest/ Wildlife Management Area

Location: In Hendry and Collier Counties, 30 miles east of Fort Myers along CR 832 (hunter check station on CR 832 and unpaved Wildcow Grade Road—26° 35' 42" N, 81° 20' 6" W)

Season: Year-round

Sites: Primitive camping year-round at 1 campground; 2 additional campgrounds for hunters with permits; walk-in campground with 2 campsites open except during "quota hunts"

Maximum length: Call for current information

Facilities: Call for current information

Fee per night: $-$$

Management: Division of Forestry, Fish & Wildlife Conservation Commission, and South Florida Water Management District

Contact: (239) 690-3500, www.fldof.com/field_operations/caloosahatchee_publicland.html, http://myfwc.com, www.floridabirdingtrail.com

Finding the forest: Okaloacoochee Slough is approximately 30 miles east of Fort Myers, in southeastern Hendry and northeastern Collier Counties. It can be accessed along CR 832, marked by the various self-service pay stations.

About the forest: Okaloacoochee Slough is a vast area of 32,039 acres. It is important as a source for thousands of miles of rivers and wetlands, including Fakahatchee Strand and Big Cypress Preserve. The ecosystem provides a large roaming area of contiguous habitat for threatened and endangered species: Florida panther, black bear, sandhill crane, wood stork, and gopher tortoise.

Campers use the miles of forest roads and a few "hidden" trails for hiking and bicycling. Fishing is excellent in the forest's canals and ponds. Hunting is popular also.

158 Dinner Island Ranch Wildlife Management Area

Location: Southwest of Clewiston and east of Immokalee in southern Hendry County (26° 30' 0" N, 81° 7' 421" W)

The Great Florida Birding Trail offers 489 sites for excellent bird-watching. It is a 2,000-mile, self-guided trail designed to conserve Florida's bird habitat.

Season: Year-round
Sites: Primitive camping; no facilities
Maximum length: Call for current information
Facilities: Call for current information
Fee per night: Call for current information
Management: Fish & Wildlife Conservation Commission
Contact: http://myfwc.com, www.floridabirdingtrail.com
Finding the campground: From I-75 in southwest Florida, take exit 111 onto Immokalee Road/111th Avenue and drive east to the town of Immokalee. Turn right (east) onto Main Street/SR 29 and in 0.50 mile turn left onto Clewiston Exchange/Immokalee Exchange Road. After 17 miles, the road swings 90 degrees north but does not change its name. Look for WMA signs and the gated entrance to Dinner Island Grade Road on the left (west). The camping area is close to the entrance on the right (north) side of the road.
About the campground: Dinner Island is in the middle of nowhere—and that is perfect for real campers. This is 34 square miles, 21,714 acres, of loneliness: pastures, sloughs, flatwoods, hammocks, snakes, and gators. Swamp—euphemistically named wetlands—on all sides. A network of graded roads and mowed trails in this WMA is open for wildlife viewing, hunting, off-road cycling, horseback riding, and hiking. This area is part of the Great Florida Birding Trail.

159 CREW Wildlife and Environmental Area

Location: CREW WEA is not a contiguous WEA and straddles fast growing Lee and Collier Counties (Gate 6—26° 27' 6" N, 81° 33' 48" W)
Season: Year-round
Sites: Primitive camping is allowed with permit at designated sites in the Corkscrew Marsh Unit
Maximum length: Call for current information
Facilities: Call for current information
Fee per night: Call for current information
Management: Fish & Wildlife Conservation Commission and South Florida Water Management District
Contact: (239) 657-2253 for permit or (239) 867-3230 for information, www.sfwmd.gov, http://myfwc.com/
Finding the campground: Take exit 123 from I-75 and drive east on CR 850/Corkscrew Road. Watch for signs to the camping area through Gate 6 on the right at about 14 miles when CR 850 makes a 90 degree turn to the left (north).
About the campground: CREW WEA is not a contiguous area, but consists of three separate units: Corkscrew Marsh, Flint Pen Strand, and Bird Rookery Swamp. Together, they total 28,540 acres, and the WEA is part of the larger 60,000-acre Corkscrew Regional Ecosystem Watershed, or CREW.

The countryside is a blend of marsh, pine lands, oak hammocks, and cypress swamps; in other words, something for everyone. A camper who gets out early and hikes might see a black bear, perhaps even a Florida panther. The Corkscrew Marsh Unit has three hiking loops that vary in length from 1 to 2 miles. The marsh trail leads to an observation deck, an excellent spot for bird-watching. Hunting is allowed during fall seasons for big game, and in the spring for wild turkeys. Fishing is permitted year-round. Kayaks and canoes are the only types of boats allowed.

160 Picayune Strand State Forest/ Wildlife Management Area

Location: 20 miles east of Naples in western Collier County (26° 09' 11" N, 81° 47' 55" W)
Season: Year-round
Sites: Rugged primitive camping
Maximum length: Call for current information
Facilities: The Belle Meade Tract has a 22-mile horse trail, 10 paddocks, nonpotable water, and an equestrian camping area
Fee per night: $–$$
Management: Division of Forestry and Fish & Wildlife Conservation Commission
Contact: (239) 348-7557, www.fl-dof.com/state_forests/picayune_strand.html
Finding the forest: Access the forest via Everglades Boulevard from the north or Jane's Scenic Drive from the east. Public parking and restrooms are at 2121 52nd Ave. SE. Limited trailer parking is available at M&H ($): (941) 455-8764.
About the forest: Most of this forest is underwater when any significant rain falls, and consequently, you want to take care camping here. As Florida has undergone fairly extreme cycles of

Pop-up, pull-behind campers are maneuverable and versatile and, for many, provide just the right compromise between roughing it and comfort.

heavy rain and drought recently, camping can be wonderful, peaceful, quiet—or damp and miserable. Bide your time and enjoy the solitude and the trails. Be sure to try the Sabal Palm Trail, a 3.2-mile trail that gives hikers an opportunity to view cypress trees—too small to harvest in the 1940s and 1950s—which are now a century old.

161 Collier-Seminole State Park

Location: On US 41 south of Naples in Collier County (25° 58' 34" N, 81° 36' 14" W)
Season: Year-round
Sites: 137, including primitive and youth/group campsites, in two camping areas: one wooded area with 19 sites, popular for tents, vans, and pop-up campers; the other with 118 sites and more suited for RVs (but including tent sites). The youth camping area, which can be reserved, is accessible from the park's hiking trail, the primitive site (first-come, first-served) only by kayak.
Maximum length: 60 feet
Facilities: Full-facility sites with electricity, picnic table, and grill. There are 3 modern bathhouses, 1 with washer/dryer; another with activity room.
Fee per night: $$
Management: Florida Division of Recreation and Parks
Contact: (239) 394-3397, www.floridastateparks.org/collier-seminole/default.cfm; (800) 326-3521, www.reserveamerica.com
Finding the campground: Driving south on I-75, take exit 101 (SR 951 and SR 84) and turn right (south). Follow SR 951 south about 8 miles to US 41. Turn left (southeast) on US 41 and Collier-Seminole State Park will be 8 miles on the right just past CR 92.
About the campground: This park has a wealth of tropical plants, and the weather varies from warm in the winter to hot in the summer. The best time for a visit, of course, is whenever you can get a reservation, but a weekend or a week in the winter will probably be a more rewarding experience than a visit in June or August.

One of the most spectacular trees in the park is the Royal Palm. This tree grows to several stories in height with a smooth trunk and thatch of palm atop a sheath, giving the appearance of a floral bouquet.

Campers can hike, cycle, fish, and canoe special trails. Canoe rentals are available, and a boat ramp provides access to the Blackwater River.

162 Big Cypress National Preserve/ Wildlife Management Area

Location: Headquarters: 33100 Tamiami Trail East, Ochopee, FL 34141; Oasis Visitor Center and general preserve information, (239) 695-1201. (25° 54' 04" N, 81° 18' 13" W). The cooperatively managed area spans parts of Collier, Dade, and Monroe Counties and borders Everglades National Park.
Season: Year-round

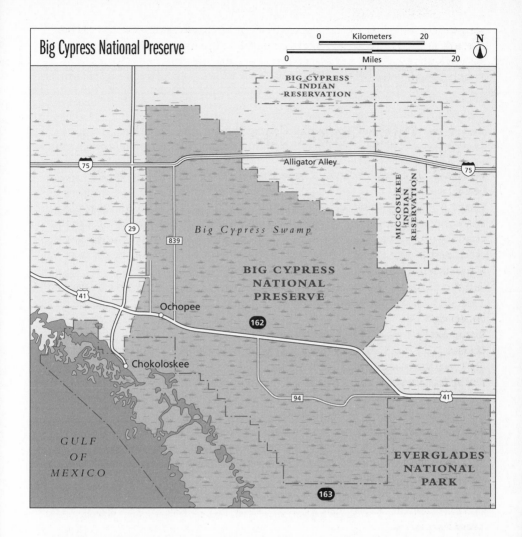

Big Cypress National Preserve

0   Kilometers   20

0   Miles   20

N

BIG CYPRESS
INDIAN
RESERVATION

75   Alligator Alley   75

Big Cypress Swamp

29

839

MICCOSUKEE
INDIAN
RESERVATION

BIG CYPRESS
NATIONAL
PRESERVE

41

Ochopee

162

Chokoloskee

94

41

GULF
OF
MEXICO

EVERGLADES
NATIONAL
PARK

163

Sites: Monument Lake and Midway campgrounds, along US 41, have water and modern rest-rooms; fees are charged for camping here. There are also 4 free primitive campgrounds within the preserve. These small campgrounds are first-come, first-served; no reservations are accepted. Campgrounds on the Loop Road are not suitable for large RVs.

Bear Island: Primitive camping all year at 3 designated, primitive campgrounds: Bear Island (40 sites), Pink Jeep (9 sites), and Gator Pit (9 sites). Pink Jeep and Gator Pit require an off-road vehicle permit. Access to Bear Island is via a secondary gravel road. No potable water or restrooms.

Burns Lake: 40 sites open September 1 to January 6, primitive camping only, no potable water or restrooms.

Monument Lake: 26 RV sites and 10 tent sites available September 1 to April 15; restrooms, drinking water, cold-water shower; no hookups for electricity, sewer, or water.

Midway: 26 RV sites with electric hookup and 10 tent sites open year-round; dump station, restrooms, drinking water, day-use area.

Pinecrest: 10 primitive camping sites open year-round; no potable water or restrooms, access along a secondary gravel road.

Mitchell's Landing: 15 primitive sites open year-round; no water or restrooms, access along a secondary gravel road.

Maximum length: Call for current information

Fee per night: 0-$$ (depending on level of service)

Management: U.S. National Park Service and Florida Fish & Wildlife Conservation Commission

Contact: Oasis Visitor Center and general preserve information, (239) 695-1201, www.nps.gov /bicy/index.htm and http://myfwc.com

Finding the campground: Big Cypress National Preserve is located in southwest Florida between the cities of Miami and Naples. I-75 (Alligator Alley) and US 41 (the old Tamiami Trail) are the primary roads traversing the preserve. Visitor facilities and most activities originate from the Tamiami Trail. The Oasis Visitor Center is located on the Tamiami Trail, 50 miles west of Miami and 50 miles east of Naples. Headquarters is near Naples and Everglades City, on US 41, 5 miles east of the SR 29 intersection.

About the campground: At more than 720,000 acres, Big Cypress National Preserve is a "vast swamp." Big Cypress WMA is half-a-million acres within the federal preserve.

Even a brief visit here gives campers a sense of the difficulties faced by people who sought refuge here. By day, the sun is unrelenting. By night, mosquito hordes have been known to choke horses and cattle. There are alligators by the millions.

In addition, this area and the adjoining Everglades are hospitable to animals released by owners who no longer wish to care for them. These exotic species have established breeding colonies in the marsh and thus Burmese pythons are abundant and permanent.

For fun you can hunt, fish, look for wildlife, paddle, hike, bike, and of course camp. In addition to the designated campsite complexes, primitive camping is allowed throughout much of the WMA (except in the Bear Island unit where all camping is limited to designated campsites). Mapped hiking trails run throughout the WMA and there are 31 miles of the Florida Trail. Bear Island is a great place to ride a bike and paddling the Turner River Canoe Trail gives a very personal sense of the land and water.

May to October is the rainy season, and the park is thick with mosquitoes, hence not the best time for camping. The dry (and cooler) season, November to April, is more inviting for outdoor pursuits and camping.

163 Everglades National Park

NOTE: Please contact the park(s) for more information regarding omitted camp specs and management as it is often changing.

General location and contact information: Headquarters: 40001 SR 9336, Homestead, FL 33034, in Dade County, but Gulf coast camping is actually in Monroe County. The northern entrance is at the Gulf Coast Visitor Center, (941) 695-3311, in Everglades City, operating daily from 7:30 a.m. to 4:45 p.m. (25° 51' 32" N, 81° 23' 5" W). The southern entrance is at the Flamingo Visitor Center, (941) 695-2945, in unincorporated Flamingo, operating daily from 7:30 a.m. to 5:00 p.m. (25° 8' 27.2" N, 80° 55' 27.1" W). Use the southern entrance for all Florida Bay sites.

Season: Year-round

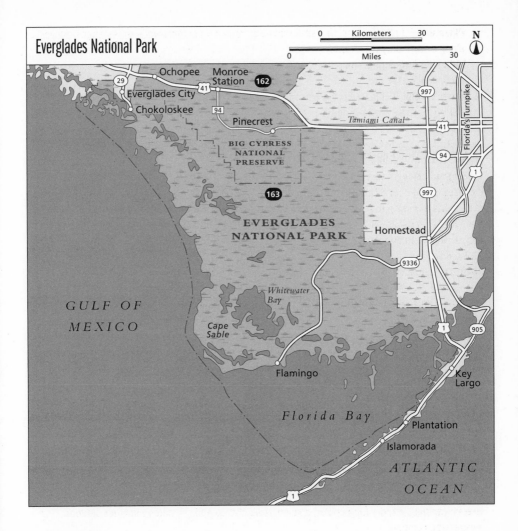

Everglades National Park

0   Kilometers   30

0   Miles   30

N

Campgrounds

There are 3 campgrounds in the park: Chekika, Flamingo, and Long Pine Key. To make reservations for Flamingo and Long Pine Key, call (800) 365-2267. Camping from May to October requires self-registration. No fees from June to August. Call (305) 242-7759 for group camping. From December to April, the drier and cooler season, campgrounds usually fill each night. Campsites are first-come, first-served, so early arrival is recommended. Checkout is 11:00 a.m. During the winter (November 1 to April 30), camping is limited to 14 days.

Chekika: Temporarily, we hope, this campground is day-use-only pending repair of damages caused by hurricanes. Located 6 miles west of Krome Avenue/SR 997 on SW 168th Street. For more information call (305) 242-7700.

Flamingo: 234 drive-in sites, including 55 with a view of the water, 4 group sites, 64 walk-up sites (20 on the water's edge). Amenities include potable water, fire grates, picnic tables, showers, and a dump station for $$ per night. Groceries are available nearby. An observation tower has been built at Eco Pond, and there are hiking trails, paddling routes, and opportunities for freshwater fishing. The campground is at the end of the main park road in Flamingo.

Long Pine Key: 108 drive-up sites for tents and RVs, and 1 group site. Amenities include potable water, fire grates, picnic tables, and a dump station for $$ per night. Nearby are a fishing pond, hiking trails, and an amphitheater. This campsite is 7 miles from the main entrance, just off the main road.

Backcountry/Wilderness Primitive Camping

Sites: 46 wilderness primitive campsites, most of which are only accessible by boat. There are 3 types of sites: chickees, ground, and beach. 6/6 indicates a double chickee and each platform is limited to one party of one to six people.

Chickees

Elevated 10-by-12-foot wooden platforms with roofs of palm fronds; over water with a self-contained toilet; free-standing tent required; insects are plentiful; and no campfires are allowed.

- Harney River: 6 people, 1 party, 1 night—toilet and dock, no tables
- Hell's Bay: 6/6 people, 1/1 party, 1 night—toilet and dock, no tables
- Joe River: 6/6 people, 1/1 party, 1 night—toilet and dock, no tables
- Lane Bay: 6 people, 1 party, 1 night—toilet and dock, no tables
- North River: 6 people, 1 party, 1 night—toilet and dock, no tables
- Oyster Bay: 6/6 people, 1/1 party, 1 night—toilet and dock, no tables
- Pearl Bay: 6/6 people, 1/1 party, 1 night—toilet and dock, no tables (ADA accessible with handrails, canoe dock, and an accessible chemical toilet.)
- Plate Creek: 6 people, 1 party, 1 night—toilet and dock, no tables
- Robert's River: 6/6 people, 1/1 party, 2 nights—toilet and dock, no tables
- Rodger's River: 6/6 people, 1/1 party, 1 night—toilet and dock, no tables
- Shark River: 6 people, 1 party, 1 night—toilet and dock, no tables
- South Joe River: 6/6 people, 1/1 party, 1 night—toilet and dock, no tables
- Sun Bay: 6/6 people, 1/1 party, 1 night—toilet and dock, no tables
- Sweetwater: 6/6 people, 1/1 party, 1 night—toilet and dock, no tables
- Watson River: 6 people, 1 party, 1 night—toilet and dock, no tables

Ground

Mounds of earth among the mangroves only a few feet above the water; insects are plentiful; self-contained toilets; no campfires allowed.

- Alligator Creek: 8 people, 3 parties, 2 nights—no toilet, tables or dock
- Broad River: 10 people, 3 parties, 2 nights—toilet, tables, dock available
- Camp Lonesome: 10 people, 3 parties, 3 nights—toilet, tables, dock available
- Canepatch: 12 people, 4 parties, 3 nights—toilet, tables, dock available
- Darwin's Place: 8 people, 2 parties, 3 nights—toilet and tables, no dock
- Ernest Coe: 8 people, 1 party, 3 nights—no toilet, tables or dock (accessible on foot or by bicycle only)
- Graveyard Creek: 12 people, 4 parties, 3 nights—toilet, tables, dock available

- Ingraham: 8 people, 1 party, 3 nights—no toilet, tables or dock (accessible on foot or by bicycle only)
- Lard Can: 10 people, 4 parties, 2 nights—toilet, no dock or tables
- Little Rabbit Key: 12 people, 4 parties, 2 nights—toilet, tables, dock available
- Lopez River: 12 people, 3 parties, 2 nights—toilet and tables, no dock
- Lost Man's Five: 15 people, 3 parties, 3 nights—toilet, tables, dock available
- Shark Point: 8 people, 1 party, 3 nights—no toilet, tables or dock
- Watson's Place: 20 people, 5 parties, 2 nights—toilet, tables, dock available
- Willy Willy: 10 people, 3 parties, 3 nights—toilet, tables, dock available

Beach

Often there are no toilets; beware of sea turtle nests, as disturbing them is a federal offense; tides vary and expose wide mud flats; insects are often quite difficult.

- Cape Sable East: 60 people, 15 parties, 7 nights—no toilet, tables or dock
- Cape Sable Middle: 60 people, 15 parties, 7 nights—no toilet, tables or dock
- Cape Sable Northwest: 36 people, 9 parties, 7 nights—no toilet, tables or dock
- Carl Ross Key: 12 people, 4 parties, 2 nights—no toilet, tables or dock
- Clubhouse Beach: 24 people, 4 parties, 3 nights—no toilet, tables or dock
- East Clubhouse Beach: 24 people, 4 parties, 3 nights—no toilet, tables or dock
- Highland Beach: 24 people, 4 parties, 3 nights—no toilet, tables or dock
- Hog Key: 8 people, 2 parties, 2 nights—no toilet, tables or dock (shallow water approach; recommended for canoes or kayaks only)
- Mormon Key: 12 people, 2 parties, 3 nights—no toilet, tables or dock
- New Turkey Key: 10 people, 2 parties, 2 nights—toilet, no tables or dock
- North Nest Key: 27 people, 7 parties, 7 nights—toilet and dock, no tables
- Pavilion Key: 20 people, 4 parties, 3 nights—toilet, no dock or tables
- Picnic Key: 16 people, 4 parties, 3 nights—toilet, no dock or tables
- Rabbit Key: 8 people, 2 parties, 2 nights—toilet, no dock or tables
- Tiger Key: 12 people, 3 parties, 3 nights—no toilet, tables or dock
- Turkey Key: 12 people, 3 parties, 3 nights—no toilet, tables or dock

Management: U.S. National Park Service
Contact: (239) 695-2945 or (800) 365-CAMP, www.nps.gov/ever/ (call no more than 24 hours in advance)
Finding the park: Everglades National Park consists of 1,508,570 acres. Once off the main roads, nautical charts are necessary for finding your way in this wilderness—and do not trust your usual Internet map source in the backcountry. From I-75 south of Fort Myers, turn south on SR 29 and drive straight south to Everglades City. From US 1 in Homestead/Florida City, turn west (right) onto CR 9336/Palm Drive. Follow the CR 9336 signs to the park visitor center and then on the long two-lane drive to Flamingo.
About the park: Camping in the Everglades can be absolutely delightful, but it often requires a special kind of endurance. The 'Glades' are an ocean of grass and the heat, the bowl of sky arching overhead, the animals and insects, make it clear that man is a guest.

The Everglades is the largest subtropical wilderness in America. Of course it has endangered crocodiles and panthers, but it also has exotic boa constrictors and is rumored, in pockets, to filled with released piranhas. A fast-spreading invasive tree is the number-one threat nent of south Florida. A native of Australia, the exotic melaleuca threatens the very e Everglades (http://plants.ifas.ufl.edu/node/264).

This vast park offers 156 miles of mapped and marked canoe/kayak and walking trails and there are 46 primitive wilderness campsites. Thus, opportunities for solitude . . . and for becoming lost—and that is not a laughing matter here—are abundant. Most wilderness campsites are accessible only by boat. (Safely exploring a wilderness by water requires careful preparation and trip planning. Permits are also required. Study the park's *Wilderness Trip Planner* before your visit.)

Because of the heat, severe storms, and an intolerable number of mosquitoes, summer (June through October) is not the best time to camp; winter months (November through April) are more pleasant, though not entirely lacking in tiny pests. The Everglades is a large, complex park with few amenities and relatively few visitors—be warned and be prepared.

164 John Pennekamp Coral Reef State Park

Location: In Monroe County beside US 1 at mile marker 102.5, south of Key Largo in the Florida Keys (25° 7' 40.3" N, 80° 24' 35.6" W)
Season: Year-round
Sites: 47, most lacking shade or privacy, but this park is so wonderful that you will hardly notice. A group camping area accommodates organized youth and adult groups up to 24 people.
Maximum length: 62 feet
Facilities: Full-facility camping. Site has fire circle, benches, picnic tables, but no electricity; restrooms and hot showers available.
Fee per night: $$$
Management: Florida Division of Recreation and Parks
Contact: (305) 451-6316, www.floridastateparks.org/pennekamp/default.cfm; (800) 326-3521, www.reserveamerica.com
Finding the campground: The park is located on US 1 at mile marker 102.5, south of Key Largo in the Florida Keys.
About the campground: John Pennekamp covers 70 nautical miles and was the first underwater park in the U.S. It was purchased to protect one of only two living coral reefs in the continental U.S. (the other is located 105 miles south of the Texas coastline in the Gulf of Mexico and practically inaccessible).

Because it is spectacular, Pennekamp is crowded. In an average year the park hosts more than a million visitors, and this speaks to its numerous natural and man-made attractions, an observation tower, for instance.

Virtually anything one can legally do on the water is available at or near Pennekamp: swimming, snorkeling, fishing, kayaking, scuba diving, and touring on glass-bottom boats. It is, after all, the coral reefs and abundant marine life that thrill most visitors. For boat tour information and reservations, call (305) 451-6300.

Two short hiking trails give you a glimpse of the mangroves and pines and the animals of the Keys. The park's visitor center has a 30,000-gallon saltwater aquarium and a theater that shows nature videos.

165 Long Key State Park

Location: In Monroe County at mile marker 67.5, 67400 Overseas Highway, in the Florida Keys (24° 48' 59.5" N, 80° 49' 24.8" W)
Season: Year-round
Sites: 60 full-facility campsites overlooking the ocean
Maximum length: 45 feet
Facilities: Picnic table, ground grill, water, electricity; centrally located restrooms with hot showers
Fee per night: $$$
Management: Florida Division of Recreation and Parks
Contact: (305) 664-4815, www.floridastateparks.org/longkey/default.cfm; (800) 326-3521, www.reserveamerica.com
Finding the campground: US 1 from Homestead to Key West is two lanes, and this park is located about halfway between the two cities.
About the campground: The fact that reservations may be made up to 11 months in advance testifies to the park's attractiveness. Set in the aquamarine waters of the Keys between the Atlantic and the Gulf, campers can haul their kayaks off the rooftop carriers and explore the beaches and mangrove swamps, the blue depths and shallow sandbars of a place the Spanish called Rattlesnake Key, because its shape resembles a snake ready to bite. And there's great bonefishing, too.

Rich people pay millions for the views you can get from your tent. And if you ever become bored with the sun and rich white sand, the scuba diving, snorkeling, and swimming, hike the two land-based trails, one leading to an observation tower. The other leads, eventually, to miles of souvenir shacks and fast-food establishments along US 1. The only drawback is that there is very little shade and at times mosquitoes, no-see-ums, and sand fleas can be pests. A breeze is always welcome.

166 Curry Hammock State Park

Location: 4 miles north of Marathon on US 1 in Monroe County (24° 44' 45.7" N, 80° 58' 57" W)
Season: Year-round
Sites: 28 along the oceanfront
Maximum length: 70 feet
Facilities: Full-facility sites, most with gravel parking areas and an adjoining sand area for tents (tents may be placed on sites without a sandbox, but the gravel is coarse and uncomfortable)
Fee per night: $$$
Management: Florida Division of Recreation and Parks
Contact: (305) 289-2690, www.floridastateparks.org/curryhammock/default.cfm; (800) 326-3521, www.reserveamerica.com
Finding the campground: The park is located along both sides of US 1 starting at Little Crawl Key, mile marker 56.2, 11 miles west of Long Key. The entrance to the facilities is on the Atlantic Ocean side of US 1.
About the campground: Any camping spot in the Florida Keys is wonderful and this park is made up of a group of islands in the Middle Keys. It offers access to swimming and snorkeling, a playground, picnic tables, grills, and showers on the ocean side of Little Crawl Key. The Keys (or "Cays")

are truly tropical in nature, and one may see a feral and exotic iguana racing across the road. Expect mangrove swamps, seagrass beds, and marshy wetlands plus great sunrises and sunsets right from your campsite.

167 Bahia Honda State Park

Location: 12 miles south of Marathon on US 1 in Monroe County (24° 39' 36.2" N, 81° 16' 25.2" W)
Season: Year-round
Sites: 86, including 6 cabins on stilts; 3 campgrounds in the park
  Buttonwood: 48 gravel sites; electricity, water, picnic table, grill. Better for RVs and pop-ups than tents. Little shade, but the largest sites in the park.
  Sandspur: 23 small sites; picnic tables, grills; water in a rare hardwood hammock habitat. 15 sites have electricity. The most beautiful camping area in the park, but sites have low clearance. Tents fit on all of these sites; and several will accommodate small pop-ups. RVs not permitted.
  Bayside: 8 sites; picnic tables, grills, water, no electricity. Bayside is the smallest campground in the park and has a 6-foot, 8-inch vehicle height restriction, as do the cabins. Vehicles must be able to go under the New Bahia Honda Bridge.
Maximum length: 71 feet
Facilities: Full-facility camping
Fee per night: $$$
Management: Florida Division of Recreation and Parks
Contact: (305) 872-2353, www.floridastateparks.org/bahiahonda/default.cfm; (800) 326-3521, www.reserveamerica.com
Finding the campground: US 1 from Homestead to Key West is two lanes. Bahia Honda is located roughly two-thirds of the distance to Key West. Watch for signs.
About the campground: Many consider Bahia Honda the most magnificent park in Florida. Its beaches, sunsets, and snorkeling are wonderful.

Campers can enjoy the breeze beside blue-green waters, relaxing or swimming in an ocean that is temperate to warm year-round. There is a boat launch in the park, and fishing is superb, but many boaters simply enjoy being out on the colorful waters or snorkeling or strapping on scuba tanks for an extended stay on the bottom or visiting the area reefs.

Kayaks and snorkeling gear can be rented and many vendors offer opportunities for fishing and other pursuits on and in the water. You can learn about the area's complex ecology at the park's nature center.

168 Dry Tortugas National Park

Location: 70 miles west of its Key West Headquarters, P.O. Box 6208, Key West, FL 33041, in Monroe County (24°37'43" N, 82°52' 24" W)
Season: Year-round

Sites: 8 primitive, first-come, first-served sites; overflow areas available; sites accommodate up to 6 people and 3 tents each. A group site (must be reserved in advance) is available for 10 to 40 people. The campground is a self-service fee area.

Maximum length: Call for current information

Facilities: No facilities except composting toilets. Campground is a short walk from the public dock and not far from historic Fort Jefferson.

Fee per night: $ per person

Management: U.S. National Park Service

Contact: (305) 242-7700, www.nps.gov/drto/, www.dry.tortugas.national-park.com/camping.htm

Finding the campground: Dry Tortugas is 70 miles west of Key West. One of the most remote parks in America, it is accessible only by boat or seaplane. For ferry schedules, prices, and reservations, contact Sunny Days, (800) 236-7937 or (305) 292-6100, http://www.sunnydayskeywest .com/fastcat.htm. For Yankee Freedom: (800) 634-0939, (305) 294-7009, www.yankeefreedom .com. Seaplane transportation is currently cancelled. Fishing and dive charters can be arranged in the Florida Keys or in Naples. For a list of services, contact the park at (305) 242-7700.

About the campground: For a remote park on a fragile island with a curious and romantic history, the Dry Tortugas is amazingly receptive to campers. The island is built on coral rubble—not exactly bedrock—and the story of how and why the fortress was built and what part it has played in history is fascinating. It is doubly fascinating once you have spent a long weekend kicking about the sand and looking out over the Gulf from the fortress's brick walls. What did they do about hurricanes? Who was prisoner here? How did they survive with little water and no shade? Campers are welcome, but do not even think of tying anything to a palm tree. In addition, the Park Service warns, there are rats and food preservation in hard-sided containers is "highly recommended."

The Gold Coast Region

C ounties: Okechobee, St. Lucie, Martin, Glades, Hendry, Palm Beach, Broward, Monroe, Dade

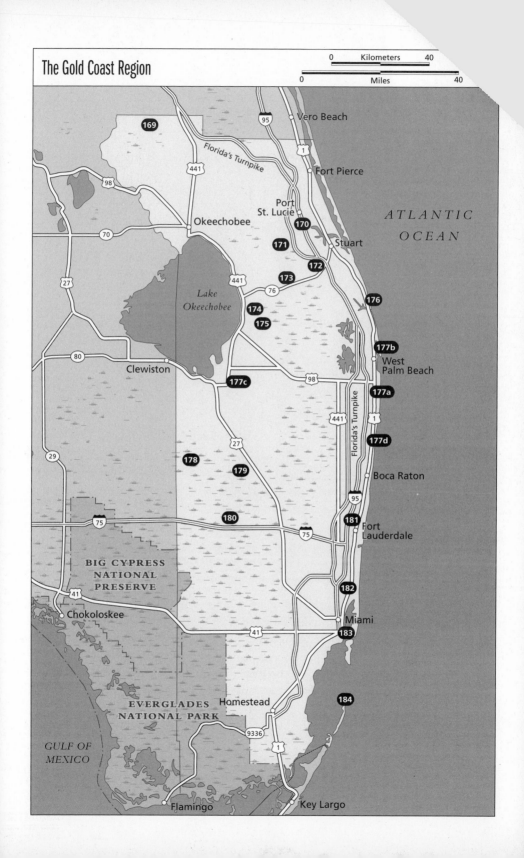

The Gold Coast Region

0   Kilometers   40

0   Miles   40

ATLANTIC
OCEAN

GULF OF
MEXICO

169

170
171
172
173
174
175
176
177a
177b
177c
177d
178
179
180
181
182
183
184

Vero Beach

Florida's Turnpike

Fort Pierce

Port
St. Lucie

Okeechobee

Stuart

Lake
Okeechobee

Clewiston

West
Palm Beach

Florida's Turnpike

Boca Raton

Fort
Lauderdale

BIG CYPRESS
NATIONAL
PRESERVE

Chokoloskee

Miami

EVERGLADES
NATIONAL PARK

Homestead

Flamingo

Key Largo

95
1
441
98
70
27
441
76
80
98
441
95
29
75
41
27
41
9336
1
75

	Hookup Sites	Total Sites[1]	Max RV Length	Hookups	Toilets	Showers	Dump Station	Recreation	Fee	Can Reserve
169 Kiss........ ....eserve State Park	35	35, T	65	WE	F, NF	Yes	Yes	HFCR	$$	Yes
170 St. Lucie County Parks	-	-	-	WE (S)	F	Yes	Yes	HFBLC	$$-$$$	Yes
171 Allapattah Flats WMA	-	-	-	-	-	-	-	HFBRC, hunting	-	No
172 Lake Okeechobee and Okeechobee Waterway	9	12	-	WE	F	Yes	Yes	FBLC	$$-$$$	Yes
173 Martin County Parks	16	58	-	WE	F	Yes	Yes	FBL	$$-$$$	No
174 DuPuis WEA	-	-	-	-	-	-	-	HFBRC, hunting	-	No
175 J. W. Corbett WMA	-	-	-	-	-	-	-	HFBL, hunting	-	-
176 Jonathan Dickinson State Park	135	140, T, C	40	WE	F	Yes	Yes	HSFBLRC	$$$	Yes
177 Palm Beach County Parks	349	369, T	-	WE (S)	F	Yes	Yes	HSFBLC	$$-$$$	Yes
178 Rotenberger WMA	-	-	-	-	-	-	-	HFBL, hunting	-	No
179 Holey Land WMA	-	-	-	-	-	-	-	HFBL, hunting	-	No
180 Frances S. Taylor Everglades/WMA	-	-	-	-	-	-	-	HFBLC, hunting	-	No
181 Broward County Parks and Rec.	299	313	-	WE	F	Yes	Yes	HSFBLRC	$$	Yes
182 Oleta River State Park	-	14, T, C	-	-	F	Yes	No	HFBC	$$$	Yes
183 Miami-Dade County Parks	240+	240+, T, C	-	WE	F	Yes	Yes	HFBLRC	$$-$$$	Yes
184 Biscayne National Park	-	40	-	-	Elliott	Elliott (cold)	No	HSFBL, scuba, snorkeling	$$	No

Key:
Hookups: W = Water, E = Electricity, S = Sewer, C = Cable, P = Phone, I = Internet
Total Sites: T = Tents, C = Cabins, Y = Yurts
Maximum RV Length: Given in feet
Toilets: F = Flush, NF = No flush
Recreation: H = Hiking, S = Swimming, F = Fishing, B = Boating, L = Boat launch, O = Off-road driving, R = Horseback riding, C = Cycling

[1] T: Almost all Florida state parks and many county parks have prepared sites with water and electricity and a primitive camping (youth or group—tent-only) area. In the more accessible primitive campsites, a spigot for potable water is available. Camping in the primitive area is sometimes regulated by site and sometimes by number of occupants or even type of group, the focus being nonprofit groups, rather than numbers per specific sites. C: cabins are available.

NOTE: Here are a few parks in this region that do not offer camping: Avalon, Bill Baggs Cape Florida, Dagny Johnson Key Largo Hammock Botanical, Fort Pierce Inlet (organized primitive youth group camping by permit only), Fort Zachary Taylor Historic, Hugh Taylor Birch (organized primitive youth group camping by permit

only), Indian Key Historic, John D. MacArthur Beach, John U. Lloyd B
num Vitae Key Botanical, San Pedro Underwater Archaeological Preserve
Preserve, Sea Branch Preserve, St. Lucie Inlet Preserve, The Barnacle Hi......,
Windley Key Fossil Reef Geological.

169 Kissimmee Prairie Preserve State Park

Location: 25 miles northwest of Okeechobee via US 441 and CR 724 in Okeechobee County
(27° 37' 1" N, 81° 4' 59" W)
Season: Year-round
Sites: 35, includes 8 horse camps, plus 3 primitive sites reached by hiking or bicycling (3.5 miles
from park office)
Maximum length: 65 feet
Facilities: Electricity, community water source near kiosk; bathhouse with coin laundry; one pad-
dock and water at equestrian sites
Fee per night: $$
Management: Florida Division of Recreation and Parks
Contact: 863-462-5360, www.floridastateparks.org/kissimmeeprairie/default.cfm; (800) 326-
3521, www.reserveamerica.com
Finding the campground: Kissimmee Prairie Preserve State Park is approximately 25 miles north
of Okeechobee. It is 5 miles north of the western terminus of Okeechobee CR 724. US 441 and
Okeechobee CR 700A intersect CR 724. The campground is 5 miles inside the park entrance.
About the campground: This is a park for stargazing. Far enough from civilization that light pollu-
tion is minimum; close enough that it doesn't cost a fortune to get there. Camping options at this
54,000-acre park are available for every rig and inclination, and recreational activities encompass
all of the state park stand-bys: ranger-led buggy tours to remote areas, bird-watching, hiking and
cycling on 100 miles of trails and service roads, palms and oaks, great sunsets, and a small, but
well-apportioned picnic area.

170 St. Lucie County Parks

Location: Savannas Recreation Area, just south of Fort Pierce on the west bank of the Intracoastal
Waterway at 1400 Midway Rd., Fort Pierce, FL 34982 (27° 22' 54" N, 80° 18' 18" W)
Season: October through April
Sites: There are 5 types of campsites, including RV sites, for general use: primitive, unimproved
(no electricity), improved (electricity and water), fully improved (electricity, water and sewage
hookup), and group (tents). Shower and restroom facilities are available to all campers. A special,
private area called Palm Island can be rented in 12-hour increments for $$$. Camping and party-
ing are allowed at Palm Island and reservations are mandatory.
Maximum length: Call for current information
Facilities: Hot and cold showers, water fill-up station, laundry facilities, public telephones

Fee per night: group: $ (per tent per day); primitive or unimproved: $$; improved, fully improved, and Palm Island: $$$
Management: Call for current information
Contact: (772) 464-7855, (800) 789-5776, www.stlucieco.gov/parks/savannah.htm, or email at Savannas@stlucieco.gov
Finding the campground: Take exit 126 from I-95 onto Midway Road and drive east for 6.2 miles
About the campground: Camping and canoe rentals are only available from October through April, although day use is an option at any time of year. Savannas outdoor recreation area provides camping, boating, fishing, and picnic facilities in an urban area. It covers 550 acres and has interpretive trails on both land and water. Activities here are fishing, bird-watching, hiking and nature trails, and picnicking. Due to unique biological and geographical features the state legislature granted it preserve status. The boat ramp limits motors to 5 HP.

171 Allapattah Flats Wildlife Management Area

Location: 15 miles west of Stuart in Martin County (Camping area—27° 11' 30" N, 80° 27' 12" W)
Season: Year-round
Sites: Primitive tent camping throughout the year; no-charge permit is required
Maximum length: Call for current information
Facilities: Call for current information
Fee per night: Call for current information
Management: Fish & Wildlife Conservation Commission (FWC), South Florida Water Management District (WMD) and Martin County
Contact: (561) 625-5122 (FWC), (561) 686-8800 (WMD), http://myfwc.com, www.sfwmd.gov, www.martin.fl.us
Finding the campground: From Florida's Turnpike, take exit 133, or from I-95 take exit 110, and drive due west on CR 714 to Allapattah Flats. Watch for signs and look for Cottage Road on the north side of CR 714 as it will lead to the camping area.
About the campground: Driving west of Florida's Turnpike, and I-95 in much of south Florida, you soon run into a slice of wet: miles and miles of miles and miles. Allapattah Flats WMA is part of this region. This 20,945-acre area is part of a "vast wetland area" that, prior to settlement and mechanized agriculture, covered hundreds of square miles. Today, it allows camping and provides recreation while protecting habitat for rare animals, particularly sandhill cranes, wood storks, and crested caracaras.

Recreation includes hiking and bicycling on a 5-mile trail system, horseback riding, primitive camping, hunting, fishing, and wildlife viewing. Horses have a 150-acre riding area and a separate trail system.

172 Lake Okeechobee and Okeechobee Waterway

NOTE: Please contact the park(s) for more information regarding omitted camp specs and management as it is often changing.

St. Lucie Lock

Location: St. Lucie Lock in Martin County (campground office—27° 06' 37" N, 80° 17' 06" W; see also Martin County Parks)
Season: Year-round
Sites: 12
Maximum length: Call for current information
Facilities: 9 RV/tent sites, 8 boat campsites with electricity and water hookups. 3 tent sites have no hookups. Additional amenities include a dump station, hot showers, public phones, a playground, boat ramp, and a picnic shelter. A large picnic pavilion located in the day-use area can be reserved.
Fee per night: $$
Management: U.S. Army Corps of Engineers
Contact: www.usace.army.mil/
Finding the campground: St. Lucie South: From Stuart, take SR 76 south. Just past I-95 (exit 101) and Florida's Turnpike, turn right on SW Locks Road. It is a little more than 1 mile to the lock.
About the campground: Campers should expect a lot of day visitors here (there were 114,600 visitors last year), especially on weekends. There are 12 campsites ($$), 9 with electricity, water, and sewer hookups, but no group sites. Located on the St. Lucie Canal portion of the Okeechobee Waterway, St. Lucie Lock Recreation Area is only a 10 to 15 minute drive from Stuart. The tropical atmosphere provides an excellent location to camp, fish, picnic, boat, or hang out watching boats and manatees passing through the lock as they travel the Okeechobee Waterway.

The campground is open year-round. Attendants are on duty and reservations are recommended, (772) 287-1382.

The city of Stuart is nearby and offers everything campers need: grocery stores, restaurants, and shopping malls. Atlantic beaches are within a short driving or even bicycling distance.

173 Martin County Parks

Phipps Park

Location: 2175 SW Locks Rd., Stuart, FL 34997, on the St. Lucie Canal in northwest Martin County (27° 06' 37" N, 80° 17' 06" W)
Season: Year-round
Sites: 58 first-come, first-served sites, limited to 6 people in a party
Maximum length: Call for current information
Facilities: Electrical hookups at sites 1 to 16 on the canal; fire rings, potable water, dump station, dumpsters, two bathrooms/shower facilities, playground, 2 pavilions, boat ramp. Campfires, if conditions permit, allowed only in the provided fire rings.
Fee per night: $$ (residents of Martin County), $$$ (non-residents)
Management: Martin County Parks & Recreation
Contact: (772) 287-6565/220-7129/288-5690, www.martin.fl.us/
Finding the campground: From I-95, take exit 101 west on SW Kanner Highway/SR 76. Turn right

(north) on SW Locks Road and proceed to the camping area.

About the campground: Located along the Okeechobee Waterway, Phipps is a 55-acre conservation and campground area. Close proximity to the St. Lucie Lock allows saltwater or freshwater fishing; many sites have a waterfront view.

174 DuPuis Wildlife Environmental Area

Location: Adjoining the J. W. Corbett Wildlife Management Area and just east of Port Mayaca (26° 59' 11" N, 80° 36' 22" W), northwestern Palm Beach and southwestern Martin Counties
Season: Year-round
Sites: Camping is permitted only at designated primitive sites and on hiking trails such as the Ocean-to-Lake Trail, at the equestrian staging area at Gate 3 (equestrian campground—30 stalls, 15 paddocks), and the drive-in campsite on Jim Lake Grade. During hunting seasons, camping is only allowed with a hunting license. Sites are first-come, first-served.
Maximum length: Call for current information
Facilities: The Jim Grade Lake site has fire rings and picnic tables; the equestrian center has restrooms with showers, a dump station, and a trailhead marking the beginning of 40 miles of equestrian trails.
Fee per night: None
Management: Fish & Wildlife Conservation Commission and South Florida Water Management District
Contact: (561) 924-5310, http://myfwc.com, www.sfwmd.gov, www.floridatrail.org
Finding the campground: The DuPuis WEA is just east of Lake Okeechobee off SR 76, 3 miles east of Port Mayaca and 25 miles southwest of Stuart.
About the campground: Although large at 21,935 acres, this wildlife unit is a small chunk of the ecosystem that once stretched to the tip of south Florida: a river of grass and water, with alligators, otters, panthers, deer, osprey, and eagles.

The visitor center at Gate 5 on SR 76 is worthy of a visit. Chances are your cell phone will not work here, and if something unexpected happens as you hike and take pictures of snakes and gators, or if you simply become thirsty . . . you are on your own.

In the rainy season, the pine flatwoods often contain standing water and roads will probably be flooded. Shade for tents is rare.

During hunting seasons access is open only to hunters and through-hikers on the Ocean-to-Lake Trail, part of the Florida National Scenic Trail. There are 35 miles of hiking trails and four loops ranging from 5.0 to 15.6 miles. Parking for hikers is located at the trailhead at Gate 2. Cycling is allowed on named roads.

175 J. W. Corbett Wildlife Management Area

Location: The southeast corner is in Palm Beach County (26° 48' 42" N, 80° 17' 36" W)
Season: Year-round

Sites: Camping at specifically designated campsites. During the archery and gene[...] in the fall, camping is permitted seven days a week; during the rest of the year, ca[...] ted only on weekends. These primitive, no-charge campsites are available first-co[...] There are 2 primitive campsites for hikers along the Florida Trail and a youth cam[...]

Maximum length: Call for current information

Facilities: Call for current information

Fee per night: Call for current information

Management: Fish & Wildlife Conservation Commission

Contact: (850) 488-4676, http://myfwc.com, www.floridatrail.org

Finding the campground: From I-95, take exit 77 and head west on Northlake.

About the campground: Between Florida's expanding Gold Coast to the east and the vast agricultural fields to the west is 60,228-acre Corbett WMA. Hunting for deer, feral hogs, turkey, and snipe is allowed during legal seasons. Here one finds pine flatwoods, cypress swamps, and a hardwood hammock. This area is hot, remote on the interior, and is usually wet, as well. The motto of the Boy Scouts is "Be prepared." That applies in spades in these primitive WMA campsites.

176 Jonathan Dickinson State Park

Location: 12 miles south of Stuart on US 1 in Martin County (27° 1' 27" N, 80° 6' 33" W)

Season: Year-round

Sites: 135 family sites in two campgrounds, Pine Grove (90 sites) and River (35 sites); 2 primitive backpack camps on segments of the Florida Trail; 3 youth group sites (for up to 30 persons each); 5-site, full-facility campground is available for horse camping and there are 12 cabins near the Loxahatchee

Maximum length: 40 feet

Facilities: Full-facility sites with water, electricity, tables, and a grill. Both Pine Grove and River have tiled bathhouses with hot-water showers, dump station; group site has tables, fire circle, and composting toilet, but no water. Cabins come in three styles and all are complete except for bed and bath linens (561-746-1466 to reserve cabin or for canoe/kayak rental).

Fee per night: $$$

Management: Florida Division of Recreation and Parks

Contact: (772) 546-2771, www.floridastateparks.org/jonathandickinson/default.cfm; (800) 326-3521, www.reserveamerica.com

Finding the campground: From I-95, take exit 96 and drive east on CR 708/Bridge Road to US 1. Turn right (south) on US 1 and the park is 3 miles on your right.

About the campground: There is a great deal to enjoy at this 11,500-acre park. It is easy to get to, and camping in the shade is easy and inexpensive. First, it offers camping opportunities for families in tents, retired couples in RVs, backpackers, and equestrians. If one has a boat or kayak, the river is scenic and full of fish.

The Loxahatchee River, which runs through the park, was Florida's first federally designated Wild and Scenic River. Rangers give tours of the 1930s pioneer homestead of "Trapper" Nelson, which trips back into an era that our grandparents would have understood but which today seems almost incomprehensible. Arrange boat tours or rent canoes, kayaks, and motorboats by calling (561) 746-1466.

When you come to Florida, bring your canoe or kayak, and your bicycle, your hiking boots, bathing suits, shotguns during hunting seasons, and cash for the theme parks.

177 Palm Beach County Parks

NOTE: Please contact the park(s) for more information regarding omitted camp specs and management as it is often changing.

John Prince Park

Location: 4759 South Congress Ave., Lake Worth, FL 33461 (26° 34' 43.8" N, 80° 4' 29.3" W)
Season: Year-round
Sites: 277 rustic RV/tent sites, group camping with reservations for non-profit youth groups
Maximum length: Call for current information
Facilities: All sites have water and a picnic table. 187 have 30-amp electricity; 90 have 50-amp and sewer. 65 sites are paved; 212 have shell-rock pads. 46 are located on Lake Osborne (no swimming). There are 4 restroom and shower buildings, 4 campfire pits, 3 playgrounds, a boules/petanque court, and courtesy phones. Firewood and ice are sold at the campground office. 24-hour monitored security gates; a gate code is issued upon check-in. Campground manager resides on-site. A dump station is provided or on-site honey wagon service ($) is available Dec through Apr.
Fee per night: $$
Management: Call for current information
Contact: (561) 582-7992, www.pbcgov.com, or email at jppcamp@pbc.gov.com
Finding the campground: Take exit 63 from I-95 and turn west on Sixth Avenue. Travel 1.3 miles to Congress Avenue and turn left. Drive 0.4 mile to the entrance on the left side of the road.
About the campground: John Prince is a 726-acre urban park, but is nevertheless peaceful and shaded. This site on the Lake Osborne chain is great for as long as you can stay, because it is

close to attractions and beaches, and if you have never strolled down Worth Avenue in Palm Beach on a warm summer evening, you must visit.

With a watercraft and fishing license, this is a place to indulge. A boat ramp is located in the campground. Prince also has a 5-mile multiuse path, a 0.5-mile wheelchair trail, 1.4-mile fitness trail, lighted tennis courts, playgrounds, rental picnic pavilions, and nature trail. Reservations are suggested.

Peanut Island Campground

Location: (26° 46' 25" N, 80° 02' 46" W)
Season: Year-round
Sites: 20 tropically landscaped, tents-only reserved campsites, and natural areas beach camping (first-come, first-served)
Maximum length: Call for current information
Facilities: Tent pad, grill, picnic table, restrooms with showers, drinking water, a picnic pavilion, and a large fire ring, but no electricity. (Open air sleeping in bedrolls or sleeping bags, and sleeping on beaches, piers, docks, picnic areas, and pavilions is prohibited). Camping is by permit only; reservations (can be accepted three months in advance) are required.

Natural areas beach camping is permitted on designated beaches on the west side of the island. Due to environmental sensitivity, beach campers are asked to only establish campsites on the sandy beach and to avoid disturbing surrounding vegetation. Open fires are prohibited but small barbecue grills are allowed. No indoor showers, but an outdoor pole shower is available at a nearby bathroom. For safety, natural areas beach campers must register at the park office and provide the names of all individuals at their site, as well as a cellular phone number (if available).
Fee per night: Reserved, $$; beach camping free
Management: Call for current information
Contact: (561) 845-4445 or toll free (866) 383-5730, www.pbcgov.com
Finding the campground: Peanut Island is in the Intracoastal Waterway east of the city of Riviera Beach at the south end of Singer Island and the north end of West Palm Beach.
About the campground: Peanut Island Campground is terrific for fishing and boating. Because it is located on a spoil island, it is surrounded by the Intracoastal beside the Lake Worth Inlet, but is accessible by powered boats, sailboats, kayaks, and canoes.

South Bay RV Campground

Location: 100 Levee Rd., South Bay, FL 33493 (26° 39' 59" N, 80° 43' 08" W)
Season: Year-round
Sites: 72 spacious, paved RV sites
Maximum length: Call for current information
Facilities: Water, sewer, electricity (30 and 50 amp), cable, picnic table, grill; also centrally located coin laundry, restroom, showers, and fire rings throughout the park. There is a pavilion with a screened picnic area, charcoal grills throughout the park, and an air-conditioned recreation room (with dial-up Internet, pool table, television, card tables, and book sharing).
Fee per night: Call for current information
Management: Call for current information
Contact: (561) 992-9045 or (877) 992-9915 (reservations accepted six months in advance), www.pbcgov.com

Finding the campground: Take exit 68/69 from I-95 and proceed west on Southern Boulevard/US 98/SR 80. Turn left (southwest) at Ninemile Bend, CR 880, and continue west through a couple sharp turns to Belle Glade where the road becomes Canal Street. Turn left (south) downtown on SR 80/Main Street and follow it to the Intersection with US 27. Turn right (north) and the park is situated about 2 miles on the right (north) side.

About the campground: South Bay is located at the base of the levee on the southeast shore of Lake Okeechobee. If you have a boat, bring it because there is a boat ramp and fishing is excellent. Kayaking the canals is boring since much is straight-line paddling, but you can put in the "big lake" across the street.

For dedicated campers, South Bay is a good place to relax. Except for the roar of motorboats or airboats, this campground is quiet. From here, you can hike, bike (take a couple of days and bike around the big lake), and bird-watch on the Lake Okeechobee Scenic Trail. Make sure you have sunscreen and bug dope. The office is attended daily, with on-site management and locked security gates (codes are provided to campers).

West Delray Regional Park

Location: 10875 Atlantic Ave., Delray Beach, FL 33436
Season: Year-round
Sites: Primitive group camping; permit required
Maximum length: Call for current information
Facilities: Modular toilets and single table picnic areas with grills, canoe/kayak launch
Fee per night: Call for current information
Management: Call for current information
Contact: (561) 966-6611/966-6600, www.pbcgov.com/parks/locations/westdelrayregional.htm
Finding the campground: From exit 52 on I-95, drive west on Atlantic Avenue/CR 806 about 7.5 miles to the park.
About the campground: This 313-acre (38 lake acres) park welcomes freshwater anglers and other water enthusiasts in non-motorized boats. Also on site: a walking trail, archery range, remote control airplane field, and remote control boat lake.

178 Rotenberger Wildlife Management Area

Location: Among a group of management and conservation areas on the north side of the Everglades in Palm Beach and Broward Counties (south side boat ramp—26° 19' 54" N, 80° 48' 48" W)
Season: Year-round
Sites: Primitive camping permitted on the Miami Canal, Manley Ditch, and Powerline levees. Camps may be set up seven days before archery season and must be removed seven days after the close of general gun season. During other times, camping is permitted on Fri, Sat, and Sun only.
Maximum length: Call for current information
Facilities: Call for current information
Fee per night: Call for current information
Management: Fish & Wildlife Conservation Commission

Contact: (850) 488-4676, http://myfwc.com

Finding the campground: From US 27, turn west at the Palm Beach/Broward County line onto the L-5 Levee. Rotenberger WMA begins in about 9 miles on the right (north side of the road), beginning about 2 miles prior to the boat ramp.

About the campground: Rotenberger is part of a complex of areas designed to save South Florida from itself. There is no office and no attendant except the occasional game warden.

The Everglades starts at the north end, which is just south of Lake Okeechobee. At 28,760 acres—and surrounded by vast wetlands on all sides—this WMA is the most northern extent of original sawgrass marsh. Here you can photograph wading birds and hunt for deer, hogs, and waterfowl. While airboats or tracked vehicles are necessary to reach the interior, the extensive network of levees and canals constructed for flood control will let you fish, gig for frogs, or hike, bike, and chill out. Bring sunscreen, a wide-brim hat, and effective bug spray.

179 Holey Land Wildlife Management Area

Location: Among a complex of management and conservation areas on the north side of the Everglades in Palm Beach and Broward Counties (boat ramp on L-5—26° 20' 6" N, 80° 38' 6" W)

Season: Year-round

Sites: Primitive camping permitted only on the L-5 and Miami Canal levees. Camps may be set up seven days before archery season, and must be removed six days after the close of general gun season. At other times, camping is permitted Fri, Sat, and Sun only.

Maximum length: Call for current information

Facilities: Call for current information

Fee per night: Call for current information

Management: Fish & Wildlife Conservation Commission

Contact: (850) 488-4676, http://myfwc.com/

Finding the campground: From US 27, turn west at the Palm Beach/Broward County line onto the L-5 Levee. Holey Land WMA begins in about 6 miles on the right (north side of the road), starting at the boat ramp.

About the campground: Calling this vast area of lowlands a WMA labels the nameless. South Florida is a miraculous area of water and wildlife, sun and wind; and humans have been little more than trouble for the glades ecosystem. So designating this flat land a WMA and regulating human activity is some small measure of restoration.

The only facilities are boat ramps at the extreme southeast and northwest corners. Nevertheless, a surprising number of campers occupy the levees—the only high ground in the 35,350 acres and none of it shaded—at one time or another during the year, but especially during hunting seasons. If it rains and you are in the interior, it is important to have 4-wheel-drive; if it rains hard, consider making your bed on the roof. Although the interior can only be accessed by airboats or tracked vehicles, the levees and canals afford plenty of opportunities for bird-watching, fishing, hiking, and biking.

Multilevel towers offer an overview of the Florida landscape.

180 Frances S. Taylor and Everglades Wildlife Management Areas

Location: In western Palm Beach, Broward, and Dade Counties (26 8' 48" N, 80 26' 36" W—the intersection of US 27 and I-75—from this point the WMA is 270 degrees around you from 90 to 180 degrees counterclockwise)

Season: Year-round

Sites: Primitive camping. In this remote area you "bring everything you need and take everything you use." Camping is permitted in the fall, seven days prior to the beginning of archery season until seven days after the close of general gun season. At other times, camping is permitted on Fri, Sat, and Sun along the L-5 and Miami Canal levees.

Maximum length: Call for current information

Facilities: No facilities

Fee per night: Call for current information
Management: Fish & Wildlife Conservation Commission
Contact: (850) 488-4676, http://myfwc.com/
Finding the WMA: Too big to miss, this group of WMAs extends from US 41, which runs due west from Miami for 50 miles and, with other conservation areas and the Everglades National Park, protects the water and natural resources of South Florida.
About the campground: Trackless except by air, the Everglades and Francis S. Taylor WMA needs to be approached carefully by campers. Still, except during hunting seasons, this 671,831-acre area is a terribly interesting place because of its size and its very remoteness. What makes this freshwater marsh ecosystem interesting is the ability to camp in utter silence. You may be annoyed, at first, to have the mosquitoes and frogs drown out the noise of your breathing, but soon the call of blackbirds and the sound of wind moving through the grass will be comforting. Airboats or tracked vehicles are necessary to reach the interior, but the network of levees and canals constructed for flood control and water supply give you quiet and affordable opportunities for fishing, frogging, hiking, biking, and wildlife viewing.

181 Broward County Parks and Recreation

NOTE: Please contact the park(s) for more information regarding omitted camp specs and management as it is often changing.
Location: Broward County
Season: Year-round
Fee per night: There are two levels of fees for camping, all in the $$$ range; one level for Tri-County (Broward, Palm Beach, and Miami-Dade) residents and a slightly higher fee for everyone else. Two forms of proof of residency are required (a photo ID and voter's registration, vehicle registration, utility bill, or proof of property ownership). A two-day deposit of $$$ is required. Sanitary dump station $. Primitive, youth, and group camping $ per night.
Contact: Broward County Parks & Recreation, (954) 357-8100, www.broward.org or email at parksweb@broward.org

Markham Park

Location: 16001 West State Rd. 84, Sunrise, FL 33326 (26 7' 48" N, 80 21' 12" W)
Contact: (954) 389-2000, www.broward.org/parks/mk.htm or email at markhampark@broward.org
Finding the campground: From I-95, or Florida's Turnpike, take I-595 west to exit 1A where the exit slides onto NW 136th Avenue paralleling the interstate, and continue west on SR 84. The park entrance is on the right (north) at the Weston Road intersection.
About the campground: There are 88 full-hookup sites (water, electricity, and sewer), each with picnic table, fire ring or barbecue grill, plus two restrooms with showers and pavilions. Primitive camping is available for youth and nonprofit groups. The park has a pool and a lake for personal water craft; tennis and racquet courts; off-road bike trail; an observatory; model boat lake; a nationally recognized rifle and pistol target with sporting clays, trap, skeet, and five-stand courses available; a playground and separate dog park; and a special airfield for remote controlled airplanes and helicopters. Reservations recommended.

John D. Easterlin Park

Location: 1000 NW 38th St., Oakland Park, FL 33309 (26° 10' 16.8" N, 80° 9' 39" W)
Contact: (954) 938-0610, www.broward.org/parks/ep.htm or email at easterlinpark@broward.org
Finding the campground: From exit 32 on I-95, head west on Commercial Boulevard/NW 50th Street and take an almost immediate left (south) on Powerline Road. Turn right (west) on Park Avenue West (formerly NW 38th Street), and once you go over the railroad tracks, take the first left (south) into the park.
About the campground: This park is a designed Urban Wilderness, and it retains a buffer of vegetation. Easterlin has 45 paved RV sites with water, sewer, and electricity (20, 30, and 50 amp); 7 are pull-through sites. Of the 10 tent sites, 6 have water and electrical hookups. Full-service restrooms with showers and a sanitary dump station are available as are a shaded playground, picnic shelter, nature trails, horseshoes, volleyball, an 18-hole disk golf course, and a scenic lake. A soda machine and ice are located at the park office. The tent-only primitive campground is set aside for nonprofit organizations, not for family camping. Reservations are recommended. A two-night deposit is required.

C. B. Smith Park

Location: 900 N. Flamingo Rd., Pembroke Pines, FL 33028 (26° 0' 55" N, 80°18' 58" W)
Contact: (954) 437-2650, www.broward.org/parks/cb.htm or email at cbsmithpark@broward.org
Finding the campground: From exit 20 on I-95, drive west on Hollywood Boulevard/CR 820. (Hollywood Boulevard becomes Pines Boulevard at Florida's Turnpike.) Turn right (north) at Flamingo Road. The entrance is less than 0.5 mile on the left (west).
About the campground: Smith is a 299-acre park with a wide range of facilities and activities. The campground has a restroom, hot shower complex, and coin-operated laundry. It features 72 sites with RV hookups (water and electricity) and a 10-site lakefront tent area with picnic tables and grills. In the youth and nonprofit group primitive camping area, no electricity is provided, but some sites have water spigots. This camping and recreation complex also includes a water park, batting and golf cages, a pier and rental boats, a miniature village to teach children about traffic and safety, racquet courts, a multiuse path, and playgrounds with basketball, horseshoe pits, and volleyball. Reservations are recommended.

Deerfield Island

Location: 1720 Deerfield Island Park, Deerfield Beach, FL 33441 (26° 18' 19" N, 80° 4' 59" W)
Contact: (954) 360-1320, www.broward.org/parks/di.htm
Finding the campground: From I-95, take exit 42 to Hillsboro Boulevard and drive east past Federal Highway (US 1). Turn north (left) on Riverview Road, just before crossing the Intracoastal Waterway. A boat shuttle for the park departs from Sullivan Park on Riverview Road.
About the campground: Once owned by Chicago gangster Al Capone, Deerfield Island is accessible only by boat or the free shuttle. The 56-acre park is bordered by the Intracoastal Waterway and the Hillsboro and Royal Palm Canals. There is a bare-bones marina with six first-come, first-served slips for small boats. Deerfield is a designated Urban Wilderness, and primitive camping is allowed by registered nonprofit groups with reservations.

The primary trails are the 0.5-mile Coquina Trail, which includes an observation platform overlooking the Intracoastal, and the Mangrove Trail, which includes a boardwalk through a mangrove swamp. There is one medium-size picnic shelter with grills, water, tables, electricity, volleyball, and horseshoes. The shelter must be reserved for use. Other picnic tables and grills on the island are first-come, first-served. The park is ADA-accessible at high tide only. For reservations and to inquire about the tide schedule, call (954) 360-1320.

Quiet Waters Park

Location: 401 S. Powerline Rd., Deerfield Beach, FL 33442 (26° 18' 36" N, 80° 9' 12" W)
Contact: (954) 360-1315, www.broward.org or email at quietwarterspark@broward.org
Finding the campground: From I-95, take exit 42 at Hillsboro Boulevard and go west. Turn left (south) on Powerline Road. The park entrance is on the right (west) side between Hillsboro Boulevard and SW Tenth Street.
About the campground: This urban recreation area has an innovative Rent-A-Tent package that allows campers to rent a site with a tent or a teepee already set up. Each of the 27 sites has a platform, and the campground fee includes running water, fire ring, picnic table, grill, and electricity. (Tepee sites include a grill, fire ring, and picnic table.) There are restrooms and shower facilities, but no RV sites. The primitive youth group camping areas do have restrooms, and there are a few spigots for drinking water. These campgrounds have after-hour security; maximum two pets per campsite.

T.Y. (Topeekeegee Yugnee) Park

Location: 3300 N. Park Rd., Hollywood, FL 33021 (26° 2' 12" N, 80° 10' 18" W)
Contact: (954) 985-1980, www.broward.org/parks/ty.htm or email at typark@broward.org
Finding the campground: From I-95, head west on Sheridan Street from exit 21. Turn right (north) on North Park Road. The entrance will be on the right (east) side.
About the campground: Topeekeegee or TY has shady picnic areas, numerous shelters, and a gazebo. The campground has 61 full-hookup RV sites and a new restroom, hot shower, laundry complex. There are two free-standing restroom buildings, a paved 2-mile multiuse path, basketball courts, swimming pool, water playground, and playground fencing. A nearby marina rents boats. TY has many picnic shelters, all with water, electricity, grills, and tables. Because this is an urban park, there are facilities for basketball and volleyball. There is a special children's play area called "Safety Town," a miniature village designed to teach pedestrian and bicycle safety. TY's restrooms are air-conditioned. Reservations are required.

Vista View Park

Location: 4001 SW 142nd Ave., Davie, FL 33330 (28° 35' 46" N, 81° 20' 48" W)
Contact: (954) 370-3792, www.broward.org/parks/vv.htm
Finding the campground: From I-595 between Ft. Lauderdale and Hollywood, take exit 18 at Flamingo Road and go south for 3.2 miles to Orange Drive. Turn right (east) and drive 1.4 miles to Boy Scout Road/SW 142nd Avenue. Turn right (north) on Boy Scout Road for 500 feet, and the park will be on your left.
About the campground: Primitive camping is allowed, and potable water is available at this 272-acre park. There is a 1.2-mile horse trail loop around the park connecting to trails in the town of Davie. The park encourages cyclists, runners, triathletes, skateboarders, and paragliders. Radio-controlled plane and glider pilots have an airstrip and there is a fishing dock.

182 Oleta River State Park

Location: 3400 NE 163rd St., Miami, FL 33160, in Dade County (25° 55' 38" N, 80° 8' 9" W)
Season: Year-round
Sites: 14 primitive cabins and a youth group campsite
Maximum length: Call for current information
Facilities: Most cabins have double bed, bunk bed, and air-conditioning, but no kitchens or bathrooms; centrally located bathhouse. Cabin occupants must bring bed/bath linens and cooking utensils. Cooking utensils, stoves, and refrigerators are not provided. Firewood is available at the ranger station. The Blue Moon Outdoor Center is open from 9:00 a.m. until 1.5 hours before sunset. There is a concession stand that rents canoes, kayaks, and bicycles.
Fee per night: Cabins, $$$
Management: Florida Division of Recreation and Parks
Contact: (305) 919-1844, www.floridastateparks.org/oletariver/default.cfm; (800) 326-3521, www.reserveamerica.com
Finding the campground: From I-95 in Miami, take any downtown exit and drive east to US 1. The park is 1 mile east of US 1 off CR 826/Sunny Isles Boulevard.
About the campground: Located on Biscayne Bay in the Miami metro area, Oleta River is Florida's largest urban park. It made its reputation from miles of off-road bicycling trails, rated from novice to challenging.

Along the Oleta River, a large stand of mangrove forest preserves native Florida plants and wildlife. Kayakers can paddle the river to explore this interesting natural area. Swimming from a 1,200-foot sandy beach and fishing are available and there are picnic tables and grills. The park has nine rental pavilions, all with water, and the largest has electricity. You can rent kayaks, canoes, and bicycles, and the park will loan you a bike helmet.

183 Miami-Dade County Parks

NOTE: Please contact the park(s) for more information regarding omitted camp specs and management as it is often changing.

These parks, operated by Miami-Dade Park & Recreation, feature some form of camping.

Camp Greynolds

Location: Downtown North Miami Beach at 18601 NE 22nd Ave., North Miami Beach, FL 33180 (25° 56' 58.5" N, 80° 9' 19" W)
Season: Year-round
Sites: Greynolds has cabins and group camping only
Maximum length: Call for current information
Facilities: Sites have campfire rings and barbecue grills. Cabins have fireplace and full kitchen. Playground, picnic shelters nearby.
Fee per night: Call for current information
Management: Call for current information

Contact: (305) 692-3079/945-3425, www.miamidade.gov/

Finding the campground: From exit 14 on I-95, drive east on Miami Gardens Drive/NE 185th Street. Turn right (south) on NE 22nd Avenue. The park is on your left.

About the campground: Greynolds, one of south Florida's finest urban retreats, lies on the west bank of the Oleta River, virtually right downtown. Still, a swath of mangroves allows herons, ibis, and egrets to flourish here. Surprisingly, the park's woods have miles of hiking trails, so expect oaks, tropical plants, wild flowers, butterflies, a heron rookery, and owls, bats, raccoons, and foxes.

Campers can wake to the sounds of birds with their traffic noise. They can scale the observation mound to look over the park or paddle the lagoon or the Oleta River. "Jock sports" include volleyball and golf.

Camp Owaissa Bauer

Location: Downtown Homestead (just west of Homestead Air Reserve Base), 17001 SW 264th St., Miami, Florida 33031 (25° 55' 13.3" N, 80° 21' 56.7" W)

Season: Year-round

Sites: Group campsite

Maximum length: Call for current information

Facilities: Dormitory-style cabins

Fee per night: $$$

Management: Call for current information

Contact: (305) 247-6016 (reservations required), www.miamidade.gov/

Finding the campground: From I-95, swing west onto the Dolphin Expressway/CR 836 at exit 3A. Watch for an early swing on the right side onto a frontage road, which parallels the Dolphin Expressway for several miles before sending you onto Florida's Turnpike headed south. Take exit 9B and swing north onto Allapattah Road/SW 112th Avenue. After only a block, turn left (west) on Coconut Palm Drive. Turn left (south) at Tennessee Road/SW 167th Avenue and right (west) on Bauer Drive/SW 164th Street. The park is on the left.

About the campground: Owaissa Bauer is a 110-acre group camping facility set amid hardwoods and pines and offering swimming plus basketball and volleyball. By accommodating 150 overnight campers in dormitory-style cabins with separate staff quarters, it is ideal for conferences, retreats, or reunions. Activities such as Eco-Adventures Camps and tours, bird and butterfly viewing, campfires, hayrides, and pool rentals can be arranged.

Larry and Penny Thompson Park and Campground

Location: Halfway between South Miami and Homestead, just west of US 1 and Florida's Turnpike at 12451 SW 184th St., Miami, FL 33177 (25° 36' 1.4" N, 80° 23' 59.2" W)

Season: Year-round

Sites: 240 campsites for RVs

Maximum length: Call for current information

Facilities: Electric and water hookups, four restroom/laundry facilities, camp store, picnic shelters, a freshwater lake with its own beach and water slide, playground, concession stand, 20-station fitness course, a jogging/bike trail . . . and more. Pets on leash allowed.

Fee per night: $$, seasonal reservations available with weekly, monthly rates

Management: Call for current information

Contact: (305) 232-1049, www.miamidade.gov/parks/parks/larry_penny.asp

Finding the campground: From exit 13 on Florida's Turnpike, drive west on Eureka Drive/SW 184th Street. The park entrance is less than 2 miles on the right.

About the campground: Adjacent to and on the south side of the Miami MetroZoo, this 270-acre park is one of the last portions of wilderness in Miami-Dade County. Here, you can find wildflowers, palmetto thickets, and rocky pinelands. The park camping area is set in natural woodland and has both horse trails and hiking paths.

184 Biscayne National Park

Location: Headquarters: 9700 SW 328th St., Homestead, FL 33033, in Dade County (25° 39' 0" N, 80° 5' 0" W)

Season: Year-round

Sites:

Elliott Key: 40 designated sites, first-come, first-served, all with picnic table and grill and designated by a "C" painted on the grill post. There is a group campsite located in the breezeway between the harbor and the ocean side of the island. Backcountry camping is allowed on Elliot Key, but you must pick up a free permit at headquarters.

Boca Chita Key: Designated campsites east of the "Chapel," first-come, first-served, all with picnic table and grill. Individual campsites are designated by a "C" painted on the grill post, the group campsite by a "G." A saltwater restroom is available (no sinks or showers).

Maximum length: Call for current information

Facilities: Primitive campgrounds, accessible only by boat. All supplies must be brought in and all trash must be packed out. Prepare for insects. The park's concessionaire provides transportation for campers to Elliott Key from Nov through May: call (305) 230-1100.

Fee per night: $$ per night camping fee on Elliott Key and Boca Chita Key (group sites $$$). The fee covers up to 6 people and 2 tents, but does not include boat transportation to the island. Boat transportation is available from the park's concessionaire from Nov through May (305-230-1100); a fee is charged.

Management: U.S. National Park Service

Contact: (305) 230-7275 to reserve group sites; reservations are not accepted for campsites; www.nps.gov/bisc/

Finding the campground: Take Florida's Turnpike south to exit 6, Speedway Boulevard. Turn left from the exit ramp and continue south to SW 328th Street/North Canal Drive. Turn left and continue to the end of the road. It is approximately 5 miles and the entrance is on the left. Or, from US 1, drive south to Homestead and turn left on SW 328th Street/North Canal Drive. Continue to the end of the road. It is approximately 9 miles, and the entrance is on the left.

About the campground: Within sight of downtown Miami, Biscayne National Park protects subtropical aquamarine waters, islands of pines and palms, and beautiful coral reefs. Outdoors enthusiasts can boat, swim, snorkel, scuba, camp, watch birds and wildlife, or just relax beside the bay.

Index

About the Author

Rick Sapp is a cultural anthropologist and freelance writer. Specializing in all things outdoors, he camps, hikes, hunts, and kayaks from the Panhandle to the Keys. He lives in Gainesville, Florida.